Powerful Profits from

BLACKJACK

Powerful Profits from

◆

BLACKJACK

◆

VICTOR H. ROYER

LYLE STUART
Kensington Publishing Corp.
www.kensingtonbooks.com

LYLE STUART BOOKS are published by

Kensington Publishing Corp.
850 Third Avenue
New York, NY 10022

All Kensington titles, imprints, and distributed lines are available at special quantity discounts for bulk purchases for sales promotions, premiums, fund-raising, educational, or institutional use. Special book excerpts or customized printings can also be created to fit specific needs. For details, write or phone the office of the Kensington special sales manager: Kensington Publishing Corp., 850 Third Avenue, New York, NY 10022, attn: Special Sales Department, phone 1-800-221-2647.

Lyle Stuart is a trademark of Kensington Publishing Corp.

First printing: January 2003

10   9   8   7   6   5   4   3

Printed in the United States of America

Library of Congress Control Number: 2002113509

ISBN 0-8184-0629-1

Text design by Stanley S. Drate/Folio Graphics Co. Inc.

This book is gratefully dedicated to my mother

Georgina S. Royer

on the occasion of her birthday
February 28, 2002

"Veni, vidi, vici"—"I came, I saw, I conquered."
—Julius Caesar

Remember this each time you go to a casino.

Contents

Preface

This book is part of a series called *Powerful Profits.* The title of this book is *Powerful Profits from Blackjack.* These are not just interesting slogans. There is a specific meaning behind these titles.

This series of books is called *Powerful Profits* because what you will find here are casino secrets that will enable you to gain profits previously available only to a select few. Your ability to gain these profits is vested in a thorough understanding of not just the game, but the entire casino environment and casino life. I have spent a large part of my life in casinos, as a casual gambler, as a professional gambler, as an employee, as a consultant to the casino industry and casino owners and operators, and as a visitor. The most meaningful thing I learned was that there is a big difference between what the books on casino games *say* and the *actual reality* of in-casino play.

Before I started to write books on casino games and gambling in general, I read all the books I was able to locate on the various casino games. I then learned how to play these casino games, and played them. I started as a mere visitor and a casual gambler, but as I became better I actually made a living gambling. During this process, which took some ten years, I discovered that what I had learned about the casino games in the books I read was not necessarily the way the games are actually played in the casino. Or, which was more correct, the games in the actual casino are not *allowed* to be played the way most of the books suggested. What this means is that the *theory* behind the games is not necessarily the way that the games are *really offered* in the casino.

Casinos are a business. This is the first thing you must understand. The corporations that own most of today's casinos are not in business to lose money. They could not build billion-dollar casino hotels and resorts if they weren't making money. The way they make money, most of the time, is from the losses that occur when people like you and me come to the casino to play the casino games. No one ever wins all the time—except the casinos. They are in the *business* of winning. The way they do that is by altering the rules of play for the casino games, from the purely theoretical to the actual, so that they always have an edge over the players. There's absolutely nothing wrong with this and nothing sneaky about it, and that's the second thing you should understand. Casinos are *not* out to "get you."

Many books on casino games seem to suggest that players are somehow involved in a war against the casino, or that the casino is somehow involved in a war against them. That is not the case. The casinos are a business, and they offer services that you purchase. The services are structured in a manner in which the casino makes a profit. This is no different from any other business. It's no different from your purchasing a ticket to a film; or going to dinner, a show, or a concert; or buying clothes, gas for your car, or anything else. If none of these businesses made a profit, there would not be any such businesses. Therefore, to suggest that the casinos are somehow in a fight against their customers is simply ludicrous. Casinos are businesses that sell entertainment, and you, as the casino's customer, purchase that entertainment when you play the casino games, stay at their hotels, and enjoy their facilities.

However, it is also an undeniable fact that the casinos want your money. So does any business that sells you something. Have you ever heard of a car dealer offering to sell you a car for free? (Well, it could happen.) Ever heard of a company that stays in business by making a loss each time they sell their product? Not likely, unless that business is some kind of a charity, which is not supposed to make a profit. So all the casino games have a house edge, and that's how the casino makes money from the services they sell, which are entertainment and a gaming experience.

Does this, however, also mean that you *must lose* money? Absolutely not. I will show you, in each book in this series, the reality of how the games are offered and played in the casino, and what you can do to reduce—and in some cases eliminate—that casino "edge." This is no pipe dream. Just as the casinos are in the business of making money, you as the player can also be in a position to make money. At the very least, you can make money by *not losing* as much as you would have otherwise. You can also make money by making *better choices* among the games you play. Finally, of course, you can make money by *winning more often*, and more consistently, than you ever could have if you did not know what I will show you.

Casinos make money by having a small-percentage override on everything that is going on at their property. Every dollar spent and every dollar wagered includes an overall general override percentage that constitutes the house proceeds. In casino games, the house edge varies from game to game and even within each game, based on the rules of play. There are good games and not-so-good games. There are good rules and bad rules. There are good bets and bad bets. All these vary depending on the game you are playing and how that game is played. Because the casino has an overall override on everything, it makes money all the time in small increments. Sometimes it's less than 1 percent. Sometimes it's more. Sometimes it's much more. The casinos' average profitability is anywhere between 10 percent and 20 percent, overall. Some casinos do much better than this and others not as much. It fluctuates, like any business, but generally remains constant at about this level.

If the casino has an edge in a game of, say, 2 percent, this means that it will "keep" an average of $2 out of each $100 wagered on that game. This may not sound like much, but you must remember that the casino has this game generating this percentage every day, twenty-four hours a day, seven days a week, the whole year round. Overall, this makes a sizable profit.

Although you, as the player, can actually play some of the games in the same manner as the casino, in games such as blackjack (as we will shortly discover), you cannot expect to make money in the same way as the casino. Even if you are able to achieve, say, a 1 percent or even a 2 percent swing against the house edge and in your favor, you are a human being and you cannot play that game 24/7/365 as the casino does. Therein lies the fallacy of any book that tells you that you will win if you get the casino edge in your favor by 1 percent or 2 percent or even 10 percent. You simply will not win in the same manner that the casino does by trying to exploit these small percentages in your favor.

Is it better to play a game where you can swing the house edge and overcome it and get a game that is actually in your favor, percentage wise? Absolutely. If you can do it, play it. I would. However, don't expect to retire after a week or a weekend, or even a month or a year, playing like that. It's a very small percentage.

Let me put this into real money for you. Assume that you are playing a game where you can eliminate the house edge and swing the percentages and odds in your favor to the level of 2 percent. This is very hard to do, but it is possible. Most casinos would be ecstatic if they could always count on a 2 percent edge. For the sake of this example, let us further assume that you have a job where you make $40,000 a year. Maybe you make a lot more or maybe less. It doesn't matter for this example, because whatever your level of income may be, you can extrapolate these figures to your specific financial status. Now assume that you want to make the same amount of money by gambling for a living. You know that you have found a game where you can make a consistent 2 percent profit over the long haul (blackjack is one game where this is possible), and you are always, and at all times, a machine-perfect player, without ever making any errors. Let us again assume that you will "work" an eight-hour day, five days per week.

Now, you need a bankroll. Gambling for a living means that you are actually a business, just like the casino. You don't need a building and an office in which to conduct your business, but you do need money to start with. How much money? Well, here's where it starts to get interesting. In order for you to make your $40,000 per year income, you will need to generate $3,333.33 per month. This equals about $833.33 per week, or $166.67 per day (five days of work, remember?). You know that you are playing a game where you can always count on a 2 percent return, and you also know that you are a perfect player at all times, and therefore always confident that this percentage will never vary (good luck if you can be that perfect, because I know of no person who actually can, but since this is only an example, we will allow that it can happen). You also know that you must make $166.67 per day, every day of your five-day work week, in order to make your annual income of $40,000. You must also factor into your daily income other "expenses," such as transportation, parking, tips, general expenses, and so on. All these are paid from your income, and will therefore diminish your actual "take-home pay." In your normal job, you don't see these general expenses on a daily basis because they are usually hidden in withholdings and general daily costs that come in bunches on paydays, rather than in bits and pieces every day, as they will now that you are gambling for a living. You must, nonetheless, be very aware of them.

To make your required $166.67 per day, from your 2 percent edge against that great game you found, you will need a daily bankroll of about $8,300. This is your *daily* bankroll. You will need a total bankroll of $41,500 for each *week*. This means you must carry a bankroll of $166,000 for each *month*! If you look at this annually, for the whole year, to guarantee yourself a "win" of $40,000, you will have to have a bankroll of $1,992,000. You must carry this large a bankroll because there will be the inevitable mathematical fluctuations in overall probability where you will lose, and lose, and lose, no matter what you do. There will be times when you will lose every day, every week, and every month. Yes, in the long run this will turn around and you will, eventually, make that average 2 percent. To do so, however, you will need to be like a business. That's why you will have to carry that large bankroll, which is your business stake. Casinos know that. Their owners don't just carry a $2 million bankroll, as you would have to do in order to win your $40,000 per year. Casinos carry bankrolls in the hundreds of millions and even billions of dollars overall, and they have access to billions more in banklines, loans, shares, bonds, and so on. Unless you are a multibillionaire, you are simply not in the same league as a casino, and therefore you cannot operate as a gambler in the way the casino operates as a business. If you had that much money, chances are you would *own* the casino, rather than play in it for a few dollars a day in combined annual salary.

That's another reason this series of books is called *Powerful Profits*. The methods of "winning" that are so prevalent in books on casino games are simply unfeasible in the real world of casino gambling. However, when you read the books in *this* series, you will find the real, workable, plain truth. I will not only explain the theory behind the games and how the games are *supposed* to work, but I will also tell you how to play each game in the real world of in-casino gambling, and how these games are *actually* offered in the casinos you will visit.

Does this mean you can't make money in a casino? Absolutely not. Winning is the essential part of the casino's business. If no one ever won, no one would ever go there. So how do you win? Well, that's why the title of this book is *Powerful Profits from Blackjack.*

When you read this book on blackjack, you will discover not only information about the game, the theory, and how to play it well, but also the reality of blackjack as it is actually played in today's casinos. Sometimes the truth hurts— but once you know it, and once you learn to expect it, and know how to deal with it, the truth will always lead to profit. There is a way you can make money from gambling, and there is a way you can make money from blackjack. One way is *not* to try to "be a gambler." The plain truth is that 99 percent of all people who visit casinos *don't want* to be gamblers. About 1 percent do, and of those a very small fraction actually *are*, but that's immaterial to the big picture.

Most people go to a casino to have a good time, play the games, and, they hope, win. Hope: it's a *wish.* I can help you forget the wishing well, and instead concentrate on winning as a reality. No, this doesn't mean that you have to become a gambler, or start to listen to those people who say that you can't win unless this, that, and the other. Yes, you must know something. You can't play blackjack without knowing anything and expect to win steadily. The best that can happen is that you will win sometimes, out of pure luck. It does happen—but for most of us, we'd rather learn something about the game and how to play it well, so that when luck does strike us we can recognize it and make it work for us. Likewise, when luck abandons us, we can also recognize that and limit our losses. Powerful profits come from several key ingredients:

1. Knowledge of the game
2. Patience
3. Bankroll
4. Persistence
5. Discipline

Many books on gambling, and particularly on blackjack, tout "money management" as a key ingredient. In my mind, this is part of "discipline." Money management is supposed to be the holy grail of gambling, but in reality it is nothing more than a little common sense. Its value is hugely dependent on what the value of your money happens to mean to you at any given moment in your life. Suppose you have lots of money this weekend and you want to have fun. What good is money management to you? Well, you could take your entire bankroll and blow it on one hand, but what good would that do you for the rest of the time? Most people have enough common sense not to blow all their money on the first hand, on the first game, in the first hour, or on the first day in the casino. Some people do this, however. What effect that has on them is again hugely dependent on what the value of their money happened to mean to them at the time.

The truth is that almost everyone who goes to a casino resort as part of a weekend trip, holiday, vacation, or visit for whatever reason comes hugely undercapitalized. They bring far less money than they realize they should have. That's why banks make so much money from offering in-casino ATMs. Is this a mistake? Some proponents of money management techniques would say that yes, this is a cardinal sin of any serious gambler. Well, if you are a serious gambler, then yes, it could be so seen—but if you are, like most of us, basically out for a good time and willing to use some intelligence to win money, then this is not so bad. If you run out of money too soon, you go get more. Just about everyone does this, and it isn't as bad a "sin" as it may be viewed by those to whom money management is somehow the key to winning. It is *one* of the aspects of *discipline*, but it doesn't have to be a chore and a grind.

I am in no way trying to indicate that it's okay to be reckless with your money. That's your choice, of course, but for most of us our money comes to us as a result of hard work, and therefore it has some value other than the face value of the currency itself. When we go to spend that money, we expect some value for it in return. In a casino, however, many people tend to get a lot looser with their money than they would under other circumstances. In a casino, a person may see nothing out of the ordinary in paying $2 for a candy bar that costs 75 cents in any convenience store, or $5.50 for a pack of cigarettes that can be bought for around $2.25 in any corner gas station. Regardless of whether you eat candy, or smoke, or whatever the actual costs may be by the time you read this book, the example simply demonstrates that in a casino environment, people tend to lose sight of the value of their money. However, that's part of the experience. It is part of the atmosphere of the casino, of the overall ambiance. To deny you the opportunity to be so free is to defeat the purpose behind going to the casino in the first place.

That's why I do not like to see books that treat gambling as some kind of a war against the casino, some kind of a job, or a grind for small percentages and meager profits. Gambling is entertainment and it is supposed to be *fun*—but being entertained and having fun do not automatically exclude making profits. Therefore my title *Powerful Profits from Blackjack* is again not just a slogan, but a directional principle. It *is* possible to have fun, be entertained by playing gambling games, *and* make a profit. How? Well, that's what this book is about.

I have spent a lot of time learning about gambling, discovering it, living it, and now writing about it. I hope you will find my book entertaining, informative, and helpful. Somewhere in this book there is something for everyone. Even if you already know blackjack, or think you do, there is new information here. I speak from the knowledge of being within the casino business itself, having been a consultant to the casino industry, as well as a casino employee, a customer, and a player. What I offer you here is what I truly believe to be the best information you can find anywhere. It is, simply, the real truth as I know it. That is the most I can say about my reasons for writing this book and the others in the series.

I really believe that what I am offering will help you. I hope it helps the gaming business as well. I wish all casino customers came to casinos with the knowledge that I share here, so that they could play better, have more fun, have better chances at winning, and be happy with the games they found. I hope that the casinos will benefit by realizing that informed players make better customers, happier customers, who will want to come back more often. I also hope that casinos will realize that customers who know how the games work and how the business of gambling works are not a threat, but an asset. No one will win all the time—but more winners will talk more about the great time they had, and so more people will come. That's good for business— and that's also good for the customer.

To you, the reader of this book, I offer the first and simplest piece of advice: Don't be afraid to have fun gambling. Life is not meant to be a grind all the time. Expect to win. Winning is not something that should "only happen to the lucky few." At the same time, don't be afraid of knowledge. Knowing more is better. Knowing the right stuff is better still. Knowing what to *do* with the right stuff is *priceless*.

Why This Book?

Why should I buy this book? That's the first question I ask when I look at a new book. What's new here that I don't already know? What's different about this book on blackjack as opposed to the other books on blackjack?

If I were looking for a book on blackjack, I would look for one that explained the game simply, gave me the basics of the game, simplified the Basic Strategy rules, and showed me the easiest way to learn the game. I would also want this book to improve my ability to play the game and maximize my chances to win. Finally, I would look for a book that would tell me the truth—not merely the theoretical, but the actual truth—of what the game of blackjack really is like in the real world of the casino. That's what I would want in a new book on blackjack. I couldn't find one that did all that, so I wrote it instead.

In this book, I will tell you the simple truth about the game, and how it is played in the casinos of today. Not some theoretical analysis of the game as it should be, but the actual game you will find when you go to play. I won't involve you in the mathematics of blackjack. I won't bore you with meaningless statistics or numerous charts. I will tell you what you need to learn, why you need to learn it, and what you should do to give yourself the best chance to win. What you do with this information is up to you. I can, however, tell you that without this simple information, you can't win, you can't beat blackjack, and you will not have fun playing it. There are now so many rules and rule variations in the game, from casino to casino, and often even within the same casino, that if you don't learn what I am offering you here, you will put your money at risk more often, and lose more often, than you really have to. I will *not* tell you that you will win with what you learn here. I *will* tell you that you will *gain the best chance to win* if you learn what is presented here, the result of more than two decades of research, work, and actual casino play.

There are many books available that claim to teach you how to actually beat blackjack. They say that if you learn how to do what is written there you will be a winner. That is simply not so. It is true that under selected circumstances and with a lot of practice, skilled blackjack players, such as card-counters, can beat the game for a small percentage gain over the long haul—provided, that is, that they can still find a game where they can do this to their advantage. These players, however, are less than 1 percent of all the blackjack players who come to casinos and play the game. It is therefore very important that you do not delude yourself into thinking that you can win at blackjack if you read some of those books that claim to teach you to be a professional winner at all times. Instead, what is far more important is that you take a few moments and read what the game of blackjack actually is today, the way you will find it when you go to the casino. This book will give you information that will provide you with the best chance to *minimize risk* when making wagers with your money and *maximize winning opportunities*, which you will learn to find and exploit.

Yes, you can be lucky. There are people who can win at any game without knowing anything about it. Those are the favored few who have their lucky star guiding them in all they do. Most of us are not among this small percentage of people. Most of us fall into the greater category of the regular person. Sometimes we are lucky, and sometimes we aren't. What differentiates those of us who win more consistently from those who don't, among our group of regular persons, is *knowledge*. For this reason alone, if none other, there is real gold in this book.

Even if you already know about blackjack, or think you know, read even the parts that tell the basics. I know from personal experience that the game changes. *What you learned last time you played, or last time you read a book on blackjack, is no longer the same.* Much of it may not even be applicable. Even the basics of the game aren't the same as they once were. I didn't write this book because I enjoy working long hours alone. I wrote it because I think it's necessary. I see thousands of people every day in casinos in Las Vegas, where I live, literally *give away their money* in blackjack because they lack the simplest understanding of the game as it is actually played in the casinos of *today*.

Some authors of gambling books will go on TV and say that they are the best gamblers in the casino. To some extent, that can be true. I can walk into any casino in the United States, walk around the casino floor, and in a few minutes know exactly which games are better than others and why; what the house withholding percentage is on the games; what the rules are and whether or not they are favorable; and what strategy to employ, when, and how. Does this make me the best gambler in the casino? I think it may make me the most *knowledgeable* person in that casino, but not necessarily the best gambler. Even very knowledgeable people don't win all the time. There are many categories of "best gambler." Perhaps it is the one with the biggest bankroll, or the one who is the luckiest. There are always people who are better "gamblers" than I am. The point is, when I enter a casino I try not to gamble at all. I am willing to play the gambling games, but gambling *at* them is not my intention. You can figure out the difference for yourself.

Finally, this book is intended to be fun. I am not trying

to create a work of scholarly learning. I am also not trying to create a bible that is to be taken word for word and never questioned. Blackjack is a game that is supposed to be fun to play, and not the grind that many other books try to make it out to be. Yes, if you want to learn the Advanced Strategies and all the various card-counting techniques, then accumulate the huge bankroll necessary, and then make playing blackjack your *job*, then yes, this is possible. Will you learn how to do this in this book? Yes, I will show you, in simplified form, how to do this. One of the books in this series is specifically about these advanced playing strategies, which I designed precisely for those players who want to make winning money at gambling their job. Even then, playing blackjack should still be fun. Look at the job you have now. Isn't your job better when you can also have at least some fun at it? So it is for professional blackjack play, and I discuss that in my other book.

Here, in this book, I want to take you on a journey of fun, entertainment, and the profit that can be had without the need for a dedicated job on a daily basis. I will assume that you are the kind of person who falls into the 99 percent of all blackjack players—the normal casino visitor, the person who is interested in winning money as well as having a good time doing it. If this is you, then I will show you how to do it simply and profitably, and without the need for a large supply of headache pills from all the studious learning. I have a great time when I play. It's a lot of fun. It's even better when I win, which happens more often for me than for others, for reasons that you will soon find out. I want you to join with me in the camaraderie of the casino, the beauty of the great game of blackjack, and all the fun that a modern casino can, and will, provide.

Of all the various forms of entertainment you can buy, gambling in a casino is the only one where you can go home with more money than you had when you arrived! Where else can you do that? The casinos are your friend. They provide you with an unsurpassed environment of pleasure, great food, great shows, great gambling games, and a lifetime of memories. On top of that, they will be happy if you play as a knowledgeable player. Casinos love winners, because for every winner who knew what he or she was doing, there are tens of millions of others who do not, and the casinos will still make money. Many of the games the casinos offer cannot be beaten, because they are made to win, always (over the long haul), for the casinos. Even that doesn't mean that you shouldn't play them. These games also pay winners. If they didn't, no one would play them and the casino would never make any money.

It is perhaps one of the greatest fallacies of modern casino literature, or perhaps merely a superstition, that casinos don't want you to win. Why wouldn't they? When a player wins, it's publicity. It's good for business. If nobody ever won anything, how many players would go there? None. Therefore, the knowledgeable blackjack player can, and will, be welcome at the casino because winners are equally as important as losers, if not more so. If no one ever won at blackjack, the game would become extinct. Of course, there are certain tricks of the trade that are used to minimize the casino's exposure to too much winning, but these can be explained, and you can easily learn how to spot them and how to avoid them.

So, I welcome you to my world!

Acknowledgments

There are many people who have contributed in some way to this book, and have influenced my life. I dedicated this book to my dear mother, because her life has been of such profound meaning, and of such complexity, that her story is a book in itself. If I were to tell you, you would simply not believe what this lady has gone through. It is an everlasting credit to her not only that she has retained her life and her sanity, but that she was able to continually contribute to and foster our family. She is by far the most deserving person to whom I can offer my thanks.

I also wish to thank my literary agents, Greg Dinkin and Frank Scatoni. Greg is an accomplished author in his own right, and Frank a widely respected book editor. Through their agency, Venture Literary, they recognized the value of what I had to offer as an author of books on casino games and gaming. Without their efforts, this book, and the others in this series, would never have come to exist.

My thanks also to Bruce Bender, at Kensington Publishing Corp., who has published this book and this series. He recognized that this book and series offer valuable insight into the casino games as they really are, and that this book will enable almost all players to finally realize a happy and profitable casino experience. I thank Bruce, and the staff of Kensington, for their help in this process, and in particular that wonderful lady Ann LaFarge, my editor.

I also wish to thank my friend, fellow author, and gaming

columnist John Grochowski, for his thoughts and help while I was thinking about the various aspects of blackjack. I have enjoyed reading John's works for a long time, and I find his words and thoughts of considerable value.

The same also applies to my other fellow columnists from *Midwest Gaming and Travel* magazine. These are Henry Tamburin and Frank Scoblete, both well-known authors of many books on casino gaming and casino games. Also, thanks to my other colleagues and staff at the magazine, particularly Cathy Jaeger and Beth Wesselhoeft. Cathy and I have known each other for a long time, and she was at one time also the editor of several other magazines in which she published my articles. Since 1984 I have published a continuous column on casino gaming in various publications, and for most of these years it was Cathy who was my editor and friend. And darling Beth, well, she always calls me and reminds me of my deadline for my magazine column; without her I would most likely have forgotten the month, and not just the day.

Now, I am fortunate also to bring you a list of my friends, and others, who have helped me and influenced my life in many ways.

I extend my gratitude and thanks to my longtime friend Tom Caldwell for the many things he has done to help me and enrich my life. I have had many discussions with Tom about blackjack, and my thoughts about the game have become more mature because of these discussions. I also send my thanks to Norreta, Sean, and Brent, for reasons they all know.

To the management, staff, and employees of Arizona Charlie's Hotel and Casino in Las Vegas, in particular those in the poker room, I thank you for tolerating my ups and downs as I was writing this book and the others and grumbled about various things, and so on and on, all of which were, at one time or another, a frustrating part of my life.

These nice people, and the many regular players and customers who also know me, have helped me in many ways, even though they may perhaps not be aware of it.

To all my other friends and associates in the gaming business, owners, managers, senior executives, hosts, and supervisors, you all know who you are, and I thank you.

To Linda Johnson and Steve Radulovich from *Card Player* magazine, and June Field from *Poker Digest,* I also send my thanks. Friends, I'm getting ready with my poker book, so it's time to run for cover!

I thank my friends in Australia, Neil and his family, Lilli and little MRM (Mark), Ormond College, University of Melbourne, the Governor of Victoria and my former Master, Sir Davis McCaughey. Also his Proctorial Eminence R. A. Dwyer, Esq. (I still have the Swiss knife you gave me more than twenty years ago), and the Alumni Association of the University of Wollongong, NSW, department of Philosophy, and Professor Chipman.

My grateful appreciation I also extend to Mr. Laurence E. Levit, C.P.A., of Los Angeles, who has been my steadfast friend, accountant, and adviser for two decades, and whose faith in me and my work has never faltered. A truer friend a man rarely finds. Also to Mr. Michael Harrison, attorney-at-law in Beverly Hills, California, whose expertise and help have made my life more secure.

To Andrew Hooker and the "Cowboys" from Vietnam, I also send my thanks. As well as to Edwin Slogar, a good friend.

I also wish to extend my sincere thanks and appreciation to Mrs. Ursula Steinberg for her valuable help and assistance.

Finally, to all those whose paths have crossed mine, and who have for one reason or another stopped a while and visited. I may no longer remember your names, but I do remember what it meant to have those moments.

Thank you!

Introduction

I have been playing casino blackjack for many years. I
played blackjack when the game still resembled that of the
1950s, 1960s, and 1970s, when the original group of blackjack theorists and authors first came up with the rules of
profitable play that later became known as the Basic Strategy. Originally conceived and published in the mid-1950s
by Baldwin, Cantey, McDermontt, and Maisel, these early
principles of blackjack playing strategy were later improved
and further defined by Edward Thorp in the breakthrough
book *Beat the Dealer.* Later, the brilliant mathematician and
computer programmer Julian Braun refined the strategies by
programming what was then the world's fastest IBM computer to simulate millions of hands of blackjack. Building
on this information, later author Stanford Wong, in a series
of books, further refined and defined principles of blackjack
Basic Strategy, Advanced Basic Strategy, and the various
point-count and card-counting systems. Most of the succes-
sion of books on blackjack since around 1960 have been
based in some way upon these principles of play. Later authors took advantage of the increasing sophistication in
computer technology to refine and improve these strategies
and to combat casino rule changes, the introduction of multiple decks, and other casino refinements designed to combat the sophisticated blackjack players. Even as far as the
late 1970s and early 1980s, most books on blackjack still

carried the same focus and philosophy that had been established over the previous two decades.

Then a funny thing began to happen. The world of the casino environment began to change. First, there was the opening and legalization of Atlantic City casinos in New Jersey. Prior to that, the casinos in Nevada, mainly Las Vegas, Reno, and Lake Tahoe, had the only legal blackjack games in the United States. Then, in the 1980s, the computers hit the casino. For the first time in the history of American legalized gambling, the slot machine took over. No longer was the pit the main focus of the casino. The slot floor took over and millions of people flocked to new slot games like video poker. Shrinking profits from table games, and the increased perception of the sophistication of blackjack players, soon led to a sharp decrease in the availability of blackjack. Among the games that were left, casinos began to substantially alter the various rules of play, such as having the dealer hit soft 17s, using two decks but cutting off 50 percent of the cards from play, later using extended playing decks of four- and six-deck shoes, and so on (more on this in later chapters).

These and other changes took their toll not only on the blackjack game as it was supposed to be, but also on the blackjack game as it was written about in most of the books available at the time. The casinos were first scared of the seemingly large numbers of players who flocked to blackjack games armed with Basic Strategy books. Later, the casinos thought that slot machines would take over entirely. Since blackjack players were now seen as more sophisticated, cutting out the tables to make room for more slots seemed the thing to do. This kind of mind-set was, fortunately, short-lived.

Casinos soon found out that most blackjack players were not nearly as sophisticated as they had assumed, since so much information on how to beat blackjack was now available. It turned out that most people did not understand the principles of playing blackjack with a professional strategy and mind-set, or they simply couldn't remember all the rules all the time and made mistakes. Since the Basic Strategy player was able to get the game to about even odds, casinos thought that these players would break them. There were many stories in the media at that time about professional blackjack players and player teams who took casinos for millions of dollars. What the majority of the casual blackjack players failed to understand, however, was that these professional players and player teams were actually card-counters, who used advanced strategies that exploited the casino's blackjack rules at the time, and not just players like everyone else who happened to read some books on Basic Strategy and got lucky. Casinos, first scared of the general player armed with knowledge of blackjack strategies, were then scared of the card-counters and their teams. Finally, they thought slots would be better since they were machines and not people. In the end, all these thoughts proved wrong.

Slots were not a source of never-ending casino profits. Yes, they did take over the majority of gaming positions in the casinos. Today, casinos consist mostly of video slots, and all slots—regardless of how they may appear—are computerized (for more information on slot machines please refer to my book *Powerful Profits from Slots*). Casinos gain anywhere from 60 percent to 80 percent of their overall profits from slots. So, in one sense, the casinos were correct in the assumption that slots would account for the majority of profits, but casinos with nothing but slots would be no more than video arcades—and that was not the answer either. However, at the time of the first boom in computerized slots, which coincided with the emergence of the knowledgeable blackjack player, no one in the early 1980s could have foreseen the impact that computers would have on everything. After realizing that slots would not be the only route to regular and steady casino profits, the casinos were surprised to find out that the popularity of table games actually increased, with the media exposure generated by the reports of huge wins by the blackjack experts, and the general availability of more and more books on blackjack strategies. Even more surprising was the simple fact that profits from blackjack also increased as more people came to play—each armed with their own book on blackjack, and the knowledge of strategy they thought they had mastered. How was this possible?

Entertainment—that is the simple, direct answer. People came to play blackjack because it was simple to learn, and it was fun. *Fun*. People were *entertained* in the casino. For the first time, the general public could find entertainment in a gambling game—the same kind of simplicity and entertainment found in video poker, which came on the casino scene in the 1980s. Prior to this social phenomenon, the casinos were thought of as somehow "dark," and their denizens were cigar-chomping hustlers out to make a score. This was the sort of image portrayed in films and books of fiction, and was a mixture of historical misunderstanding and a lot of misconceptions about gambling in general. Fortunately, the last vestiges of this pseudoreligious stigma were about to crumble.

Many people learned at least something about blackjack, and they came to Las Vegas and Atlantic City casinos to try it out. Many lost money because they didn't learn the game as well as they could have. Many others lost money because they became caught up in the casino atmosphere, with the free drinks, shows, dinners, and so on—the general ambiance of the casino scene that is so overpowering. Still others lost money because they weren't able to practice their skills in reality as they were able to do in the privacy of their homes, or in the various blackjack clinics and clubs that sprang up. There were others who lost money playing black-jack because they knew nothing about the game, but found so many people playing it and seemingly having a good time that they tried it out themselves. Some won money. Some won because they were lucky, very few because they actually did learn how to play the game to win—but these winners were so few, overall, that the casinos found out they didn't have to be afraid of them. On the contrary, with all that was going on in the media about blackjack, the game actually increased in popularity to such a level that today it is still, by far, the most popular casino *table* game on the gaming floor. Every casino that has a full casino license will have more blackjack tables than any other table game.

What the majority of these blackjack players had in common was not so much that virtually all of them lost some money. Instead, what all these people actually had in common was the fact that they had a great time. Here, in black-jack, they found a simple game that was easy to play, with some rules that were likewise easy to learn, and a game that provided them with a whole bunch of great times and stories to tell their friends back home. Thus the legend of casino blackjack was born, reinforced time and time again across the past decades by countless stories by countless millions of casino visitors who played blackjack and had a great time, win or lose. Mostly lose. Surveys conducted among casino visitors asked what was more important: winning money, or having a great time. Many of these surveys indicated, time and again, that players wanted to have a good time more than they cared about winning money. These are the casual players, and about 96 percent of all casino visitors fall into this category. This doesn't mean that each person thus defined has to come only twice a year and stay for the average three-days-four-nights. This can mean anyone, even a person who lives next to a casino and plays every day. What defines a casual player is the fact that the person enters the casino for reasons other than purely winning money. Many go there for the food, the shows, the music, the entertainment, the bowling, the movies, the conventions, the meetings, and gambling. Although they may say that they go to the casino for reasons other than gambling, all these people say that they *will* gamble. At the same time they will also state categorically that winning money is secondary. If they get lucky, so much the better. If not, ahh, well, maybe next time they will. Even those who say they go to a casino specifically to gamble also say that winning money is not the first priority—having a good time is. What we can learn from this is what the casinos have learned: that gambling to win money is the aim of only the very few and very knowledgeable people, while gambling for fun and not to win money is the overwhelming choice of the vast multitudes who visit casinos.

The purpose of this book is also to diminish this gap between those who wish to be entertained but don't expect to win at blackjack, and those who always expect to beat blackjack and care little about the other accouterments of the casino environment. There is a balance that can be struck. Blackjack does not have to be intimidating, and it does not have to be a losing proposition. Likewise, blackjack does not have to be a "job" without any of the entertainment. Blackjack is a game that looks simple, but is not. For that reason, many people mistakenly think that they can play it with little or no information or knowledge about the game. This is another reason I have written this book.

Having fun at blackjack doesn't mean that you have to lose money, and it certainly doesn't mean that you have to assume the studious nature of a Harvard scholar. You can gain both profits and fun from blackjack by at the very least becoming aware of some of the simplest fundamentals of the game. For instance, if you were dealt a pair of 3s (3,3) against the dealer's upcard of 3, what would you do? Here's the answer: If you were playing on a shoe game, you would split this hand if the casino allowed you to double your bet after splits. If you played the Modified Basic Strategy (MBS), then you would split, based on the strategy suggested (more on this later). Does this sound simple, or does it sound complicated? If you answered "yes" to either part of this question, then you need to read this book. If you didn't know the answer to the 3,3 hand, then you most definitely need to read on. What if you already knew the answer, and were correct? Were you correct also for a single-deck game? For Strip rules, or Downtown rules? For Atlantic City? For tribal casinos? For riverboats? For two-deck hand-held games? The point is that everyone needs to have a little more knowledge than they think they do. Every day is a new day in a lifetime of learning. Blackjack is changing, rules are changing, the game is played differently in different casinos. Your whole life is a process of learning. Here, in this book, you can invest a little effort and gain a lifetime's worth of knowledge. It seems like a pretty good bet.

Powerful Profits from

BLACKJACK

1

A Short History of Blackjack

I enjoy history as a subject, and I also enjoy knowing the history of the gambling games about which I write. However, I do understand that many of you may not share my passion for finding out the true origins of a particular gambling game. Instead, you are anxious to read the salient truths about blackjack so that you can quickly go to your favorite casino and start winning money. I can appreciate that, so if you wish, you may skip this short chapter on the history of blackjack and go on to the next chapter, where we begin the serious discussion of the game and how to win playing it. For those of you who decide to remain here with me for a few pages, I will share with you some of the interesting aspects of how blackjack came to be the game we know today.

Most people don't know that the famed Italian dish of spaghetti was actually invented in China. Historians believe that it was Marco Polo who brought the Chinese version of pasta back to Italy with him, and from that time we have come to think of it as an Italian dish. The ancient Chinese also invented gunpowder and writing paper, among many other things that we take for granted today and think they came from other nations, or are more recent inventions. Conversely, what most Americans today consider "Chinese food" was actually invented in San Francisco in the 1800s. These are some of the curious quirks of history.

Given the fact that the Chinese were such hugely enlightened and inventive people, it is no wonder that the invention of playing cards is also credited to them. Sometime around 800–900 A.D., in China, or Hindustan, historians believe that the first playing cards were put into common use. The Chinese, who also invented paper money, began playing games by shuffling this paper money and placing it into different combinations. In China today, the name for playing cards still means, literally, "paper tickets." Later, around the mid- to late thirteenth century, playing cards appeared in Italy, and a few decades afterward, similar playing cards were found in France, Germany, and Spain. By the sixteenth century, playing cards had acquired what we now call their "suits." They were named after the French words describing a pike, a clover leaf, a heart, and a square, although the latter became known as a diamond because of the way it was originally drawn. What we now know as the fifty-two-card deck was first introduced by the French sometime in the early seventeenth century and became known as the "French deck" or "pack" as the word was used at that time. This was the way the playing cards became adopted by the English, who then spread the use of these cards in that format throughout the world during the following centuries of British colonization—and that's how the cards came to America.

Gambling itself dates back much further. Ancient Egyptians used a form of dice made of bone, which look remarkably like the dice we now use in the game of craps. This was some 6,000 years ago or so, give or take a few centuries. Dice made of bone were also found among other ancient cultures, and that's one of the reasons that the dice in craps today are still sometimes called "bones." Historians theorize that these dice were used by the ancient Egyptians and other ancient cultures, more for religious and ceremonial purposes than for games of chance and gambling as we now know it. As far as I know, the earliest record of actual gambling was made about 4,000 years ago, sometime around 2,500–2,000 B.C. by the Chinese again. In later years, the ancient Greeks were very fond of gambling, and since our civilization takes much of what we now consider to be our Western culture from the Greeks, we also acquired a historical and sociological interest in gambling as a means of entertainment and of making a profit. The ancient Romans also gambled, as we all know from the biblical story of the Roman soldiers casting lots for the cloak of Christ. It was because of this one mention of gambling in the biblical story that later societies, led by religious zealots, took gambling to be a sinful activity. This was simply not so, not in history and not even at the time of Christ, and not even for Christ himself. This was an erroneous perspective given to this one passage in the Bible by later revisionist theologians.

By the time of the First World War in 1914, the games of cards using the suited fifty-two-card deck, so structured by the French and later adopted by the English, were in common use around the world. Among the games that became hugely popular during the First World War was a simple game played by the trench-bound soldiers called "vingt-et-un." This was the French word which meant, translated literally, "twenty-and-one." This was the first recorded playing of a game called "21," which became known as "blackjack." At that time, this game became hugely popular among the English, Australian, and New Zealand soldiers of World War I, prior to the entry of America into that war. The Australians and New Zealanders had already played their own version of this game, and they called it "pontoon." This was probably a linguistic perversion of the various names that the Australian, English, and New Zealand soldiers gave to the game that the French were playing. The French called theirs "vingt-et-un," which the non-French-speaking allied troops first corrupted into "Van John," which later became "vontoon," and later "pontoon." The various games that these soldiers were playing were all very similar, with some differences. For example, the Australian game had a 3:1 payoff on a first three-card combination of three 7s, which was then called "royal pontoon." There were other subtle variations, such as calling the first two-card hand of an Ace of Spades and a Jack of Spades the "Black Jack," which paid either 3:1 or 3:2, depending on which allied soldier you were playing against, or with. When the Americans joined the war in 1917, they became exposed to these various versions of the game. They began calling it "blackjack," after the two-card hand of the black Ace of Spades and Jack of Spades. However, they began to pay off for any two-card hands of any black Ace and any black Jack, and later any black 10-value card, and later still for any two-card hands of any Ace and any 10-value card.

This didn't happen overnight, nor did it happen only in the trenches of World War I. The Americanization of the game of "vingt-et-un" took some time, but by the decade of the 1920s the various illegal casinos in the United States, and the various legal casinos in the Caribbean, played the game known primarily as "blackjack," and with virtually the same standardized set of rules that we now know as our game of blackjack. So it was that the most popular casino game of today found its way onto the casino floor of your favorite casino and into our hearts and minds, thanks to some interesting thinking and fortitude on the part of American soldiers in World War I. And that, dear friends, is about as much history as there is time to tell.

Can *You* Beat Blackjack?

I am posing this question to you directly—*you*, the reader of this book. It seems to me that you bought this book primarily for two reasons: First, you wanted to know the latest information about blackjack and how it is really played in today's casinos—the casinos where *you* will actually play. Second, you wanted to find out how to beat the game of blackjack and win money. If this is correct, then we are on the same page and we will be able to carry on a discussion with meaningful purpose. If you didn't buy this book for either of these reasons, then you probably bought it because you wanted to learn something about blackjack and because you wished to be entertained by the game and your experience in the real casino. If this is so, then we are also speaking on the same terms. I want to make sure that those of you reading this chapter understand that I wish to speak to *all* of your aspirations. By the act of buying this book you have shown a desire to learn something about a wonderful and entertaining game, and to that end all my efforts are here directed.

Can *you* beat blackjack? You will know the answer to this question after you have read the whole book. How well you do in understanding what is written here, learning it, and applying it to your actual in-casino play will determine your answer. At the end of this book I provide a quick Blackjack Quiz Show, where you can practice what you have learned, and how well you have learned it. No peeking now! Wait till the end. It'll be fun for all of us when we get there together.

The truth is that you *can* beat blackjack. Actually, *you* can beat blackjack. There is no magic to it and no special potion or self-sacrifice. *You can win* at blackjack, and you don't have to do it professionally, like a job. Of course, if you do want to make winning money at blackjack your job, then my book on advanced strategies is for you, but in that case you should definitely first know everything that is found here, in this book. For those of you who treat blackjack first as a game of fun and excitement, who wish first to be entertained by it and the experience of playing it, and then to make this experience even more worthwhile by winning money, well, you are also about to join me in the quest for knowledge and the empowerment of learning how to do all this simply and easily.

Speaking now generally, blackjack in its purest form is a game that can inherently be beaten, because of the simple fact that it is clearly defined by its rules, and by the mathematics imbedded within the game in conjunction with those rules. It is one of the few games in the modern casino where figuring out what the odds are is not nearly so difficult as in other games.

Blackjack is played with a deck of fifty-two cards. There are, therefore, four of everything. Four Aces, four Kings, four Queens, and so on. The cards rank from the Ace through the King, this way: Ace, 2, 3, 4, 5, 6, 7, 8, 9, 10, Jack, Queen, King. That's thirteen cards in a suit, therefore fifty-two cards

10
J | 4 x 4 = 16 card.
Q
K |

Can You Beat Blackjack?   47

total (13 × 4 = 52). Since there are thirteen cards in a suit, we also know that there are thirteen Spades, thirteen Clubs, thirteen Hearts, and thirteen Diamonds. Suits do not factor in blackjack and are, therefore, not used. The only exception may be in games where there may be special side bets, or promotions, involved, such as when you receive a blackjack hand and the first two cards are a suited Ace and a King (or a Queen, or whatever). Otherwise, you need not be concerned about the various suits since they will not affect your success in blackjack (although it doesn't hurt to learn what they are and how they rank; the suits rank, from the lowest to the highest, as follows: Clubs, Diamonds, Hearts, and Spades).

So, in a simple single-deck game, we can easily learn to spot what cards have been played and which ones still are left to play. For example, if we have seen four Aces played, we now know that there are no more Aces left, and therefore no more blackjack (or 21) hands are possible on the first two-card combination. The only 21 hands that are now possible are those containing more than two cards, such as hands of, say, 9,2 (which is 11) plus, say, a Queen (which is a 10-value card), for a total of 21. We also know that in this case we can no longer expect to hit the bonus pay of 3:2 on the first two-card hand of blackjack. Also, as we see other cards played, we can easily tell which of their like are still left. For example, if we have seen three Kings, four Aces, two Queens, and four 5s dealt, then we know that the remaining deck has only one King, no Aces, two Queens, and no 5s left—and so on for all the other cards in the single fifty-two-card deck. That is the basis for what we will eventually discuss as Basic Strategy and card-counting.

Knowing what is left to be played in the deck is the primary reason that blackjack can yield an actual player-positive expectation. This simply means that if you know what to look for and how to look for it and how to track it and how to play your hands accordingly, you can, and will, be able to win more and more often than would otherwise be possible. This is not all, however; you also need to know the principles of what to do with your hand once you receive the first two cards that the dealer will deal to you, as well as what to do with the subsequent totals you get if you have to hit and draw more cards. These decisions often seem puzzling to many players, but in reality there are simply no decisions to be made. Such decisions have already been determined by decades of research into the game of blackjack, and by millions of simulated hands on supercomputers. This is possible because blackjack is easily programmed, and the mathematics involved in the game are simple enough so that a sampling generated by such tests can actually yield a workable plan for blackjack decisions that can be easily learned, and actually applied, in a real-world environment of authentic in-casino play.

There are some 550 decisions in blackjack. Basic Strategy was developed to quantify these decisions and format them into a framework that can be applied to the actual game. There are various deviations from these standards for decisions, but these will be explained in more detail later, as will the various stratagems themselves. It may seem like a lot to learn, but they are actually quite simple and easily understood. Playing blackjack according to these rules of decision, based on your two-card hand (or the subsequent total of your hand when you must draw) and the dealer's upcard, you can play blackjack anywhere from an almost even game, to a game where the house has only a 0.5 percent edge against you, to a game where you can actually gain anywhere from a 0.01 percent to a 0.5 percent edge over the casino, just by applying these Basic Strategy standards for decisions according to the rules of play for blackjack in that particular casino. Most casinos today have games whose rules, and methods of playing, will not enable you to gain a long-term edge over the house by applying only Basic Strat-

egy. Other, more involved methods of play and hand decisions are required. However, this is largely for those whose
desire it is to play blackjack more like a job than like a vacation.

For those who wish to achieve a better game and gain
more chances to win, the Basic Strategy, with its easy rules
for making decisions for the stipulated hands against the
dealer's visible upcard, is the best way to approach the
game. Even if you don't want to learn all the decisions, there
are simplified versions of what you ought to do that will
give you a better chance at winning than you would have
without such knowledge. There are variations required for
Basic Strategy, depending on where you are playing blackjack, how many decks, what rules, how far into the deck
the cut card is placed (called deck penetration), and other
factors. These we will explore later on.

This book, however, is not just about Basic Strategy.
There have been many books written on blackjack that have
outlined the Basic Strategy theorems and charts for making
the correct decisions. Unfortunately, the rules of the game
have changed so much that many of these charts and Basic
Strategy facts are no longer applicable and no longer useful.
Also, many of these Basic Strategy charts either fail to account for changes in the game or the variations required for
different regions, casinos, and rules, or are too complex and
complicated because they offer too many variations and
changes. All this then becomes more of a headache than it
should be, and takes away from the inherent simplicity of
the game and the fun factor that should be of primary importance to anyone who wants to play blackjack in a real casino.

In order to beat blackjack, you absolutely must gain an
understanding not only of the game and its rules, or its theory and theoretical opportunities for profit, but also of the
reality of the game as it actually exists. Also, you must abso-

lutely master Basic Strategy at the very least. Without either of these requirements, you will be nothing more than a twig in a storm, either lucky or unlucky, based purely on fate and chance, and not based, instead, on your inherent ability to use your mind to learn something.

In this book I have taken the various Basic Strategy concepts and simplified them into two categories: the Modified Basic Strategy (MBS) for all blackjack games, and a simplified version of the MBS. The Modified Basic Strategy is the full and complete chart, showing all the decisions that are necessary to make the game as even as humanly possible under actual in-casino conditions of today's casino blackjack games. This is the complete Basic Strategy as I have modified it to apply to the vast majority of all blackjack games found in United States casinos in the twenty-first century. The MBS, as I have written it, is also applicable to American-style casino blackjack elsewhere in the world, as well as on cruise ships. I have done this to create a simple, easy-to-use, and easy-to-follow format that anyone can learn, and that can be used in any casino anywhere. For those who wish more details, I have also included information that shows the Basic Strategy chart and card-counting methods in more detail, based on the derivatives that can be found among the various games, casinos, and regions of the world.

Second, I have also taken the Modified Basic Strategy for all blackjack games and created a simplified version with only a few decisions to be learned. This is done so that even if you do not wish to learn all the various decisions required, you can at least learn some of the key ones that determine your chances of winning.

Finally, I have also created a short-form as a stratagem card. As part of my license to readers of this book, I am permitting you to photocopy this one part of this book—this specific stratagem guide—so that you can carry it with you when you go to the actual casino's blackjack table. You can easily carry it concealed in your hand, in your shirt pocket, or some other simple way, and be able to refer to it quickly if you need to. If you wish, you can have it laminated, and then you will be able to carry it with you for a long time and refer to it any time you need to refresh your memory about any blackjack decision you may encounter.

If we take our journey together through all these means, and learn all that we are able to accumulate in this quest, we will all be able to go to the casino and play blackjack like winners. We will win more—and more often—than others who do not know what we have learned, discovered, and put into practice. That's how we make *Powerful Profits from Blackjack*.

Blackjack 101

This is the part where the fun starts, and as with everything else that begins, we have to start somewhere. It is best, therefore, to lay a solid foundation of information so that we all know the same things in the same way. That way we will not be confused and will gain understanding of the game of blackjack in the way we should to expect our positive results. Because all parts of blackjack knowledge are intertwined at most levels, there will be occasions here when I will refer to some other parts of the information. These items will, therefore, be covered in more than one section, as they relate to each other. Consequently, if you come across something that may not seem to contain all the information, don't be concerned. Later, those parts will surface again, and because the entire book is designed to give you a solid understanding of the game, all these parts will eventually come together to form this foundation.

If you already know something about blackjack, I would still encourage you to read these pages. You may be able to refresh your memory. Perhaps you will find something that you have forgotten, or perhaps you no longer remember it quite the way you thought you did. Read through these pages even if some of this information may sound familiar. Blackjack has changed. What you learned, or read, last week, last month, or last year may no longer be valid. This book is intended to provide a complete framework for your success at blackjack as it is now being played in the casinos you will visit, and therefore all the information is necessary for you to be able to gain the benefits. In the remaining sections of this book, I will therefore assume that you have read this chapter thoroughly, and I will no longer make descriptions of the actions, or information, but instead focus on the application of the basic knowledge of blackjack, which we are going to discuss here.

OVERVIEW

In recent years, blackjack has undergone significant changes in how it is played in today's modern casino. Most of these changes have been to the player's detriment and designed to boost the casino win. Chief among these changes is the introduction of shuffling machines. Initially touted as designed to speed up the game, the truth is that they were introduced to combat card-counting, human error in shuffling by the dealers, and "clumping," and basically to further take the "human" elements from the game. In some, but not all, casinos, these and similar changes in the dealing of the game, shuffling, playing options, and methods of dealing have basically reduced the game to no more than a "slot machine" with cards.

Nevertheless, blackjack is still a great game, and a game that can be beaten—not only with pure luck, but definitely with correct play. However, the methods of dealing the game that are now prevalent in many casinos have rendered most of the old books and strategies on the game virtually obsolete. For example, you will no longer find a single-deck game dealt first-card-to-last, unless this is a special casino gimmick that has several "catches" to how the game is played. Even if you find a good shoe-dealt game, most casinos will no longer "cut" only one-third off one deck, but will cut fully 50 percent off the shoe. There are many other such subtle rule deviations that can cost you money if you don't know what to look for, or how to play the game under those conditions. These, and other similar situations, are a *trap for the unwary.*

In the final analysis, the way to winning—or at the very least the way to greater enjoyment from the game—is to play in casinos that offer you most of the better choices and playing options that blackjack can offer: playing options that you will learn to spot once you have read this book. To be fair, there are many casinos that will offer you the better games. These games may be in the higher limits—$5 per spot and up—but it is definitely worth your while to seek such games out. Then really *know* what to do when you sit down to play. Almost all casinos will have at least a few tables where you can play blackjack to your best advantage—based on the rules offered and methods of dealing. The information I am sharing with you in this book is designed to give you the best, simplest, and easiest-to-learn knowledge of how to make your gaming dollar go farthest when playing blackjack.

Because the game of casino blackjack has undergone so many changes in recent times, I will first begin with some of the most important basics. A thorough understanding of the basics is essential to any casino game, but particularly to blackjack. If you have never played casino-style blackjack, this opening section will provide you with some of the most important information that you must know in order to be a successful blackjack player. Even if you are already familiar with blackjack, I will again recommend that you read through this part, even if you think you already have this knowledge. Often a refresher course can be helpful even if you have played blackjack before. In addition, throughout this text I comment on aspects of blackjack play that have important impact later in the discussions, and this will help you when you read these sections.

TERMINOLOGY OF CASINO BLACKJACK

Before we begin the process of discussing blackjack in all its forms and details, it is important that we grasp some of the key terminology. Gambling has a language of its own, and some of this jargon may be unfamiliar to you. As it applies to blackjack, here are some of the key words and terms, and their meanings, that you will encounter at a blackjack game in any major casino in the United States:

Blackjack The name of the game, also called "21." This also refers to the hand that is a combination of an Ace with any 10-value card, for a two-card total of 21, and is also referred to as the "natural." This usually pays 3:2.

Stand To keep your first two cards, without drawing any other cards. Also to remain on whatever card total you have achieved, without going over 21, after you have drawn cards. In games where cards are dealt face down, you indicate that you wish to stand by gently sliding your cards under the wager, making sure that your hands never touch the wager or cover it in any way. In games that are dealt face up, you indicate that you wish to stand by waving your hand, palm down, from side to side with your palm outstretched over your cards.

Hit To ask for another card. This request may be repeated as many times as you wish, as long as your continued running total of the value of your hand does not exceed 21. Also known as "draw." In games where cards are dealt face down, asking for a hit is indicated to the dealer by a "scratching" motion of your cards on the table's felt covering. In games where the cards are dealt face up, the same "scratching" motion is normally used, but this time you do it with your hand or fingers, palm down, without touching the cards.

Bust   When you draw cards and the last card you draw places your hand total over 21. This also applies to the dealer when he draws cards and goes over 21. Also known as "breaking."

Split   To separate your matching first two cards into two hands. For example, when your first two cards are of the same value, such as 8,8 or A,A, you can separate them into two hands—which is what splitting them means—and then wager additional amounts on the second hand and thus play two hands instead of one. You will receive additional cards on each split hand, beginning with the hand to your far right (dealer's left), which is completed first, and then the other hand. Sometimes you will be able to play in casinos where you can split and resplit hands, which is a very good rule. In the above example, if you were first dealt 8,8 and you split them, and on the second card drawn to the first hand played (the one on your right), you received another 8, you could split that hand again and now be able to play three hands 8, 8, 8, each receiving additional cards from your right to your left. All such hands will then be in action in accordance with the rules of the game at that casino. The only exception to additional cards for split hands is the A,A hand where, even with resplit, you will receive only one more card to each Ace. More on this later. There is no 3:2 payoff for a blackjack on a split hand; it merely counts as 21.

Bet   This is what your wager is called. It also describes the act of wagering.

Chips   Also known as "checks," these are the brightly

colored casino tokens that are used in table games. They
have denominations clearly marked on them and their value
in actual currency is equal to the value shown on them.
They can usually be used at any game in the same casino,
although they cannot be used for purchases in the gift
shops, for example. You can cash them in at any time at the
casino cage, where you will receive cash money for all your
chips.

Double-down   To increase your wager by an amount
equal to your original bet and thus ask for only one more
card. This can be done only on the first two cards dealt to
you. (Unless you are in a casino that is offering special, or
promotional, rules, whereby you are allowed to double-
down on either the first two cards, the first three cards, or
any number of cards. Usually, these offers are combined
with some kind of a gimmick or other subtle alterations to
the house rules; therefore this is not only very rare, but playing in these games is quite often counterproductive. Consequently, I will only refer to the regular blackjack games
where doubling-down is permitted only on the first two
cards.) Doubling is usually done on totals of 10 and 11; however, in most casinos you can double-down on *any* first two-
card total. For example, say that you have wagered $10 and
your first two cards are an 8 and a 3, for a total of 11, and
the dealer's upcard is a 6. This is about the best set of circumstances you can hope for, and you can therefore double
your wager by adding another $10 to your bet and saying
"double-down." This indicates to the dealer that you have
chosen to double your bet and receive only one more card.
In most casinos this card will be dealt to you face down. Of
course, you are hoping for a 10-value card, which will give
you an automatic total of 21, and therefore you are quite
likely to win, and win two bets instead of one.

Hard Hand   Any hand that does *not* contain an Ace, and
whose total value is 12, 13, 14, 15, 16, 17, 18, 19, or 20.

Soft Hand Any hand that *does* contain an Ace, and whose value is less than 21.

Stiff Any hard hand of 12, 13, 14, 15, or 16.

Push To tie. To have the same hand value as the dealer and not lose.

Upcard The first card that the dealer deals himself and that is turned face up. (In some casinos, the process of which card will be the dealer's upcard and which card will be the hole card can be reversed. Again, this will depend on the house rules of that particular casino, but this rule does not affect the percentages of the game. You will simply play your hand according to the strategy indicated for whatever the dealer's upcard will be.)

Hole Card The other card that the dealer deals himself and that is face down under the upcard.

Flat Bet A wager of the same amount. Usually used when consecutive wagers are consistently of the same amount.

Rank In blackjack, the numerical value of each card. All cards in blackjack count for their numerical value, except for the face cards (Kings, Queens, and Jacks), which count as 10, and the Ace, which can count as 1 or as 11, depending on how you want to rank it in combination with the other card or cards in your hand.

Insurance A side bet that usually pays 2:1 and can be made when the dealer's upcard is an Ace. You may wager half of your original bet on insurance, so that if you win your insurance bet—but lose your original bet—you actually push. Basically, if the dealer has an Ace up, you are wagering that he has blackjack, and are insuring your bet against losing. It is a very bad bet.

Surrender This is not widely used or widely available, but this is a player's option available only on the first two-card hand total. Surrender means that the player indicates to the dealer that he wishes to relinquish, or surrender, his hand. By so doing, you are giving up half your bet, but will get to keep the other half without risking the entire hand. This is mostly done when you have a stiff, such as 15 or 16, and the dealer is showing a power card of 9, 10, or Ace. Surrender, when available, can be used against any dealer's upcard as long as you make that surrender decision based *only* on the *first two cards* dealt to you. Once you draw more cards, or hit, you can no longer ask for surrender. There is also a difference between "early" surrender and "late" surrender, and this we will discuss later in this book.

Dealer   A casino employee who deals the game. Remember that you are *not* playing against the dealer. The dealer just works at the casino; your action is *against the casino*, not the dealer who deals you the cards. Therefore, when you read in this book, or in any other book, sentences where writers describe actions to take based on what the dealer's card may be, or refer to actions "against the dealer," these are just expressions signifying the action against, or with, the employee dealing the game. Any such references are not to be taken personally, because they are just that: references to the person employed to do that job. Your action is entirely against the house, the casino, and not the person dealing you the cards. Many players get angry at the person dealing the cards, which is unfair. These employees are people, just like you and me, and they work very hard for their meager wages, so don't blame them for your cards or your actions. All they do is give you the cards. What you do with them is up to you.

Toke (*Tip*)   A gratuity. Most people don't know how hard a job it really is to be a dealer, or the fact that dealers are mostly paid only minimum wage. Or that these meager wages are usually taxed and taken away from them under draconian tax rules that punish these poor people who work hard for the lowest wages possible. Therefore, all casino dealers support themselves and their families on the tips that casino players give them. So, when you are having a good time, don't forget the person dealing you the cards. Even if you are not winning, give something. It all adds up. Of course, if you are winning, give more. If it weren't for the dealers, you would not have a game to play, and dealers won't work in this job if they can't make a decent living. Just a few thoughts for you to remember next time you are having a good time while these people work hard to make your entertainment enjoyable and profitable.

Cut   To separate the deck into two parts, which are then exchanged, back part to front and front part to back. This is done at the end of the shuffling, to further assure randomization and to prevent stacking of the deck.

Cut Card   This is the colored card-shaped plastic insert that the dealer uses to cut the deck, and then places partway into the deck to signify where the next shuffle point will be. The farther the cut card is into the deck, the better it is for the player, since more cards will be dealt.

Burn   To set aside one or more cards from a freshly shuffled deck. This is done to take the first few cards out of action in order to prevent anyone from glimpsing the first sequence of cards to be dealt. In some casinos, depending on the house rules and the number of decks in play, this can consist of one burn card, or a number of burn cards, sometimes about six cards in all. This is arbitrary, dependent on whatever the house rules dictate; however, the fewer burn cards there are, the better it is for the players.

Nickel   A $5 chip.

Quarter   A $25 chip.

Dime $1,000.

Strategy   A method used to decide what to do once you have received your first two cards and have seen the dealer's upcard. Often called Basic Strategy, this is the set of rules that we will learn later in this book, as well as other derivatives to these methods of determining your actions in a profitable approach to playing blackjack.

Card counter A person who employs Basic Strategy combined with Advanced Strategies and methods or systems for keeping track of the cards that have been dealt. These are methods, or systems, developed to give an indication—a sort of "prediction"—of what kinds of cards are left in the deck. This knowledge then determines the actions and levels of wagers that these players will make. More on this in later sections.

THE BEGINNING

In the game of blackjack, you are first dealt two cards. These cards may be dealt to you face up, as is common with shoe games, or face down, as is common with single-deck and two-deck hand-held games. Whether this will be one way or the other will largely depend on the house rules of the casino where you happen to be playing. For example, in Atlantic City casinos, you can never touch the cards. In Las Vegas casinos, you can often touch the cards regardless of whether they are dealt face up from a multiple-deck shoe or from a hand-held single- or double-deck game. Sometimes the casinos in Las Vegas may ask you not to touch the cards, which are dealt face up, and other times they won't care. It will depend on the casino in which you are playing, since most casinos have their own peculiarities regarding the touching of cards. It's really mostly a matter of protocol for that particular casino, and you shouldn't be concerned with it. Whatever this may be, it will not have any effect on either the value of your first two cards, or any subsequent cards, or your ability to win the hand. Similar such small changes to the way the game is dealt and played can be found in different casinos.

In the past, much has been said about what the actual

purpose of the game of blackjack is supposed to be. Some say that it is the drawing of cards as close as possible to the total of 21, without going over. Even I have so stipulated in past writings. However, to be more precise, the actual object of the game of blackjack is to *win*. This does not necessarily have to be accomplished by having the best hand, but merely the *winning* hand. Does this sound like splitting hairs? Well, no. You see, it all depends on what you do with the cards you get, and what the dealer's upcard is. You can win by having your final-hand total beat the dealer's final-hand total. There may be some drawing of cards involved here for you or the dealer, or both, and that also determines what your final-hand total will be, and whether or not you will win—but more on that later. For now, remember that the object of playing the game of blackjack is to win. This can be accomplished by either you having the better hand at the final showdown, or by the dealer breaking (busting) his hand before reaching the final showdown. Therefore, in blackjack, there are the following possibilities:

1. Your hand total is higher than the dealer's hand total at showdown, and you win.
2. Your hand total is set, and you stand, and the dealer draws and breaks, and you win.
3. Your hand total requires you to draw, and you break, in which case you lose.
4. Your hand total is set, but the dealer's hand total is higher than yours, and you lose.
5. Your hand total is the same as the dealer's final hand total, in which case you tie (push): no loss and no win.

In blackjack all cards are counted at their face value, with the exception of the Ace. Simply put, cards whose printed numerical value is 2 through 10 are counted as having precisely that value. Therefore, if you are dealt one 2-value card, one 8-value card, and one 9-value card, your total is 19. Face cards—Jacks, Queens, and Kings—are counted as having a value of 10. Therefore, if you are dealt one Queen and one 8-value card, the total value of your hand is 18. The Ace is different. This card can have, at your discretion, either a value of 1 or a value of 11. The best possible hand in blackjack is a combination of an Ace with a 10-value or face card. This is an automatic 21, when counting the Ace as an 11, and is called "blackjack," or a "natural." It cannot be beaten, but if the dealer also has the same combination, the hand is a "push," a tie—you neither win nor lose. There is, however, a way you can win even with a blackjack against the dealer's blackjack, under certain circumstances, and that is called "insurance." More on this later.

HOW TO START PLAYING

When you first approach a table you have the choice of sitting in any available seat. If the game is already in progress with other players present, sit at any open seat of your liking. When the hand currently being played is over, you can ask the dealer for "change" by placing your money on the table and pushing it toward the dealer. Asking for "change" means you are requesting that the dealer convert your cash currency into gaming chips. However, be careful not to place the money in the betting spot in front of you. If you do this, the dealer may assume you are making a cash bet, known as "money plays," and may deal you cards before you have a chance to ask for change. If this happens, you are stuck, and the money you placed on the table will "play" on the next hand dealt.

Naturally, if you do not want to change your cash into chips, you can simply say to the dealer "money plays" and then put whatever amount of money you have in your hand in the betting circle, and that will be your bet. The dealer will most likely announce this action to the pit boss, so that they are aware that you are playing cash instead of chips. However, you will probably not be allowed to play only some of your cash, and keep some other cash in front of you. Normally, casinos will request that you either wager all the money you brought to the table as a "cash bet," or if you only want to wager some of it, to convert all that cash into gaming chips, at which point you can choose whether to wager all the chips, or just one at a time.

There are many reasons that casinos like to convert all cash into gaming chips. One is the psychological effect. People tend to treat chips differently than cash currency, and therefore are likely to wager more money in chips than if they actually were able to see and touch the cash currency itself. The second is that the chips are more easily tracked, either for player evaluation for comps, gifts, and so on, or for the purpose of keeping an eye on the level of the action. Actually, many casino chips today have tiny computer chips inside them, and the tables are wired so that whenever a bet is made in the betting circle, or area, the amount of that wager is automatically registered on the pit computer. This makes it a lot easier to track players' actions and thus offer them extras, comps, free rooms, dinners, and so on, depending on their level of play. It also helps prevent the introduction of fake casino chips. However, although these items of information may be interesting to learn, none of this actually affects your hand at all, nor how you should play your hand, or your potential to win.

After asking for change, the dealer will then give you an assortment of gaming chips with which to play. Depending on the amount of currency you are changing, dealers often anticipate the kind of bets you will make and give you gaming chips accordingly—but you can ask the dealer for any combination of gaming chips you like. After you are given the chips, you select the amount you wish to bet on the next hand. This has to be at least the minimum amount for that table and can be up to the maximum bet amount for that table. The maximum and minimum betting limits are displayed on a sign, usually at the dealer's right (player's left), and normally it will say something like "Minimum $5 Maximum $500." These limits vary from table to table, and from casino to casino. Simply put, this tells you what level of betting this table is set up to play. If all you want to play are small bets, say, $1 to $5 per hand, don't sit at a table whose sign indicates limits higher than that. You could get caught in a game where the stakes are higher than you can afford.

After you have received your gaming chips in exchange for currency, place the chips you wish to bet in the spot in front of you, and the dealer will deal the next hand. All cards are dealt left-to-right of the dealer (player's right-to-left). You will receive your cards in turn with all other players on the table, depending on which position at the table you occupy.

SEATING POSITIONS

The first position at the blackjack table is called "first base," and it is the seat immediately to the dealer's left. It is so called because the player sitting in that position will always get the first card out. The seat at the opposite side of the table, at the far end and dealer's right, is called "third base," because the player sitting in this position will always get the last card dealt to the players in the round of dealing, and the one just before the card that the dealer deals to himself. The general perception is that the third-base position at the blackjack table is important because the player in that position controls, to some degree, the cards the dealer will receive in the event that the dealer must draw more cards. The third-base player's decisions as to how he plays his hand can, therefore, determine whether the rest of the players at the table, including himself, will win or lose. This makes the third-base position a very powerful one for the knowledgeable player. Similarly, a poor or unskilled player in that position can often cause the other players at the table to lose if that player's play is anything other than nearly perfect.

However, the general random nature of the cards in the deck means that the third-base player will most likely not have a great effect on the rest of the players, or on the dealer. His actions actually affect only his hand—unless that player is a skilled professional player, such as a card-counter, who will know the likelihood of a particular value card coming out. Such skilled players, of whom there are very few, may under special circumstances be able to anticipate that the remainder of the deck is, for example, composed mainly of high cards, and therefore will be able to alter their strategy decisions accordingly. It is a player of this skill who will be the one to benefit the most from the third-base position at the blackjack table. For most of us, the methods of playing blackjack profitably in the short term, on our visit to the casino, may not necessarily involve such detailed play. Our overall success rate will not be substantially affected if we don't sit at the third-base position, or if someone who sits there makes an error in Basic Strategy play. Therefore, don't get upset if this happens to you. Also, if you happen to be sitting in the third-base position, and you make what other players think of as a mistake and they get angry at you, simply remind them that the general random nature of the cards and events means that the overall statistics will eventually equate, and that just because on this occasion your "error" appeared to cause the table a loss, on another occasion the same action may actually provide a winner. This way you will impress the other players with your knowledge, skill, and ability to analyze the game, and they should thereafter leave you alone. Plus, you can remind yourself of this analysis any time you feel like getting angry at the third-base player.

NEW GAME ON AN EMPTY TABLE

In the casino, a blackjack table is considered "open," or ready for players, if there is a dealer standing (or sitting in some cases) behind the table, with the chip rack uncovered. This signifies to the customers that this table is ready for play, even if at that particular moment there are no players playing. If you approach such a table where there are no players, you can sit at any seat. Don't be afraid of sitting at a table where there are no other players. Many novice players make this mistake and often try to crowd into a blackjack game already in progress. Safety in numbers may be good for other games, such as craps, but not for blackjack. If you can get a one-on-one game with the dealer, this is the best game you can hope for.

The one-on-one game is best because when you play at least Basic Strategy (see later chapters for details), you will not only get practically an even game with the house, but as the only player in the game you will also get all of the players' blackjacks, and all of the other good players' cards and streaks of winners, without having your sequences interrupted by others. It is also a faster game, when you know what you are doing, and that is also better for you. There are many other reasons that a one-on-one game with the dealer is the best, particularly when you are trying to maximize your profits and are able to exploit the game of blackjack to its best potential. We will discuss more of these situations later. For now, remember that any time you can get one-on-one with the dealer, you will be getting the best the game of blackjack can offer. Don't be intimidated by the prospect of sitting at an empty blackjack table.

SHUFFLE, CUT, AND BURN

When you approach a "new game," as an empty table is sometimes called, the first thing you will probably hear the dealer say is, "Shuffle." Dealers say this to let the pit boss know that a player has come to this game and that a "new shuffle" is about to begin. After the cards are shuffled, the dealer will ask you to "cut" the cards. For this you will be offered a colored piece of plastic the same size as the playing cards that you can place in any position within the deck. There are usually two such "cut cards" used for any blackjack game. These cut cards are just plain pieces of plastic in the same shape as the rest of the cards so they fit in the deck. They are usually red, but they can be yellow, or any other color. They are used only for three purposes:

1. To cut the deck.
2. To be placed within the freshly cut deck to indicate the next shuffle point.
3. To "seal" the bottom of the deck so there is no possibility of dealing cards from the bottom (a cheating procedure).

To cut the deck means to place this colored cut card somewhere in the deck, after which the dealer moves the stack of cards above the cut card to the bottom of the deck. The dealer then places one of the colored cut cards into the deck about one-third of the way from the bottom, then places an extra colored cut card at the bottom of the deck to "seal" it, then "burns" (sets aside) the top card of the shuffled and cut deck and begins the game. During the course of the game the dealer will eventually reach the cut card he placed in the deck. At this point the cards dealt become the last hand before the next shuffle.

The point of "burning" the top card is to avoid "funny shuffles," or cheating, and to take that card, or cards, out of play in case some players have caught a glimpse of it. Some casinos burn several cards, all dealt face down in front of the dealer and then placed into the discard tray where all exposed cards are placed after each hand. When blackjack games were still being dealt first-card-to-last, card counters took advantage of knowing which cards were left, so this rule and others like it were introduced to combat this player advantage. However, in the current way of dealing blackjack, burn cards have little effect, particularly for the casual player.

There is a famous story of a card counter who was playing blackjack in a casino when casinos still offered a single-deck game dealt from first card to last. This player knew exactly what cards were left, and would bet accordingly. At the time neither the dealers, nor the pit bosses, nor the casino owners knew about the detailed methods that could be employed by the knowledgeable card counter to beat the game as it was then offered. Therefore, dealers would give this player funny looks whenever he did something out of the ordinary that we now know was a strategy play based on the running count (more on card counting in later sections of this book). To make a long story short, in this particular situation this blackjack player was dealt two 10-value cards for a total of 20, which is usually a very powerful hand and would under normal circumstances never be hit and never ever doubled. There was only one card left to be dealt from that deck, and our player wanted to double-down on his total of 20, with a very large bet. A commotion ensued. The dealer, convinced that this player was a total idiot, tried to talk him out of it, particularly since his upcard was showing a 10-value card, normally an indication of the dealer's strength. This went on and on between the player and the dealer, with the player insisting that he wanted to double-down. Eventually, the pit bosses and other customers and employees began to crowd at the table, all trying to convince this player, who they thought was making a bad decision, not to double his bet. Finally, totally exasperated, the player banged on the table and yelled, "Gimme that goddamn Ace of Spades!" The room fell silent, the dealer turned over that last card, and bingo! It was the Ace of Spades, giving the player a total of 21, against the dealer's 20, because the dealer had another 10-value card under his upcard.

Needless to say the crowd gasped in amazement, the player was promptly asked to leave the casino, and from that point on casinos became aware of how card counters can know what cards are in the deck. This then led to modifications in the way blackjack was played and dealt, and as a result we have the game that we find in the casinos today. The game we have now may not be the same game they had then, but it can still be exploited for good wins, if we know how to make the game work for us, instead of against us. This story is part of the blackjack folklore, and there are many others like it. Suffice it to say that if you learn how to play blackjack from what I show you here, you may be able to start a few stories of your own.

Good and Bad
Blackjack Rules

Blackjack may look like the same game in every casino you visit, but that is only an illusion. The game may have the same basic core of rules, and be played with the same number of cards, but there are many differences in the various subtle rules of the game. Each casino can, and does, alter the rules to suit its own particular situation. There's nothing inherently wrong with that, since any business has the right to offer their services however they wish. Whether these services will sell will eventually depend on the customer's willingness to buy. In the case of playing blackjack, whether the casino will succeed in selling their particular rules of blackjack play will depend on whether you, the player, are willing to play at their tables.

Other than the fact that blackjack is dealt from a fifty-two-card deck with four suits, and that the numerical values of each card are exactly as stated—that face cards count as 10 and that the Ace card can count as either 1 or 11—the remainder of the rules of blackjack are entirely up to the casinos to determine for themselves, and alter as they wish without prior notice. This means that just about every casino has some kind of a rule differential, often offering blackjack games with different rules within the same casino.

Sometimes the rule variations are simple, such as offering one-deck games on one table, two-deck games on other tables, and a six-deck shoe game on other tables. Also simple is the placement of the cut card. On some games the cut card is placed two-thirds into the deck, leaving only one-third as unplayed cards. On other games, the cut card may be placed in the middle, cutting off fully 50 percent of the deck from play. On other tables, the cut card can be placed deep within the deck (called deep penetration), and therefore more of the cards will be in play for that deck before the next shuffle. Other simple rule variations may be in the timing of the next shuffle. Some casinos will shuffle a single deck after each hand is dealt. Others will deal two and three hands, or more if only one or two players are present. Some of these simple rules do not have an overridingly devastating impact upon the players. However, there are many others that do have an effect on the players, and are specifically introduced to combat player expertise, or simply to increase the average house edge over the game.

These sets of rule alterations vary considerably from game to game and from casino to casino, depending on the geographic location of the casino, its clientele, the competition, and a myriad of other factors. Therefore, if you are serious about learning something meaningful about the game of blackjack, you should at least learn what these rules are, how they are changed, what effects such rules and rule changes may have on your ability to win, and how to spot these rules and act accordingly. You should not necessarily always avoid blackjack games that are played with most of the unfavorable rules. Perhaps the casino nearest you is the only one there, and you don't have much of a choice. Well, if you want to play blackjack in that casino, fine, do so, but at least be aware of what these rules mean to you, what you will be giving up in overall casino edge, and how this will affect your ability to come away a winner.

It is important not only to learn, or become aware of, the various rules of the game, but also to be conscious of what these rules are designed to do. In most circumstances, any rules imposed by the casinos over the game of blackjack are imposed so that the casino can assure itself of a steady win from the game, and therefore diminish the overall risk of offering it. Again, casinos are in business to make money, so this is not entirely bad—but some games have been so restricted by various unfavorable rules of play that you simply cannot win there. You are, therefore, being largely victimized in these places, and are not getting a fair shake. For this reason, if no other, becoming aware of what these rules are and how they can, and will, affect your money is very important indeed.

SOFT AND HARD

Many novice players don't know what is meant by a "soft hand," and many experienced players often forget what to do with one when it is dealt to them. This knowledge becomes even more important when you are dealt hands such as a "soft 17" or a "soft 18," or any number of the other "soft hands" that give blackjack players so much trouble. Do you hit such a hand? Do you double-down on it? Or what? Well, in a little while we will discuss all that, but for right now here's what the "soft hand" means.

A "soft hand" in blackjack means a combination of an Ace with any card other than a 10-value card. For instance, an Ace with a 3-value card dealt to you as the first two cards is called a "soft hand," and is so called because you can count the Ace as either 11 or 1. In this example, you can have 14 or 4, depending on how you choose to tally these values. Of course, the reason the two-card combination of an Ace and any 10-value card is *not* called a "soft hand" is that it is blackjack, the natural, the 21 hand, an automatic winner under most circumstances and a hand that you would never hit or double-down. (The only exception to this may be in a blackjack tournament, where, under very specific circumstances, it may be more advantageous to treat this as a "soft hand," and thereby count it as 11, and use the double-down play to increase the amount of your tournament chips. However, this play is very dangerous in the real world of in-casino cash play, and you should *never* do this when risking your own money in a live game.)

The importance of a soft hand is that it gives you more options with which to make your decisions. Most important is the fact that with a soft hand you can take a "hit" without any danger of going over 21. This is very important, because it offers you a chance to get closer to 21, and closer to a winning hand, especially if the dealer's upcard shows a probable hand better than the one dealt to you. Also, you can do so without the danger of "busting" with the draw of just that one additional card—as would be the case if this hand were a "hard 14."

In our example, you can count the A,3 as 4 and receive a hit of, say, 9. If you did not have a soft hand, and instead had a "hard 14" (also known as a "stiff"), a hit of 9 would have put you over 21, a "bust," in which case you would automatically lose the bet. However, by counting the Ace card as a 1, and receiving a hit of 9, this combination of Ace and the 3 and the 9 will give you a 13. Although not a good hand, this nonetheless offers you yet one more chance to draw another card. In this instance you may draw a 7-value card, giving you a final value of 20 for that hand. In effect, by using the Ace as a 1, you gave yourself two more chances to win. Many times you can substantially improve a bad hand by doing this, and even make a double-down bet in the correct circumstances. Doubling-down, splitting, and receiving a blackjack are your three main advantages over the house in blackjack play.

Soft hands are so important that many casinos try to eliminate this option for the players as much as possible. Although the rules cannot be altered to a point where players would not have this choice at all, because players would then categorically refuse to play the game, many casinos will require that their dealers 'hit soft 17.' The number 17 is crucial in blackjack because it can be either the worst hand for you, or the dealer, or the best of a bad hand for you. As in craps, where the number 7 can be either the player's friend or foe, so in blackjack the number 17 can make or break your hand.

Some casinos may also restrict the double-down option to hands of 10 and 11, and sometimes hands of 9, 10, and 11, which means that they will not allow you to double-down on soft hands. These casinos are therefore eliminating a very large portion of hands with which you can make the most money. Consequently, it is never a good idea to play in casinos that make such restrictions and rule alterations regarding soft hands.

Many casinos offer blackjack games where the house rules, painted on the felt cover of their blackjack tables, indicate that "Dealer must *stand* on all 17s." These are favorable rules for you, and mean that even if the dealer gets an Ace with a 6, a soft-17 hand, he *must* count the Ace as 11, and therefore the total hand as 17. This means that the dealer will have *no options*, and must play this hand as 17, and consequently cannot take another card (or cards) to potentially improve his hand and thus beat players who "stand" on their own 17 hands. In blackjack it is important to remember that the player is the only one with choices. The dealer, playing for the house, must play each hand in accordance with the house rules—with no exceptions! This, therefore, makes the "Dealer must stand on all 17s" a better game for the players, especially for a player making educated choices and decisions.

In the case of soft hands, you have so many options that in casinos where the rules allow dealers to hit a soft 17, that one factor of hitting a soft 17 gives the house a much higher percentage edge against you, and in many cases, combined with other unfavorable rules, can double the normal percentage edge over you. Players' choices, house rules, and house expected win percentage all make the 17 hand a crucial point in the game. Consequently, if you are playing in a casino that clearly states that "Dealer must *hit* soft 17s," you are giving up part of your edge, a portion of your choices, and therefore are not playing a game as favorable to you as others you can easily find in other casinos, or even at other tables in the same casino (some casinos provide both styles of dealing the game).

Hitting a soft 17 will give the dealer a chance to make a better hand. If, for instance, you are dealt an 18 on such a table (not one of the best hands you can hope for but usually a fairly respectable hand in blackjack), you do not automatically have a winner if the dealer has a soft 17. In casinos where the "Dealer must *stand* on all 17s," you would automatically win—but not at this table. Here the "Dealer must *hit* soft 17s," and although you are sitting pretty on 18, the dealer can easily draw a 2—or any other card or even a series of cards that can improve his hand—and beat you. Even if the dealer draws a 9, a bust card if the dealer's hand were to be hard 17 (at which point in the real world he would never take another card), in a game where "Dealer must hit soft 17s," he now has 16 and therefore has yet another opportunity to draw another card. He may draw a 4 and make a 20 and beat not only you, but all the other players at your table as well. All because the house rules dictate that the dealer must *hit* soft 17s.

Time and time again I have seen dealers make better hands from a soft 17 when allowed to hit them by the house rules. This is not good for the player—not at all. By dictating to the dealer to hit a soft 17, the house takes the choice-derived edge away from you. In all other circumstances, where the "Dealer must stand on all 17s," it is the player, exclusively, who has all the choices to make.

Once again it is important to remember that it is not the *dealer* who is playing against you, but the *house*. The dealer is merely the front man, the soldier on the line, and he deals the cards and plays mechanically (as much as possible by a human being). The way a dealer plays his hands is totally determined by what the house rules are. The dealer could, in effect, be just a robot, and the outcome of all hands dealt would be just the same.

DOUBLE-DOWN RULES

In addition to the 17 variances, you'll be wise to find out whether the casino where you are playing imposes other restrictions on the blackjack games dealt there. For example, some casinos will allow you to double-down only on 10- or 11-value combinations of the first two cards dealt. This means that if the dealer is showing, say, a 6 as the upcard (normally an indication of a possibly bad dealer hand) and you have a first-two-card total of 9, you cannot double-down, even though this is typically a good time to do this. To double-down is another choice that the informed player can make, and, therefore, offers you an additional advantage.

In the above example, if the dealer has an upcard of 6 and a down card of 10, and then draws another card of 6, he has 22, a bust hand. All the players who are still in the game at that point win, and if you were able to double on your first-two-card hand of 9, no matter what extra card you drew, you would win twice the amount of your original bet. By eliminating this choice on all two-card values except 10 and 11, the casino further reduces players' choices, and hence your ability to win more money. Of course, some of these casinos will also allow you to double-down on that 9 but restrict all these options to the 9, 10, and 11. As mentioned earlier, this eliminates all the double-down options for soft hands, and this will have a very negative impact on your ability to win. Stay away from games like these.

SPLITTING AND RESPLITTING

A similar situation applies to splitting cards. In all casinos you will be allowed to split the first two cards *if these cards are of the same value*, say, two 8s. By splitting, you will, in effect, play two hands, and thus have to place a bet equal to your original bet on each of the two hands you are now playing. The dealer will then deal cards to the first of the two hands, and then the second, and you play each hand individually in accordance with all the rules in the same manner as if you had placed two bets originally.

The exceptions to the way casinos allow you to play your hands when splitting cards are splitting Aces and resplitting cards. Most casinos will allow you to split Aces, but if you do, virtually every major casino that allows this will deal you only one additional card on each of the two Aces. Normally, if you split, say, two 9s, and received a 3 on the first hand, you can still hit the hand and get another card, or as many cards as you want to ask for, until you make 21, bust, or choose to stand. In that example, if you get, say, another 9, you can split this again, and again if another 9 is dealt (and so on up till all the 9-value cards are out, if they were grouped together in the shuffle). In most instances it is not unusual to receive three and even four of the same value card, giving you an opportunity to split and resplit these cards, if this is allowed by the casino rules.

This is not the case with Aces in most casinos. What if you split two Aces, and then get an Ace dealt to you on the first of your two hands? Naturally you want to split these two new Aces again, to make an even better hand and win more. The majority of casinos will not let you do this—but some do. In these casinos you can split and resplit Aces as many times as they are dealt to you in such sequential groupings. This is a distinct advantage, but the house often counters this by offering this option to split and resplit Aces only on the shoe games. However, such a game is still a much better option for you than other games that do not allow this.

The same applies to any first two matching cards that are dealt to you. Those casinos that offer rules that allow you to split any first two matching-value cards may also offer the resplit option on any such combinations, including Aces. Rarely, however, will you find single-deck or two-deck games that offer all these options *together*. Players who want to play blackjack with all, or most, of these options must usually settle for the shoe game. Even with the extra number of decks, it is still to your overall advantage to seek out these favorable rules.

SUMMARY OF FAVORABLE RULES

For your overall best advantage, look for blackjack games that offer the majority of the following rule options:

1. Always look for a table where "Dealer *must stand* on all 17s."
2. Play tables offering "double-down" on *any* first two cards.

3. Look for tables offering "split and resplit" on *any matching first two cards.*

4. Play tables where you can "split and resplit Aces."

5. Avoid games using the mechanical shuffling machine wherever possible.

Ultimate Basic Strategy

Don't be afraid of the word "basic" in "Basic Strategy." In this case, the word does not mean "cheap" or "simplistic." The word means what it always meant, before the introduction of "generic" products called "basics," which have tainted its meaning. The word "basic" actually means "essential" or "fundamental," something that is absolutely "must-have."

As a result of work done by numerous blackjack theoreticians, and authors and explorers of mathematical probabilities, a set of rules for actions to be performed in the game of blackjack were developed. These rules were called Basic Strategy, because they came to completely quantify all the actions and decisions in the game of blackjack, based on the probabilities calculated from the study of event occurrences. Many people can be credited with beginning this process, which took shape over some thirty years, from the early 1950s through the 1960s and into the 1970s, when many of the refinements to the original Basic Strategy were made publicly available. All of us who play blackjack, and who use Basic Strategy or any of the refinements on this method of play, and who write about blackjack, owe a great debt of gratitude to those people who, over so many years, devoted themselves to the quantification of blackjack decisions, and the resultant application of such gained information into the stratagems for betting and winning.

Of all those persons, who are too numerous to credit in my small book but whose names and works can easily be found in anthologies, libraries, and research centers, there is one man who is universally acknowledged as the father of the modern game of blackjack, particularly the modern stratagems we now call Basic Strategy. This was the late Julian Braun.

Most people don't know very much about Julian Braun or his contributions to the game of blackjack. Although he was known and respected in academic and research communities and among the select group of blackjack professionals who were his contemporaries, when he died recently, very little mention of him was ever made—and almost no mention of his contributions to blackjack. Julian Braun was a mathematician, a theorist, and a probability enthusiast who worked as a programmer for IBM in the 1960s. At that time, IBM owned and operated the world's biggest and fastest computers, what we would today call "supercomputers." By today's standards, any home PC is better and faster than those huge two-story monsters made out of tubes, wires, and transistors. At that time, however, those computers were the cutting edge of technology, and not many people had access to them, much less knew how to operate them or program them to perform specific tasks. That's where Braun came in.

After reading Edward Thorp's book *Beat the Dealer,* in which Thorp first proposed a series of decisions for actions in the game of blackjack based on the dealer's upcard, Braun became interested in the mathematical probabilities inherent in the game of blackjack, and how they could be quantified to produce a series of predictable outcomes, within the mathematical model of probability calculus. Since blackjack was a game with very definable rules, and therefore easily quantified, it became the primary focus of Braun's research into mathematical probabilities. The key focus was, of course, the improvement of computer mechanics, inclusive of software, hardware, and, particularly, memory capacity. Blackjack offered such salient and inviting sets of quantifiable principles that its very nature made it not only an interesting exercise in the mathematics of probabilities, but also a useful tool for the advancement of computerization.

Braun programmed the entire rules of the game of blackjack into IBM's supercomputer and played some eight million hands. This was an enormous undertaking at the time. Today a software program can be bought for under $100 that can play millions of hands on your home PC equally well, but at that time this was quite an accomplishment. After this was completed, Braun found out that based on the probabilities of hand decisions produced by his test, there was a set of precise actions that a player could take, based on the information provided by the dealer's upcard. The resultant probability of the potential value of that dealer's hand, when performed consistently and accurately, produced a winning series of events. That's where Braun should be credited the most for his efforts, because he had done this research from the perspective of attempting to devise a series of decisions for the player in order for the player to *win*! Mathematical studies that would compute the events in a blackjack game may serve as an interesting exercise in probabilities, but do nothing in the real world of playing blackjack in a casino. Braun, however, assumed at the very beginning that the purpose of blackjack was to win, and therefore his program was designed to reach a sequence of decisions that would help the players of blackjack do just that.

This took several years. All the possible hands of blackjack and their respective combinations relative to the possibilities of the dealer's upcard, and the probability of the dealer's hand based on the upcard, and so on, had to be programmed, quantified, analyzed, and structured into a meaningful and understandable format. It would have been no good if it were so complicated that no ordinary person could understand it. Or if it were so complicated that, even if understood, it could not be used in the real world of blackjack play. Braun, and the series of his contemporaries who undertook further developments of his findings, were finally able to get these blackjack decisions down into a simple and easy-to-understand chart. This, then, became the Basic Strategy for blackjack.

WHAT IS BASIC STRATEGY?

Shown in charts in many books, Basic Strategy is simply a set of predetermined actions that the player should take based on the information available to him from the total of his hand versus the visible dealer's upcard—and that's it. That's all there is to it. Well, almost.

Once the Basic Strategy calculations were completed, and began to be used by players in the late 1960s and 1970s, casinos began to combat this player's edge by changing the game and altering the rules. We will discuss the modern game of blackjack in the casinos of the twenty-first century a little further on in this book, but for right now we should focus on the Basic Strategy as the framework for all our blackjack playing decisions.

The simple rules for when to stand, when to hit, when to double-down, and when to split are the core of the Basic Strategy for blackjack, as most widely and commonly available in various forms. There are also subtle refinements based on whether the Basic Strategy is to be applied to a single-deck game, a two-deck game, a shoe game, an Atlantic City game, a Las Vegas game, or a Reno/Tahoe game. These various locations, or house rules in these casinos, require small and subtle changes for some of the decisions that Basic Strategy indicates the player should make in the circumstances identified. Many of these subtle alterations in the Basic Strategy are, however, worthless in the modern casino.

When Julian Braun and his contemporaries and successors first began to develop what eventually became the Basic Strategy we know today, they were basing their results largely on the single-deck game, and mostly on rules that allowed the game to be dealt first-card-to-last, without cut cards or frequent shuffles. Today many casinos no longer offer the single-deck game, and even if they do they will not allow it to be played to its theoretical potential. Also, some casinos shuffle the single deck after each hand, or after two or three hands. Still other casinos use shuffling machines, including a new monster called the "continuous shuffler" and an even newer one called "the randomizer," which not only continuously shuffles the decks but also randomly switches cards from one deck to the other (more on these later).

All of these situations had a profound impact on what the Basic Strategy was initially designed to do. Frankly, all these changes in the way that blackjack is now being dealt have meant that so many variations to the various decisions within Basic Strategy had to be included in the last decade or so of books on blackjack, that the original purpose of providing a simple set of decisions was largely defeated. That was precisely the purpose behind all those various rule changes and alterations to the game made by the casinos.

Now, when you pick up a book on blackjack and look at

the various charts for Basic Strategy, you will also find several pages of additions and modifications, based on the variances in rules of play, or where you are playing. There's nothing wrong with studying these charts, but the process becomes confusing, and the number of decisions to be learned by players has grown exponentially. What Braun, and the others, had first intended was to quantify a *simple* series of decisions, so that the average person would be able to memorize them easily, and thus be able to use them perfectly in the actual situations of real casino play—but this did not happen quite that way. Casinos weren't stupid, and they realized that players could beat them if they all played the same game of blackjack the same way. After all, the casino was only one, and the players were many. Any small but consistent loss would add up to a very large loss to the casino. Frankly, I don't blame them. They are in business, and so they did what any business would: they changed the service. Subtly, in small pieces, but enough so that the Basic Strategy now required many other details and additions, and so on and on, and this has resulted in the current series of various Basic Strategies and variations to them, so that to learn all of it—and then be able to actually perfectly remember it in the real casino play—is all but impossible, and certainly impractical.

MODIFIED BASIC STRATEGY FOR BLACKJACK

I am going to call this the MBS, an acronym for the most essential portion of this title, which is Modified Basic Strategy. In what I call Figure 1, I present to you a chart that combines all of the numerous modifications to the various blackjack strategies, and gives you a single format for all your blackjack decisions. This chart will teach you what to do, wherever you are and whatever blackjack game you may be playing. This will apply to any blackjack game where the basic game is the same, such as being dealt from a fifty-two-card deck, with each card valued at its stated value, each face card (K, Q, or J) counting as a 10-value card, and each Ace able to be counted as either 1 or 11. The reason I am stipulating this is that there are also a number of blackjack derivatives available in various casinos. These are *not* blackjack, even though they may *look* like it or be advertised as "blackjack." These modifications are gimmicks, and mostly they are designed to eat your money, with the house edge often over 20 percent. No matter what they may be called, they are not blackjack, and therefore it is important for you to remember that what I am speaking about here is the *traditional* game of blackjack, with the basic rules as I have stated. If you find a game that is called "blackjack," but where some cards have been removed from play, such as a game called "Spanish blackjack," or any other game where the game is not of the traditional style, these are not blackjack games, and therefore no strategy that you will find in any book on blackjack will apply (other than those books that also include sections on these deceptive gimmicks).

The MBS I have devised will allow you to make the best decisions in any traditional game of blackjack. Once you learn this simple series of decisions, you will know exactly what to do and when to do it. You will be able to play blackjack mechanically, just like the casinos. You will no longer be faced with any decisions or agonizing thoughts, wondering what to do. Remember that blackjack is mathematics in practice, with cards substituting for sequences of binary numbers, like computers. The results, once the deck has been shuffled, cut, burned, and put into play, are predetermined. The only way you can win is by exercising your choices in what to do with the cards you are dealt—and these choices are yours to make, but the decisions are set. You can choose to make that decision, or not, but the decision itself should not be subject to question.

If you learn this, and learn to play this way, you will level the field between yourself and the casino. You will in effect become just like the casino. You will play mechanically, because you know the decisions to be made. You will also know when to make these decisions and when to choose to make others. By learning my MBS, you will get the game virtually even between you and the casino. In some cases, you will have a small edge over the casino, based on the rules, of somewhere between 0.01 percent and 0.5 percent. At other times, depending on the rules, the casino will have a small edge over you, of somewhere between 0.02 percent and 0.5 percent. Basically, variables included, you are getting a statistically even game. The minute fluctuations within the applied percentages are too small and too insignificant to have an impact on your wins and losses in the short term, or to be of any ideological or practical significance.

In addition to my MBS chart, in chapter 12 I also offer you a digest that I call the "Essential MBS." This is a series of key decisions that you should always employ in your game without ever changing the way you do it. These are the most basic and most important keys to keeping blackjack as even a game as you can make it, under these simplified strategy decisions. If you make mistakes in the overall MBS as I presented it, you will give up some of your wins, and this will have the effect of increasing the house edge over you in the game. However, if you consistently make mistakes in the *key situations*, you will start losing more and more, and the house edge over you will climb and climb. You won't win as a result of your expertise, although you may win in the very short term through pure luck—but such luck is fleeting, and if you continue to ignore these simple principles of blackjack play you will wind up a loser. Sorry, but that's the real truth.

If you don't want to think of yourself as a loser, and want

to be a winner consistently, or at least more often than you have been in the past, or want to start playing blackjack with a solid grasp of being a winner overall, then my MBS is necessary for you to learn, and the Essential MBS is a *must* for each and every circumstance of those events. Otherwise, there's no point to the game. You won't win, you won't have fun, and your ability to function as an intelligent human being, with the capacity to learn something and act accordingly, will have been wasted.

THE WHOLE MBS

Well, here we are. This is the crux of what this book is about. This is not the most fun part of this book, but it is the most valuable. Here you actually have to learn something. This is the part where you will have to become a student for a little while. I know you probably won't like this. Although my whole life has been spent in the pursuit of more knowledge, even I feel apprehensive each time I am about to begin the process of learning something new. Learning is not always easy. Often it is very hard, but I do it because I know the value of it, and I try my best to have fun doing it. Therefore, I now advise you to take a close look at Figure 1 (on the next page), and *learn* that chart. I have used real words to describe what you should do, rather than a "legend." I did this so that it will be easier for you to remember what to do. I want there to be no confusion about anything that is in this chart. In chapter 14, this is presented in the form of a strategy chart, but by that time you will already know all this, so reading that chart will be easy.

The MBS should be easy to learn. I estimate that it can be fully learned in about one to two hours. Practicing the decisions so that each one is always correct may take longer—perhaps a day, maybe a week, depending on your own personal abilities. You can have fun practicing these

decisions by taking a deck of cards, or more than one deck
if you so wish, and then dealing out hands of blackjack to
yourself, or to your friends, and then making the required
decisions and comparing them to the chart. This way you
can have fun learning. After a while, you will find out that
you are getting better and faster at it, and pretty soon you
will discover that it has become second nature to you and
there will no longer be any kind of a mystery about what to
do in any game of blackjack. Once you reach this point, it
will become even more fun, because now you will be the
one driving the game. Now you can fully enjoy the game,
and the ambiance and atmosphere of the casino and all that
is provided there, and you will never be at a loss as to what
to do in any situation in the game of blackjack. *That* will
feel really great!

ABOUT FIGURE 1

This is the simplified MBS chart as I have created it. Before
I began writing this book, I did considerable research into
the various versions of Basic Strategy that were available
over the past thirty years. I was amazed at how complicated
these versions of Basic Strategy had become. I mentioned
this earlier, but the various changes to the way blackjack is
being played have led to so many required alterations to the
various parts of Basic Strategy that it has become overwhelm-
ingly complicated. When I was researching these versions
of Basic Strategy, I gasped at the length and complicated
derivatives that these showed. It would take even an expert
several years to master all these variations and complexities. Even I had become befuddled by some of these versions
of Basic Strategy, and it took a lot of looking and searching
to find the understandable common denominator. So I set
myself the task of simplifying everything into this one chart,

Figure 1

YOUR HAND	2	3	4	5	6	7	8	9	10	A
					**Dealer's Upcard**					
YOUR DECISION										
5-8	Hit	Hit	Hit	Hit	Hit	Hit	Hit	Hit	Hit	Hit
9	Hit	Hit	Double Down	Double Down	Double Down	Double Down *	Hit	Hit	Hit	Hit
10	Double Down	Double Down	Double Down	Double Down	Double Down	Double Down	Double Down	Double Down	Hit	Hit
11	Double Down	Double Down	Double Down	Double Down	Double Down	Double Down	Double Down	Double Down	Double Down	Hit

Hard Hands

YOUR HAND	2	3	4	5	6	7	8	9	10	A
12	Stand	Stand	Stand	Stand	Stand	Hit	Hit	Hit	Hit	Hit
13	Stand	Stand	Stand	Stand	Stand	Hit	Hit	Hit	Hit	Hit
14	Stand	Stand	Stand	Stand	Stand	Hit	Hit	Hit	Hit	Hit
15	Stand	Stand	Stand	Stand	Stand	Hit	Hit	Hit	Hit	Hit
16	Stand	Stand	Stand	Stand	Stand	Hit	Hit	Hit	Hit	Hit
17-21	Stand	Stand	Stand	Stand	Stand	Stand	Stand	Stand	Stand	Stand

Soft Hands

YOUR HAND	2	3	4	5	6	7	8	9	10	A
A-2	Hit	Hit	Hit	Double Down	Double Down	Hit	Hit	Hit	Hit	Hit
A-3	Hit	Hit	Hit	Double Down	Double Down	Hit	Hit	Hit	Hit	Hit
A-4	Hit	Hit	Double Down	Double Down	Double Down	Hit	Hit	Hit	Hit	Hit
A-5	Hit	Hit	Double Down	Double Down	Double Down	Hit	Hit	Hit	Hit	Hit
A-6	Hit	Hit	Double Down	Double Down	Double Down	Stand	Hit	Hit	Hit	Hit
A-7	Hit	Hit	Double Down	Double Down	Double Down	Stand	Stand	Hit	Hit	Hit
A-8	Stand	Stand	Stand	Stand	Stand	Stand	Stand	Stand	Stand	Stand
A-9	Stand	Stand	Stand	Stand	Stand	Stand	Stand	Stand	Stand	Stand
A-10 (BJ)	Stand	Stand	Stand	Stand	Stand	Stand	Stand	Stand	Stand	Stand

Pair Hands

YOUR HAND	2	3	4	5	6	7	8	9	10	A
A+A	Split	Split	Split	Split	Split	Split	Split	Split	Split	Split
2+2	Hit	Hit	Split	Split	Split	Hit	Hit	Hit	Hit	Hit
3+3	Hit	Split	Split	Split	Split	Hit	Hit	Hit	Hit	Hit
4+4	Hit	Hit	Hit	Hit	Hit	Hit	Hit	Hit	Hit	Hit
5+5	Double Down	Double Down	Double Down	Double Down	Double Down	Double Down	Double Down	Double Down	Hit	Hit
6+6	Split	Split	Split	Split	Split	Hit	Hit	Hit	Hit	Hit
7+7	Split	Split	Split	Split	Split	Split	Hit	Hit	Hit	Hit
8+8	Split	Split	Split	Split	Split	Split	Split	Split	Hit	Hit
9+9	Split	Split	Split	Split	Split	Split	Stand	Stand	Stand	Stand
10+10	Stand	Stand	Stand	Stand	Stand	Stand	Stand	Stand	Stand	Stand

* The decision to double-down on a total of 9 against a dealer's upcard of 7 is marginal. The generally accepted advice is to hit. However, I think that the difference between the decision to hit or double-down is statistically insignificant, and therefore I defer to the policy of getting more money into action in situations that are at least realistically opportune. This position will no doubt be disputed, but it is my opinion that the disputes are merely hairsplitting, and that the correct decision is to double-down, especially given the fact that the remainder of the strategy allows for the cumulative effect of winning, rather than focusing only on individual events, as is the case with most other recommendations in situations similar to this. To my mind, any time I can get more money into action in a situation where the likely outcome can result in twice the winner, then I think it's a good move. Of course, this applies only to games where the dealer must stand on all 17. In games where the dealer must hit soft 17, the decision is easily to only hit, and not double-down.

applicable to any blackjack game anywhere (based on the majority of rules as used in the casinos in the United States).

Once you learn this chart, you will know exactly what to do in any circumstance of any hand in blackjack that you will ever be dealt. If you do this consistently, you will gain a virtually level game with the casino. Later, if you really want to become a serious student of blackjack, and you really do want to invest the years it will take to master the game, and you really want to eke out that extra 0.5 percent advantage, or perhaps even a 1 to 2 percent advantage over the house, you can learn some of the derivatives that are available for Basic Strategy play, and that I list later in this book. I will also show you how you can apply the knowledge and skills gained from learning this MBS chart and begin to exploit the advantages you will now have to make yourself a winner at blackjack.

In this chart, you will see three headings:

1. Your Hand
2. Dealer's Upcard
3. Your Decision

The column titled "Your Hand" signifies the numeric total of any number of cards, beginning with any two-card hand total. What this number is depends on the cards you are dealt. Each hand of blackjack will begin with you receiving two cards. These two cards are your starting total. Whatever total these two cards have when added together is the number that corresponds to the number in the column "Your Hand." For example, if your first two cards are a 2 and a 4, your total is 6. Therefore, look at the chart to find the total of 6 under the heading "Your Hand." Then look to the right of that number under the heading "Dealer's Upcard." Then look to where the row of "Your Hand" intersects with the column of the "Dealer's Upcard." This is Your Decision and tells you what to do. In our example, your decision for a first two-card total of 6 is, of course, to hit. Let's say that you hit and receive a 9. Now your hand consists of the three cards: a 2 and a 4 and the 9, for a total of 15. So now you will look in the column "Your Hand," find the row that says "Hard 15," then move to the column titled "Dealer's Upcard," and see where they intersect—this will then tell you what to do. And so on for any total of any number of cards, beginning with the two cards you are initially dealt. Do remember, however, that the decisions stipulating "Double-down" apply only to the first two-card hand. Therefore, if you are initially dealt, as in our example above, a 2 and a 4 for a total of 6, and then you hit and draw a 4 for a three-card total of 10, you are no longer permitted to double-down. In that case, you will simply treat your three-card hand as a total of 10 and will hit it instead.

This is the correct way to play in the traditional game of blackjack. Some casinos may be offering a game called "blackjack," but instead it is a gimmick. In these games, you may be able to double-down on more than just the first two cards. If this is the case, you are probably not getting the best blackjack game you can, and therefore the majority of the decisions concerning this blackjack chart, or any other chart, may not apply. If you are savvy enough to be able to judge for yourself what kind of a game you are getting, even if the casino does offer this gimmick, you may be able to continue to apply the MBS; however, I would caution you against playing any games of this nature since they are, mostly, not to your advantage even though they may seem appealing.

In all of the traditional games of blackjack, the simplest rule to remember is that if at any time your hand reaches a total where it would normally be a candidate for a double-down situation, *and you already have more than just the first two cards you have been dealt*, you *cannot* double-down. The option is, therefore, in all such cases, to hit, and then consider the total value of the hand after receiving that hit and act according to what that total dictates in the MBS chart.

You will also notice that we begin with the hand value of 5. This is because the hand value of 2 can be achieved only when you are dealt two Aces, which would then be counted as 1 each, for the total value of 2. Since this is a pair, we will treat this in the section called "Pairs," under the column titled "Your Hand." The hand total of 3 can be achieved only with the two-card combination of any Ace with the number 2-value card. This is called a "soft 13," meaning you can count this hand as either 3 or as 13. Hands with an Ace are called "soft" hands, and are therefore shown in the section called "Soft Hands," under the column "Your Hand." The hand total of 4 can be achieved two ways: either as a pair of 2s, in which case this hand is shown in the section called "Pairs" under the heading "Your Hand," or as the combination of any Ace with any 3-value card, in which case this is called a "soft 14," meaning that you can count this two-card hand as either a 4 or as a 14, and this hand is therefore shown in the section "Soft Hands."

If any of these examples or explanations seem a little simplistic to some of you, please forgive me for doing it in this way, but I want to be absolutely certain that all my readers are able to understand these hands, and this chart, so that we can all gain the correct benefits from learning it.

Well, there it is. That is all you will need in 99 percent of the blackjack situations you will encounter. Once you know this, you will be a winner more often than before, and certainly better prepared for casino blackjack than most of the other players in the casino with you. Practice this at home, by dealing cards to yourself and then comparing your decisions against the dealer's upcard. It won't take long, but once you "get it," you will most likely never forget it, and it will become second nature to you. Later in this book we will discuss the "Big Secret," which is a method of play that I have developed that will allow you to use this MBS chart knowledge along with a method of betting designed to increase your win potential.

MBS Decisions Step by Step

Now that you have seen Figure 1, we will tackle each and every decision by itself and the reasons behind it. These two sections—the chart in Figure 1, and this step-by-step analysis of each decision—will be your keys to continued expertise in blackjack. Any time you think you are falling short in your abilities to accurately make the required decisions, you can always come back to this chart and this chapter and regain your information and proficiency.

I will now break the MBS chart down action by action and offer my comments on why this is the appropriate decision under that specific circumstance.

WEAK HANDS

These are hands that do not contain an Ace as part of the first two cards dealt, are not composed of a pair, and are not generally a candidate for a double-down situation. Although after you take action on these hands they may, in fact, contain an Ace thereafter, the totals so achieved will mostly fall under the category of "soft hands," discussed later. Or, if you wind up with a hand of 12 through 16 after hitting these hands, those totals are then considered "hard hands," which are discussed in their own section, below.

YOUR HAND	DEALER'S UPCARD	YOUR DECISION
5	2, 3, 4, 5, 6, 7, 8, 9, 10, Ace	Hit

When your card total is 5, there is no risk to you to hit this hand, and no value to try to double-down on it. It is not a good hand, and needs at least two more cards to improve to anything worthwhile. Basically, there is nothing you can do with this other than try to improve it. After you hit this hand, add the next card total to it and see what you have. Then look at the chart for that total, and do what is indicated. Only under very specialized circumstances would you ever try to do anything with this hand other than to hit, so don't even think about that. Just remember that hitting this hand cannot break you, so go and do it and then face the decision based on what the other card, or cards, will be.

YOUR HAND	DEALER'S UPCARD	YOUR DECISION
6	2, 3, 4, 5, 6, 7, 8, 9, 10, Ace	Hit
7	2, 3, 4, 5, 6, 7, 8, 9, 10, Ace	Hit
8	2, 3, 4, 5, 6, 7, 8, 9, 10, Ace	Hit

These three hands are about as good as the 5 hand, above, and therefore the comments to that hand also apply here. Only under very special circumstances would you deviate from this and only for the two-card hand of 8. This would work for you only if you are a knowledgeable player, an expert, or possibly a card-counter, and are able to know that the likelihood of the next card out is a 10-value card, or an Ace, and only against the dealer's upcard of either a 5 or a 6. Then, and only then, would you consider to double-down on that 8, but even then I would shudder to try this because the percentage gain is just too small to justify the risk. Nevertheless, there are some circumstances where this may be a good play, but for right now and for the best of the most common results, I definitely suggest that you try to play simply and in accordance with the MBS, and not try any of these "fancy" moves no matter how appealing they may seem, or whatever else you may have read about this play.

YOUR HAND	DEALER'S UPCARD	YOUR DECISION
9	2, 3	Hit

If you have a two-card total of 9 against the dealer's 2 or 3, your safest choice is to hit. If you draw a 10-value card, then you have 19, and that is a fairly good hand in blackjack. If you draw anything less than a 10, you will protect your investment by not increasing your bet against cards that the dealer can improve. Even if the dealer has a 10 hiding under that exposed 2 or 3, there are many cards that he can draw that will improve his hand. To any 12 he can draw either a 9, 8, 7, 6, or 5 to have a standing hand, any one of which can beat you unless you draw better. To a 13, he can draw 4, 5, 6, 7, or 8 and wind up with a standing hand. So it's not worth the added risk of extra money to double-down against the dealer's 2 or 3, even though some books may recommend that you do so. To my mind, these are not the best of the potential dealer's "bad" cards. However, you can't hurt your hand by hitting, you can only improve, and therefore the action is obvious. Once you draw the next card, then you will have a total higher than 9, and it is at this point that you will need to refer to the MBS chart for the decision covering that total.

YOUR HAND	DEALER'S UPCARD	YOUR DECISION
9	4, 5, 6, 7	**Double-down**

Your circumstances improve dramatically when you have a two-card total of 9 and the dealer's upcard is either a 4, 5, 6, or 7. Now it is safer to increase your bet, and it is one of the several advantageous positions where you can double-down and gain a chance to win more money. Remember that the dealer cannot double-down, since he plays mechanically, only for the house and only in accordance with the house rules. Therefore, as a player, it is by far to your advantage to exploit situations where the dealer's cards indicate a potential weakness, because it is in these situations that you can make the most money. Any time a dealer shows the upcard of 4, 5, or 6, this is the time to go for the gusto and try to get as much money in action as you can, especially in double-down—or split—situations, such as shown here.

In the case of the 9 hand, the only contentious issue may be the dealer's upcard of 7. This could be troublesome, because if the dealer must stand on all 17s, and he does have a 10-value card under that upcard of 7, then you will need to draw at least an 8 to your 9 to tie. Therefore, the double-down recommendation for the 9 hand against the dealer's upcard of a 7 is marginal, as I mentioned earlier. Although the differences in overall statistics are insignificant, it could look as if you were getting hurt if you doubled down and did not draw a better hand than the dealer. In these situations, against the dealer's upcard of 7, you are doubling-down on the 9 because you are wagering on the success of the following two possibilities:

1. That you draw a card that will make your hand better than the dealer's.

2. That regardless of what card you draw, the dealer's hand will require him to draw more cards and subsequently break him, or cause him to have to settle for a hand total lower than yours.

These two circumstances apply equally well to any double-down situation. It is for these reasons that you are making that extra wager, plus, of course, the main reason, which is to make as much profit as possible in situations where the dealer shows a possible weak hand, with a significant statistical probability that indeed this will be so.

YOUR HAND	DEALER'S UPCARD	YOUR DECISION
9	8, 9, 10, Ace	**Hit**

Your 9 hand against any of these dealer power cards is in trouble. The best you can make from a single-card-draw is a 19, if you draw a 10-value card, or a 20 if you are lucky and catch the Ace. If you don't catch that Ace, and if the dealer has a 10-value card under his upcard, you will win with his 18 (his upcard of 8 plus his down card of 10), push with his 19, and lose to everything else. Consequently, these are situations where you just hope for the best and try to remember that playing with this strategy is designed to make you a winner *overall*, and that you won't always win every hand even if you make the correct decisions. Sometimes the dealer will win. Your goal is to play your hands the best that you can in accordance with the MBS, and make as much money in your advantageous positions as possible, while limiting your losses in situations such as this, where you have a marginal hand at best to start with, and the dealer shows power cards.

YOUR HAND	DEALER'S UPCARD	YOUR DECISION
10	2, 3, 4, 5, 6, 7, 8, 9	Double-down

This is the first of the most powerful two-card drawing hands you can get in the game of blackjack. This is a power hand for you, because if you get a two-card total of 10 against any of these dealer's upcards, then you are in the ideal position to make the most money. Only the 11 hand and, naturally, any blackjack are better ways for you to make the most money with the least potential risk. In this situation you want to double-down because here you can get more money in play with one of the best possibilities to make a winning hand. As a player, you have the option to double-down, and this gives you the opportunity to make twice as much money on this one hand in these favorable situations. The dealer can't double-down in favorable situations such as these, and it is for that reason that the players can gain a positive expectation in blackjack, even when facing a house edge of a few tenths of a percent.

A dealer's upcard of 2 through 9 is a weak hand against your two-card 10 and your double-down bet. If the dealer has a 2, 3, 4, 5, or 6 showing and a 10-value card in the hole, then he will have a stiff and must draw more cards. This gives you the chance of winning either with the dealer busting, or with the dealer having to stand on a hand whose total will very often be lower than yours. If you double-down on your two-card total of 10, and draw a 10-value card, then you will have a total of 20, which can be beaten only by the dealer's total of 21. Since the dealer cannot possibly have a blackjack (an Ace plus a 10), because his upcard is in the sequence shown above, then the only way he can beat your hand is to draw more cards and make perfect hits.

Further, you may in fact draw an Ace to your 10, and this will give you a powerful 21. You simply are the favorite all around. In fact, by doubling-down on your two-card 10 you will win about 73 percent of the time overall. If the dealer's upcard is 7, 8, or 9, you still are in the power position, because if you draw the 10 or the Ace on your double-down

10, then the dealer can't beat you. In fact, you can draw any one of five cards that will give you either the better hand or, at the very least, a very respectable standing hand. Therefore, it is always to your advantage to use your option and double-down on this hand against this set of dealer's upcards.

YOUR HAND	DEALER'S UPCARD	YOUR DECISION
10	10, Ace	Hit

A dealer's upcard of any 10 or any Ace is a red flag. No matter how much you like your two-card hand of 10, when the dealer shows an upcard of either of these two cards, you should expect the worst. At best, you can tie the dealer in most circumstances, and beat him only very rarely. If the dealer's upcard is any 10, and he has a 10 in the hole, then the best you can hope for is to draw an Ace to win or a 10 to tie, or to draw multiple cards to reach either the 21 or the 20 total. Any other cards will be a losing hand for you. What if you draw a 9? You have 19, but the dealer shows he can have a 20. What do you do? Well, you can't hit a hard 19, unless you know the next card out, which means you either know something you shouldn't, know something because you are a very skilled player (or perhaps a card-counter), possess foresight, or are really, *really* lucky. Under all normal circumstances, whenever the dealer shows a 10 or an Ace against your two-card 10, it's time to hit and hope for the best. Most of the time you will lose. Sometimes, when the dealer has a stiff card under the 10 or Ace, you may win. Overall, this is a bad hand against any of these dealer's upcards.

Also, often the dealer will in fact have a blackjack. In most casinos, when the dealer shows either a 10 or an Ace as his upcard, the house rules dictate that the dealer must check to see if he has a blackjack hand. This is done by the dealer, either by him peeking at the hole card, or, which is more common these days, by him sliding the down card to a card-reader mounted on the table in front of him. This scanner then lights up if the card is one of the others needed to make the blackjack hand. If this happens, the hand is over and the house wins, and you lose. Doesn't matter what you have, or could have had, it's done, dead, over.

Therefore, your best option is to hit this hand against any of these dealer's upcards, and hope to gain a winner despite the odds against you. Your hand is still not a bad hand, overall, but will now require you to draw cards, and perhaps more cards, to improve. Even the improvement may not be enough. So the correct play here is to risk only the original bet, and not try to hammer the house by doubling-down against the dealer's power cards. It's a safer play to hit and try to make as decent a hand as possible, and, basically, to forgo this bet and get ready for the next one. If you're lucky, and you win or push, count this as a blessing and move on. Don't linger over either the success or the failure of your play on this hand against these dealer's cards. It happens. Whatever the outcome, remember that you played the hand as best it can be played, and get ready for another. That will save you a lot of aggravation and self-reproach.

YOUR HAND	DEALER'S UPCARD	YOUR DECISION
11	2, 3, 4, 5, 6, 7, 8, 9	Double-down

Ahh, the sweet 11 hand! All blackjack players should be excited when they receive a first two-card total of 11. This is the second of the two best double-down hands; the other is the 10 hand discussed above. This 11 hand is the better of the two. Here, with the draw of only one more card, you can reach the perfect total of 21. By having an 11 as your first two cards, you are in the power position. If you draw any 10-value card to this total, you will have an automatic winner most of the time. The only way you can lose on a hand of 21, made with a one-card-draw to this two-card hand, is if the dealer has a blackjack. This can happen only against the dealer's upcards of either any 10 or the Ace. More on these two hands immediately below.

In the case of the dealer's upcards of 2, 3, 4, 5, 6, 7, 8, or 9, you are in the best position to win a larger amount of money with greater win expectations and diminished risk. In fact, you will be a winner about 78 percent of the time when your first two cards are a total of 11, and therefore by doubling-down on this hand against any of these dealer's upcards you are adding extra value to your overall wins. A little lower percentage for some cases, depending on the various house rules.

Now you are in the best position in which you can be to exploit the dealer's weakness, and you have the choice to do something that the dealer can't—increase your bet. The dealer cannot increase his "bet" because he plays for the casino and does not have a bet to make. Plus, he has to play his hand the same way every time, and therefore must draw if his running total is anything less than 17. So, by doubling-down on your bet, you will now put more of your money into action under the most favorable circumstances found in the game of blackjack, and with the best and highest possible win expectation for these situations. The truth is that you won't win all the time, because sometimes even with the best odds, the reality will go against you. You will, however, win about three times out of four when you do this, and these are the best situations as far as I'm concerned.

YOUR HAND	DEALER'S UPCARD	YOUR DECISION
11	10	**Double-down**

Here we will discuss the dealer's upcard of 10, and below the Ace. There is still some debate among blackjack players and writers about the correct method of handling the player's two-card total of 11 against the dealer's upcard of 10. Should we double-down, or should we hit? If the dealer's hole card is a 10-value card, and we draw any 10, then we win. If we draw a 9, we push (we have 20). If we draw anything else, we lose. What if the dealer's hole card is not a 10? Well, if we draw a 10, a 9, or an 8, our totals are either 21, 20, or 19, which are three of the four best hands in blackjack (the blackjack 21 hand, the natural, is the best overall).

Of course, if the dealer does indeed have a blackjack, in the event that his hole card is an Ace, then our decision is moot. In this case, we would never get to the decision of whether or not to double-down on this hand, because in all modern casinos the dealer will check the hole card for a possible Ace *before* any other action takes place. Consequently, we know that if we get to the point where we get a decision to make, then the dealer absolutely does *not* have a blackjack. Now we can be safe in knowing that the best possible hand he can have is a total of 20, with his 10 showing and the other 10 in the hole. Plus, depending on the number of decks against which we are playing, we can reasonably assume the relative odds of whether or not he has a better hand than we can make. It is in these circumstances where professional or very experienced players, and perhaps even card-counters, can find most of their edge. More on this later.

For now, we are aware that the dealer does not have a blackjack. So, now that we are faced with this decision against the dealer's upcard of 10, a definite power card for the dealer, what do we do? Some experts advise us to hit this hand, rather than double-down. The reasoning is that there are too many opportunities for us to draw a bad card, and conversely an equal number of opportunities for the dealer to make a better hand. It is true that by being limited to the draw of only one more card on any double-down situation, we are faced with the possibility of being stuck with a very bad hand—but the same goes for the dealer. In our case, we can choose to stand on any cards, even stiffs, while the dealer must hit anything less than 17. For these reasons the odds tend to equate in overall generalities.

Also part of these discussions is the money aspect. Simply put, is it worth the risk of doubling the bet against a dealer's power card? If you are an experienced player, or perhaps a card-counter, and you know with at least some reasonable accuracy that the rest of the deck is rich in 10s, then maybe the risk isn't as high, or at least your perception of that risk may not be that high—but even that is not an exact science, as we will find out in later chapters. Generally speaking, the debate over this hand is about 50-50. Statistically, you can expect to win about half the time and the dealer will win the other half. Actually, your odds of winning are just a little bit better, but it is basically a statistical dead heat, at least when considering the real world of the actual casino game instead of a theoretical model.

As I mentioned in the Preface, the purpose of this book is not only to shed light upon the truth of the real game in the actual casino, but also to find situations for making powerful profits from blackjack. This is one such situation where the "profit" part comes in. By doubling-down on this hand, when you win you will win twice as much in a situation that is generally favorable to this kind of play against this dealer's card. In those situations in which you lose, you will lose less than half the time in overall financial losses, because part of your losses will be when the dealer does in fact have a natural blackjack. Therefore, here you will lose only the original bet and will never place the double-down bet in action because you never get to that point in the process of that hand. Consequently, you will wind up with more money won, overall, by doubling-down on this hand against the dealer's upcard. Yes, the overall profit is small, but it is better than to wind up with an overall loss, which is what you will suffer if you always only hit this hand. Plus, when you wind up in a situation of "streaks" where the dealer is "cold," you will be far better off to always play this hand as a double-down situation. When you do run up against such an unlucky dealer, you will never even think twice about what to do with this hand and will thus make the best of the potential profits that this hand allows you to make. For these reasons, I recommend that this hand always be treated as a double-down situation against the dealer's upcard of 10.

YOUR HAND	DEALER'S UPCARD	YOUR DECISION
11	Ace	Hit

This part of the decision is much easier. If the dealer shows an Ace, hit this hand. Don't risk your money against a hand with which the dealer can make a whole lot of better hands. If he has a blackjack, for which he will check immediately, then you have lost already and don't have to sweat the decision. It happens. Take the loss and move on to the next hand. There'll be plenty of other chances for you to catch the dealer with worse cards than his Ace. If he doesn't have a blackjack, then hit the hand. You can't bust on the first hit, so you risk nothing. What if you do hit that magic 10? Well, it may not win. It may only push—and any other cards you may draw can indeed lose. What if the dealer has a 3 in the hole? Now he has an Ace and a 3 for a total of either 4 or 14. In this case, the dealer will draw more cards. What if he draws an 8? Well, a hard 14 would have busted him—but, since he has that Ace, now he can count that original two-card hand of that Ace and that 3 as a 4 and add the 8 and now he has a total of 12. Still not a good hand, but he must draw another card. What if the next card is a 4? Well, now the dealer has a stiff hand of hard 16, but since the rules say that he must hit anything less than 17, he now has to draw yet another card. What if the next card he draws is a 5? Well, now he has made 21. Your hit of 10 on your two-card total of 11 has gone nowhere. You push. What if you had a 20, a 19, or anything less than 21 but more than 17? Well, now you lose. Therefore, these are the situations where you simply grit your teeth, hit the hand, and hope for the best. If you win, great. Be happy. If you push, likewise be happy. If you lose, take a deep breath, realize you lost only the original bet and not a double-down bet, be grateful for your knowledge of the game, and move on to the next hand. You will retain your sanity a whole lot longer in this way, as well as keep more of your money.

For these reasons, the dealer's upcard of any Ace, regardless of the times he actually does have a blackjack, is a powerful card. Many times the dealer will make a series of hits just like the ones I described, and this will lead him to stand on the best hand, or at least on a tied hand; therefore, to double-down on your two-card hand of 11 against the dealer's upcard of any Ace is not to your advantage. Sometimes you will get lucky. Other times you won't. Overall, don't push more of your money into risky situations against the dealer's all-time power card of any Ace. Save it for a more advantageous situation later in the session. There is no need to try to win everything on every hand. This is not the time to feel adventurous. Rather, be practical. Realize that in these situations, it is the dealer, and not you, who has the best chance to make a good hand. Since you can't lose by taking a hit, take a hit—but don't risk a double-down investment. If you draw anything other than a 10 to your two-card 11, check the MBS chart for the decision on how to play that total. Do so, and then see what the outcome turns out to be. In the final analysis, *expect* to lose any hand you may have against the dealer's Ace, and so if you don't lose, when you push or win, take that as a bonus and move on to the next hand. There will be plenty of other hands far better for your added bet value.

HARD HANDS

"Hard" hands are the series of hand totals of 12 through 16, which are generally considered the worst hands in blackjack. They are considered the worst hands because any two-card total of these values (12 through 16) can be busted with the draw of just one card (any 10-value card). This means that these hands are dangerous for the player, and as a result are mostly losing hands. However, this is not so all the time. Even these hands can win, and to know what to do with them is the subject of this section.

Also, it is important to remember that a hard hand can be made up of more than just the first two cards dealt. Any time you are dealt hands such as in the section immediately above (a 5 and a 2, for example), which you must hit, you can draw a card that will then make your hand into a hard hand (such as drawing a 6 to the above example, for instance, in which case your total is now a hard 13). Whenever you have any number of cards whose totals are 12 through 16 that do *not* contain an Ace, then you have a hard hand. The following describes what to do with them.

YOUR HAND	DEALER'S UPCARD	YOUR DECISION
Hard 12	2, 3, 4, 5, 6	Stand

This is the first of the series of "stiffs." In many books you will find discussions of what to do with this hand, particularly against the dealer's upcard of 2 or 3. In some situations, you will find recommendations to hit this hand against the dealer's upcard of 2, and also against the dealer's upcard of 3. To my mind, any stiff is a bad hand, and therefore, against any of these dealer's upcards, I'd rather place the burden of the act of hitting *on the dealer*. If the dealer shows any of these upcards, and you have a total of 12, then you are stuck. Any 10-value card will break you. Any card other than a 9 may not give you the winning hand. My recommendation is, consequently, simple: Stand. Let the dealer take the hits. Many times the dealer will bust, giving you a winner that you might not have been able to achieve even with a series of non-breaking hits to your stiff 12. In this case a wait-and-see attitude is far more profitable, overall.

Any time you have a stiff, expect to lose. It happens. It's part of the game. You won't lose all the time, but why make the effort to make yourself into a loser by taking the action away from the dealer, and frustrating yourself in the process? Sit back and see what happens. If you lose, well, you expected it. If you win, it's a bonus. Thank yourself for not doing more than you had to, and move on to the next hand. This way you will be much calmer at the table, have much more success at the game, and even be able to enjoy it more. My simple motto is: Don't force it. In these situations if it's there for you, it will be there without your pushing yourself into any action. Let it be, wait and see, and then go on.

YOUR HAND	DEALER'S UPCARD	YOUR DECISION
Hard 12	7, 8, 9, 10, Ace	Hit

The difference between holding a hard 12 against the dealer's upcard of 2, 3, 4, 5, or 6 and his upcard of 7, 8, 9, 10, or Ace is profound. While against the 2, 3, 4, 5, or 6 you can let the dealer take the onus of action and sit back and wait to see what happens, which gives you a small advantage in some situations, now the situation is completely reversed. Here you are sitting with a stiff against the dealer's upcard of 7, 8, 9, 10, or Ace and you've got to do something about it. If the dealer has a 10-value card in the hole, then with any one of these upcards he has a standing hand, and this means that your 12 hand has already lost. So, you *must* hit it, because you have to assume that you have already lost. Your only hope of coming away with anything other than an automatic loss (most of the time) is to hit your hard 12 and hope to draw something that will make your hand better than the dealer's standing hand, or at least improve your hand to something that may have some kind of a chance of surviving the dealer's draw, if he must draw.

At the very best, in a situation with your hard 12 against any of these dealer's upcards, you should already admit to yourself that your hand will most likely lose, and dismiss it as one of those situations where you can do very little about the ultimate outcome. So, if you are lucky and you draw a hand that wins, or wind up standing on a higher hard hand and the dealer busts, consider that a bonus and move on to the next hand. In the event that you actually do lose, don't give it too much thought. Just remember that you played the hand correctly, and that, overall, playing hands of this kind in this way will make you a winner.

YOUR HAND	DEALER'S UPCARD	YOUR DECISION
Hard 13	2, 3, 4, 5, 6	Stand
Hard 13	7, 8, 9, 10, Ace	Hit
Hard 14	2, 3, 4, 5, 6	Stand
Hard 14	7, 8, 9, 10, Ace	Hit
Hard 15	2, 3, 4, 5, 6	Stand
Hard 15	7, 8, 9, 10, Ace	Hit
Hard 16	2, 3, 4, 5, 6	Stand
Hard 16	7, 8, 9, 10, Ace	Hit

Any of these hands, which are the series of stiffs, you can consider the same as the 12 hand described immediately above. All the comments for the hard 12 also apply to all these other hard-hand totals. These are simply hands that can't be helped very much. If you stand on them and never hit, you will lose about 77 percent of the time. If you hit against any of these dealer's upcards as shown, you will lose about 70 percent of the time (give or take a percentage point depending on the game, decks, and house rules at the place you are playing), which means that by hitting these hands in the designated situations, you will lose about 7 percent *fewer* times, and that's why these hands are indicated for a hit.

YOUR HAND	DEALER'S UPCARD	YOUR DECISION
Hard 17	**2, 3, 4, 5, 6, 7, 8, 9, 10, Ace**	**Stand**

Well, there you go—now you've done it. You've got yourself a hard 17 and no place to go with it. What do you do? You can't hit it. Any card higher than a 4 will bust you. So you must stand—but this is the worst standing hand in blackjack. The hard 16 is the worst hand overall, but at least you've got a decision to make with that one—hit it. With a hard 17, well, you are stuck with it and that's about all that there is to say. If the dealer has an upcard of 2 through 6, for possible "stiff" hard totals of 12 through 16, you might have a chance. You might push the hand if the dealer winds up with a draw to a 17, or you might win if the dealer busts. Most of the time when you get a hard 17 you just close your eyes, stand, and hope for the best. If you're lucky, maybe you'll win a few times. Most of the time you won't, but it does happen.

If the dealer's upcard is a 7, hope that he has a 10 in the hole because then you have a push and you won't lose. This is about the only time when you have a standing hand that you are rooting for the dealer to actually have a 10 in the hole. Anything else, except an Ace, and he must hit. If he hits, you have a chance that he'll bust, but mostly he has the better chance of making a winning hand. If he has an Ace in the hole, he will stand on the soft 18, and your hard 17 is toast.

If the dealer has an 8, 9, 10, or Ace showing, chances are that you are already dead meat, and therefore you can do nothing more than to hope for the best. Now you hope that the dealer's hole card is *not* a 10, and *not* an Ace (except when he shows an Ace and does not have a 10 in the hole), because if the dealer has anything other than a 17 or better this means he will have to draw cards. As long as he must draw cards you still have a chance that he will bust and make your miserable 17 into a winner, or at least that he will have to settle for his 17 and then you will tie.

Basically, a hard 17 is a very bad hand to have against any dealer's upcard. There's just no way around it, and nothing that you can do can help you in any meaningful way. In some situations, you could surrender this hand (if surrender is available; more on this later), or even chance a hit if you are a skilled player, but even card-counters will not do this and certainly not very often. Any discussion of these actions with a hard 17 is simply splitting hairs. Just grin and bear it, knowing that you are making the right decision no matter what happens. There are plenty of other hands to consider, and many better opportunities will come about.

YOUR HAND	DEALER'S UPCARD	YOUR DECISION
Hard 18	2, 3, 4, 5, 6, 7, 8, 9, 10, Ace	Stand

A hard 18 is about as good as the hard 17. However, it is marginally better as a standing hand because only a near-perfect dealer's draw or hole card can beat you. Otherwise, treat it as you would the 17.

YOUR HAND	DEALER'S UPCARD	YOUR DECISION
Hard 19	2, 3, 4, 5, 6, 7, 8, 9, 10, Ace	Stand
Hard 20	2, 3, 4, 5, 6, 7, 8, 9, 10, Ace	Stand

Of the four best hands in blackjack—the hands most likely to win—these are two. The others are a total of 21 made through drawing more cards, and, of course, the blackjack, which is the 21 hand made on the first two cards only. Therefore, these are power cards for you, regardless of whether they were dealt to you as your first two cards, or you drew to these totals with hits on previously mediocre hands. Whenever you have these two totals—the 19 or the 20—*stand*. You are in a very favorable position to win against the dealer's cards of 2 through 8 for your 19 hand, and dealer's cards 2 through 9 on your 20 hand. Against the dealer's cards of 10 and Ace, your 19 total is marginally worse off than your 20 total, but overall the differences in percentages are too insignificant to make any difference in the real world. Only math geeks may get excited about these figures, but for the rest of us it's practically a wash, so we should be happy with what we have achieved.

Under no normal circumstances is either of these hands a candidate for a hit, or a double-down. These are "pat" hands, meaning two of the best standing hands in blackjack, and therefore to do anything else is to incur the wrath of the very large person next to you who will not take kindly to your silly plays if you hit or double-down on these hands. (The only time you may consider hitting or doubling-down on these hands may be in *tournament* blackjack, when you are low on chips toward the end of the tournament and must make bold moves to improve your stack. These are *very rare* situations, however, and even then they are inadvisable. Since these are discussions for a different subject, I would hope that you will never ever consider hitting or doubling-down on these hands in the regular casino game of black-jack.)

YOUR HAND	DEALER'S UPCARD	YOUR DECISION
21	2, 3, 4, 5, 6, 7, 8, 9, 10, Ace	Stand

If you have this hand on your first two cards, this can only mean that you have received an Ace with a 10-value card, and this is, therefore, blackjack, the natural, the best hand you can ever get in this game. You win automatically on this hand if the dealer shows as his upcard any card 2 through 9. If he is showing a 10-value card, he will check to see if he has an Ace in the hole. If he does, your hand will push and not lose. If he does not have an Ace in the hole with a 10 showing, he will then immediately pay your hand accordingly (3:2).

If the dealer's upcard is an Ace, and you have a black-jack, then the dealer will always ask everyone in the game whether they wish to purchase "insurance." We will talk more about this later, but this is a very bad bet for the player. If you are holding a blackjack, and the dealer asks you for insurance because he is showing an Ace as his upcard, you may wish to consider asking for "even money," which is a verbal decision that tells the dealer that you wish to give up your 3:2 payoff and settle for an immediate even-money, or 1:1, payoff without risking a push in the event that the dealer does, in fact, have that 10-value card in the hole under his exposed Ace. After all, a blackjack hand is the best you can get, and your money-making opportunities are largely vested in the fact that the casinos pay you at 3:2 for this hand, so asking for even money, which is basically the purchase of insurance on this hand, is giving up one-third of your potential profit on this hand.

For example, if you bet $10, you would normally get a payoff of 3:2 on this hand (1.5:1), or $15 plus your $10 bet back, and therefore make a profit of $15. However, if you buy insurance, either by making the insurance wager or by asking for "even money," you will only get $10 profit, and are, therefore, giving up the extra $5, which is one-third of your potential profit on this hand. In most circumstances it is better to simply refuse the insurance and the option to ask for even money, because on those occasions when the dealer does *not* have a blackjack, you will be paid that extra money, and this will add up over time. In fact, this is the source of most of your winnings, so giving it up reduces your overall profitability. Also, remember that if you have a blackjack hand, and the dealer also turns over a blackjack hand, then you will *push*, and *not lose*. You are not risking your money by refusing to buy into the insurance scam and be talked into giving up the profits to which you would normally be entitled. Even though it may appear to you on some occasions that the dealer seems to have blackjack after blackjack against your blackjack hands, this is only an illusion. Even in short-term slices of the events you may experience in any session, or in any visit to the casino, being confident and standing on your blackjack hand with the full expectation of receiving the valued 3:2 payoff will prove the right decision. You literally have nothing to lose and everything to gain. Remember that and be confident that you are playing this hand in this situation perfectly, no matter what anyone else may say. The truth of this will show itself in the extra money you will win.

You can also make this favorable total of 21 by starting with a poor hand and drawing to this total. Let's say, for example, that your first two cards were a 3 and a 5, for a two-card total of 8. A lousy starting hand. So you look at the

MBS chart and see what it says for this hand. It says to hit, so you hit and get, say, a 7. Now you have a total of a hard 15. Now you look at the MBS chart under the hard 15 and find out what the decision is, which is to hit (assuming in this example that the dealer's upcard is either 7, 8, 9, 10, or Ace). So you hit this hard 15 and get the perfect 6, and now you have a total of 21, made by drawing cards. This is still as good a total as you can get.

If the dealer makes a total of 21 by also drawing more cards, then you push and do not lose. If the dealer checks the hole card and *does* have a blackjack, then you will never get to make any decisions because the hand ends there with a loss for everyone. If the dealer has anything else, you win, regardless of whether you drew cards to that magic 21, or had it dealt to you as a blackjack. Whenever you have a hand whose total is 21, you are in one of the most favorable positions you can possibly be in in this game. You are, therefore, an overwhelming favorite to win this hand, and will do so most of the time. Only in very rare circumstances will you push or lose. Overall, this is your bread-and-butter hand. Eat it up. It's mighty good!

SOFT HANDS

Now we are into soft hands. These are hands that contain an Ace along with any other card, other than any 10-value card. These soft hands may eventually contain any number of cards, and are always called soft hands as long as their combined total can be counted as less than 10 when counting the Ace as 1.

For example, if you have a three-card total of 16, made up of the first two cards of, say, an Ace and a 2 for an initial dealt hand of 3 or 13, and then draw a third card of, say, a 3 for a combined three-card total of 6 or 16, you would still call this three-card hand a soft 16, because you can still count that total as a 6 with the Ace counted as 1. Let's say that you now draw the fourth card and it is a 2, so now you have a total of 8 or 18. Depending on what the dealer's up-card may be, the MBS chart may suggest that you hit again; therefore you would consider the hand as an 8, now count-ing the Ace as 1. Here you may draw a fifth card without the fear of busting and hit, say, a 3. Now you can change the value of the hand, and count it as an 18, plus the 3, and therefore you now have a five-card total of the perfect 21. This was made possible because you were able to use all of the four cards up to that point and still be able to count your hand as a soft hand, thereby giving yourself added chances to draw better cards without the fear or risk of busting. Of course, you won't always draw perfect cards like this exam-ple, but you will make many of these, and similar such hands, when you have an Ace and any card, or cards, other than the 10. Therefore, all of these soft hands give you added opportunities to make winning hands, and in some situations are also candidates for a double-down opportu-nity.

YOUR HAND	DEALER'S UPCARD	YOUR DECISION
A,2	2, 3, 4	Hit
A,2	7, 8, 9, 10, Ace	Hit

A two-card hand of A,2 is not the best of the possible soft hands. It is either a 3 or 13, and neither is a good hand. There are too many possibilities that this hand may not turn into a good hand, and therefore this hand is not a good can-didate for a double-down, regardless of what the dealer's upcard may be. Remember that the only time a double-down opportunity can be considered is if either you can make a very good hand with just a one-card-draw, such as a double-down hand that, with the draw of one card, can make a 20 or 21; or in situations where the dealer's hand can break with the draw of just one card (such as in the situation shown below for the 5 and 6).

In this case, with your A,2 hand against any of these dealer's upcards, you can only hit and hope to make a decent standing hand. Whatever total you achieve after you have taken a hit, look at the MBS chart and it will provide you with the correct decision on what to do with the three-card total you now have. Proceed with the hand accordingly, and you can rest in the confidence that no matter what happens, you have played this hand correctly. The same applies to the dealer's upcards of 7, 8, 9, 10, and Ace.

YOUR HAND	DEALER'S UPCARD	YOUR DECISION
A,2	5, 6	Double-down

When you have any soft hand whose total is 18 or less, always double-down against the dealer's upcard of 5 or 6. These are indications of the two worst possible two-card hands for the dealer, either a hard 15 or a hard 16, and since the dealer must hit anything lower than a 17, these are the situations where the draw of only one more card can bust the dealer, thereby making you a winner no matter what you have. Therefore, in these situations, you want to get as much of your money into action as you can, because these are also the situations where you will make the most of your profits. You risk nothing by doing this because your hand cannot bust with the draw of any one card. Plus, you may draw a card from any number of possible cards that can make your hand into one of the power hands.

For example, to your two-card hand of A,2, against the dealer's upcard of either the 5 or the 6, you can double-down and draw, say, an 8, in which case you make the perfect 21 by counting your hand as 13 and drawing the 8 to make the hand of 21. You would *never* do this with a *hard* 13 against the dealer's 5 or 6, because then your chances of breaking would defeat the purpose of wagering the extra money. The risks of doubling-down on a hard 13 are simply too high. But with a *soft* 13, as in this example, you cannot break no matter what card you draw, and that's why this is such a good opportunity for you to make the most of your bets. This also applies to all the soft hands whose values are 18 or less, against these two dealer's upcards.

YOUR HAND	DEALER'S UPCARD	YOUR DECISION
A,3	2, 3, 4	Hit
A,3	7, 8, 9, 10, Ace	Hit

As in the above comments for the A,2 hand against these dealer's upcards, the situation is the same. Hit with no fear of breaking, and then do what the MBS chart recommends for the hand total you achieve.

YOUR HAND	DEALER'S UPCARD	YOUR DECISION
A,3	5, 6	Double-down

This is the same situation as in the comments for the A,2 hand, against the dealer's upcard of 5 or 6. Treat the strategy accordingly.

YOUR HAND	DEALER'S UPCARD	YOUR DECISION
A,4	2, 3	Hit
A,4	7, 8, 9, 10, Ace	Hit

The A,4 hand against any of these dealer's upcards can be played in the same manner as the A,2 hand. You will notice, however, that the 4, 5, and 6 hands are not included in this part of the MBS chart. This is because the A,4 hand also becomes a better candidate for a double-down opportunity against the dealer's upcard of 4, in addition to the 5 and 6. More on this immediately below.

YOUR HAND	DEALER'S UPCARD	YOUR DECISION
A,4	4, 5, 6	Double-down

Now we have entered the area of profitable situations. The A,4 hand against the dealer's upcard of 4, 5, or 6 is one of the better candidates for a double-down situation, for reasons already explained above. Any time you have a chance to gain a bigger win without the risk of busting with the draw of one card, and with the dealer showing one of the weak upcards, that's the time when you should, and must, go for the most wins you can get. By increasing your bet in these situations, you will start adding money to your wins. Although you won't win every time, overall each time you do win, you will gain more money for that hand, and therefore over the session, or visit, your wins will be greater by doubling-down in these situations. These comments also apply to the following soft hands against the dealer's upcard of 4, 5, or 6:

YOUR HAND	DEALER'S UPCARD	YOUR DECISION
A,5	4, 5, 6	Double-down
A,6	4, 5, 6	Double-down
A,7	4, 5, 6	Double-down

All of these hands give you the best chances to make the most money out of what otherwise would be mediocre hands. This is so largely because you cannot break with the draw of that one extra card to your double-down, and also because you likewise have a chance to improve the hand to beat the dealer's final total. What's most important, however, is that you are also a favorite to win because the dealer is showing a potentially weak hand, with a significant chance of breaking, thus giving you an automatic win no matter what your final total may be.

YOUR HAND	DEALER'S UPCARD	YOUR DECISION
A,5	2, 3	Hit
A,5	7, 8, 9, 10, Ace	Hit

An A,5 is a soft 16, and here you have only a marginally better shot at improving this hand than you would with a hard 16. Yes, there are many opportunities for you to draw a whole series of cards to make something out of this, but the point is that more often than not you will be forced to settle for a total that will not be good enough. The best you can do here is not risk any more money, and not double-down against any of these dealer's upcards. Hit the hand instead, as many times as you can in accordance with the MBS for whatever running total you may achieve as you continue to hit, and then see what happens and hope for the best. Sometimes you will win, other times you won't. It's the best of a mostly bad situation. Relax in the knowledge that no matter what happens, you have played this hand correctly against any of these dealer's upcards.

YOUR HAND	DEALER'S UPCARD	YOUR DECISION
A,6	2, 3	Hit
A,6	8, 9, 10, Ace	Hit

The A,6 for a two-card total of soft 17 is about as good (or bad, if you will) as the above situation for the A,5. Really, any 17 is not a good hand. If this was a hard 17, then you would have no choice but to stand. However, when you have a soft 17, you can't hurt what is largely a bad hand to begin with. So your hope is to improve the hand. Since you cannot bust by the draw of any single additional card, hit this hand against any of these dealer's upcards. Whatever card you get, consider that total, then check the MBS chart and this will tell you what to do with the hand thereafter. Treat the hand you get accordingly and see what happens. If you need to draw more cards, according to whatever total you have achieved and after you have checked that total against the MBS chart, then do so. Once you settle on a hand, then that's the best you can get. Let the rest of the reality fall where it may. Basically, what you are doing here is making the best of a bad situation. By doing this you will make yourself a winner more often than you would otherwise.

YOUR HAND	DEALER'S UPCARD	YOUR DECISION
A,6	7	Stand

The only time you would stand on a soft 17 is against the dealer's upcard of 7. This is because in most casinos the dealer must stand on all 17s, and therefore here you are playing for the non-loss, namely the push, the tie. Here your play is not to lose, as opposed to trying to win.

In some casinos, the dealer will be required to hit soft 17. Only in these casinos would you treat this hand as if it were the soft-17 hands described immediately above. This is the only variance you should keep in your mind, and I mention it only because this is a situation that you will find most often in the casinos you will visit. Only here would you hit this hand against the dealer's upcard of 7—in the casinos where the dealer must *hit* soft 17—and then continue to play the hand out according to whatever total you will achieve in accordance with the decisions as shown in the MBS chart for those totals.

YOUR HAND	DEALER'S UPCARD	YOUR DECISION
A,7	2, 3	Stand
A,7	7, 8	Stand

No choice here. You have a soft 18. Why try to break it up? It's a fairly decent hand, although not the best that can be had. Against the dealer's upcard of 2 or 3, hitting this hand will very quickly become financial suicide. The dealer can break easily enough with these cards, and often will draw to hands on which he must stand and these will be lower than your "pat" hand of 18. Also, against the dealer's upcard of 7, your 18 may already be an automatic winner. If the dealer's hole card is a 10, he will therefore make a hard 17 on which he will have to stand. In the event of the dealer's upcard of 8, you are anticipating that he will have a hard 18, on which he will have to stand, and therefore in this situation you are trying not to lose and save your bet with the push, so why wreck this and try to hit the hand? As weird as it seems, there are some people who may tell you to hit this hand against these dealer's cards. It's nonsense, and you should never do it, unless you are simply reckless with your money and don't care. If you do care, then treat these hands as shown here and you will be a much happier person.

YOUR HAND	DEALER'S UPCARD	YOUR DECISION
A,7	9, 10, Ace	Hit

Here are the only situations where you would hit the soft 18. It's a bad hand against any of these dealer's upcards because you have to assume that your 18 total is already beaten. If the dealer shows any of these upcards, and has a 10-value card in the hole, your hand is history. (Of course, if the dealer has A,10 you won't get to hit because he has a natural blackjack.) The Ace as a dealer's upcard is always a power card, and whatever total the dealer eventually gets will often easily beat your hand. Therefore, to hit is your only chance of making this troublesome hand into something better. Most of the time this is a bad situation, and you will not win—but you will win enough times to make this play the correct one overall, and therefore no matter what the smirks may be from the other players at your table, be confident that you have played this hand correctly, and move on. Don't sweat the results from these situations. There are other hands that will be much better, so keep that in mind.

YOUR HAND	DEALER'S UPCARD	YOUR DECISION
A,8	2, 3, 4, 5, 6, 7, 8, 9, 10, Ace	Stand
A,9	2, 3, 4, 5, 6, 7, 8, 9, 10, Ace	Stand

When you have any total of soft 19 or soft 20, *stand*. Always! Never, ever, hit or double-down. No matter what. If you do, you will wind up a loser and no amount of writing about the game of blackjack, or teaching you the correct decisions, will overcome just one silly play like that. *Stand!*

YOUR HAND	DEALER'S UPCARD	YOUR DECISION
A,10 (BJ)	2, 3, 4, 5, 6, 7, 8, 9, 10, Ace	Stand

Okay. This is the hand. *The* hand. Any two-card total of an Ace and a 10-value card is the blackjack, the natural, an automatic winner most of the time. It's over, done with, you've won. Don't ever think of hitting it. As crazy as it sounds, I've seen people do this and it is the most boneheaded play of all bonehead plays ever seen in the casino.

PAIRS

Most people who play blackjack, even players who have played the game for some time and may be considered veteran blackjack players, seem to have a recurring problem with pairs. The most common questions about pairs are: "When to split?" and "When to double-down?" Of course, "When to hit?" is also part of these questions, but the two shown here are by far the most troublesome for just about everyone. I have seen people at the blackjack table agonize over these decisions, yet the fact is that these are among the simplest decisions you can make in the game of blackjack.

The main reason these hands seem so confusing is that it is unusual to find yourself with a pair of anything. We, as human beings, are naturally predisposed toward seeing, and seeking, patterns in our lives and in our universe. All of our sciences are based on this, and all of mathematics is based on this. The search for patterns and order is the driving force of the human spirit seeking the ultimate understanding. In blackjack, and in our gambling games in general, this human tendency is easily manifested in just about everything. Players look for patterns in all the games. They are usually called "streaks" or "trends," but they are the indubitable pattern-recognition manifestations of the human mind.

So, when we get a pair in blackjack, it looks nice. We are thrilled to see such a pair, because they are two of the same—a pattern. It delights us—but then we are soon faced with the stark reality of the game of blackjack, and have to make a decision about what to do with them. Sitting there at the blackjack table admiring the pair isn't going to do us much good and will, most likely, anger the rest of the players at the table who just want to get on with it, regardless of how interesting you may find your pair. So these are the primary reasons why most of us are not only delighted to find a pair, but are equally perplexed as to what to do with it as it specifically applies to blackjack. Fear no more, dear friend, here are all the answers.

It is also important to mention, so that there is no misunderstanding, that this section on actions concerning pairs *applies only to the first two cards dealt*, or to any hand whose first two cards are of the same value (such as 3,3 for the initial hand, or the 3,3 3,*x* in the case of another same-value card being dealt, which will then be resplit into two hands, and perhaps even resplit again if another of the same value card is again dealt).

Such hands of any *pair* can be achieved only on the first two cards regardless of whether it is the original such hand dealt, or any subsequent number of split hands achieved after a split of the initial pair. No "pair" hand is possible when more than the first two cards are of the same value (if you split the first two cards and then get another of the same value card and resplit, this is not a three-card first hand, because you now are playing *two* hands, or more in the case of subsequent resplits). A "pair" is just that—only the first two cards of the same value.

What follow are the various possible combinations of the first two cards combining to make a pair, and what actions should be taken. My comments are designed to apply to the most widely available blackjack games in American casinos, and can be used equally well in any game whose majority rules are those as played in American casinos in the twenty-first century.

YOUR HAND	DEALER'S UPCARD	YOUR DECISION
A,A	2, 3, 4, 5, 6, 7, 8, 9, 10, Ace	Split

This hand is either a 2 or a 12, if counted as a soft hand. However, it is quite a bad play to so consider this hand, because any time you get two Aces dealt to you the decision is simple and automatic—*split!* By so doing you not only get more money into action in one of the better opportunities to win, but you are also making a very bad hand into two hands that can both win. Also, even if one of your hands wins and the other loses, you will get a push overall, assuming, of course, that you split the cards with an equal bet on each hand, which in most casinos is mandatory. By splitting the Aces, you will receive only one more card to each split Ace in most casinos, and these are the hands on which you then must stand.

However, this one card, which you will receive to each split Ace, can be any number of cards to make a winner. To each Ace, you can draw a 10-value card. This then gives you a 21. However, remember that if you split Aces, and do receive a 10-value card to each Ace, or to at least one of them, this 21 total is *not* a blackjack, because to gain the bonus 3:2 payoff this hand must be achieved *on the first two cards dealt.* In this case, you have received two Aces as your first two cards, and therefore no blackjack hand is possible. What is possible, though, are two very good hands of 21 each, when you split the Aces and receive any 10-value card on both.

What if you don't receive a 10-value card on these split Aces? You may still get any one of the following cards to make a very good hand: any 9 for a total of 20, any 8 for a total of 19, any 7 for a total of 18, or any 6 for a total of 17. Plus, of course, all of the other cards in the deck, none of which can break your hand. (Remember, you cannot hit these hands because you get only one more card to each split Ace. In some casinos you may be allowed to hit hands made from split Aces, but if you find such a place usually you are not playing the standard blackjack game, and could be caught in a promotion, a derivative, or a gimmick whose overall odds are much worse than standard blackjack games. If this is so, ask to see the rules of the game, and then make your decision about continuing to play at that table. To be sure, however, the vast majority of casinos will *not* allow you to hit the hands made from split Aces.)

This series of five cards, the 6, 7, 8, 9, and 10, drawn to your split Aces, will make you a decent standing hand. Therefore, your hands are a favorite against the dealer's upcard of 2 through 6, marginally good against the dealer's upcard of 7, 8, or 9, and reasonable against the dealer's upcard of 10 or Ace. If the dealer's upcard is 10 or Ace, you should still split these Aces because if you don't, you have a 2 or a 12 and can achieve very little with this total.

However, the option to split these Aces against the dealer's upcard of an Ace is a touchy subject. Many experts disagree about what to do in this case. I don't sweat the argument. Any time I have a reasonably favorable opportunity to make a better bet, I like to take it. Even in this case, you should know that the dealer's odds of getting a blackjack hand with an Ace showing are the same as your odds of getting a blackjack. In fact, the dealer will actually bust about 25 percent of the time when showing an Ace as the upcard. I really don't think that the dealer's Ace as his upcard is the kind of danger card that many people think it is, in *this* situation. So, whenever you get two Aces, split them regardless of the dealer's upcard, and you will win more overall by doing so. On a few occasions, your hands may "wash" (one wins and the other loses for a break-even situation). If you do lose both hands, just remember that you played the hand correctly, chalk it up to the inevitable fact that you won't win every time, and try to remember those times when you won on stiffs, when the odds were most definitely against you. It's all part of the overall game of blackjack, so remember that and move on to the next hand, and be conscious of the fact that no single hand will ever define your success as a blackjack player, or affect your overall winnings if you continue to play correctly.

YOUR HAND	DEALER'S UPCARD	YOUR DECISION
2,2	2, 3	Hit
2,2	7, 8, 9, 10, Ace	Hit

This is a pretty bad hand against any of these dealer's upcards. If you split these 2s against any of these dealer's upcards, chances are you can wind up with a hard stiff, and then what? Well, you'll have to treat the hand as a hard hand, and then do what is correct. Most of the time, you will not succeed, because this hand is among the worst hands in blackjack. If you split, you may wind up with two hard-12 hands. It's not a pretty sight. With the dealer showing a 2 or a 3, he can draw a multitude of cards, all of which can beat your hand, particularly if you split and wind up with a stiff. You simply face losing more and gaining little by splitting two deuces in these situations. Your choice, therefore, is to hit. Even if you wind up with a hard 14, and that is quite possible, treat the hand as that total. Sometimes the dealer will bust with a 2 or a 3 as his upcard. Since you cannot break your total of 4 by hitting it, do so and then stand when appropriate, based on whatever total you achieve and the respective decisions as covered by the MBS for that total. If you win, count your lucky stars and move on.

Against the dealer's upcard of 8, 9, 10, or Ace, this hand is in trouble no matter what. It's most definitely a very bad play to split. The best you can hope for is to hit and draw several cards to a hand that will, at the very least, be a non-stiff standing hand. Ultimately, however, consider this hand already a loser against any of these dealer's upcards, and if you do wind up with a win, *remember that* the next time you lose a hand that you should have won (statistically speaking). It all works together, so don't belabor this hand in these bad circumstances.

YOUR HAND	DEALER'S UPCARD	YOUR DECISION
2,2	4, 5, 6	**Split**

Now the situation has changed quite dramatically against any of these dealer's upcards. Not because your hand has suddenly become any better, but because the dealer's possible hands have become potentially worse. The reason you split the 2,2 hand against any of these dealer's upcards is that you are now betting that the dealer will bust. In fact, with an upcard of 4, 5, or 6, the dealer will bust a combined average of about 45 percent of the time. This means, therefore, that your play in this situation is not only to achieve a better hand total than the dealer, but also to get more money into action in a situation where the dealer will break more often than in other situations in the game of blackjack. It is here, in this situation and others like it, where you need to exploit your opportunities to gain more wins with your hands. It's also important to keep in mind that when you split any hands other than the A,A, usually you *can* continue to hit the hand totals you get. It is only when you split the A,A that you are stuck with a one-card-draw (except, of course, in those few, rare, casinos which allow you to resplit Aces). This, therefore, makes splitting the 2s in these situations, against any of these dealer's upcards, an even better opportunity to make more money.

Remember also that the dealer, playing for the house, cannot double-down or split, and therefore whenever you have a generally favorable situation to exercise your opportunity to get more money for any win, that's the time to try for it. There are many such opportunities in blackjack, and although none of them is a guaranteed winner and none wins all the time, the wins achieved by players playing these situations correctly are cumulatively larger than those achieved by players whose play is driven merely by hunches. There is no question about this hand, or any other hands of this type, against any of these three dealer's upcards. The choice is simple and automatic—*split!* You will make more money by doing this than you will if you don't.

YOUR HAND	DEALER'S UPCARD	YOUR DECISION
3,3	2	Hit
3,3	7, 8, 9, 10, Ace	Hit

Your 3,3 against the dealer's upcard of 2 is a troubled hand, because the dealer has too many chances to improve, and therefore your 3,3 is not a candidate for a split in this situation, much the same as the 2,2 hand against the dealer's same set of upcards. Against the dealer's 7, 8, 9, 10, or Ace, your hand may already be a loser. The best you can achieve if you split the 3,3 is to draw an Ace to each hand, thus giving you a total of a soft 14—but then you have to hit again. The same is so for any hard total that you may get, such as when you get a 10 with either of the split 3s.

The better action is to bite down hard and hit the 3,3 hand and hope to draw several cards whose added value will provide you with a reasonable standing hand. This is the best decision under these circumstances and will contribute toward diminishing your overall losses, and that is about the best that can be said about this hand in these situations.

YOUR HAND	DEALER'S UPCARD	YOUR DECISION
3,3	3, 4, 5, 6	Split

Again, as with the 2,2 hand, the situation improves dramatically against any of these dealer's upcards. The same reasons described in the comments for the 2,2 hand apply here. In addition, the 3,3 hand is also a candidate for a split against the dealer's upcard of 3, as well as the dealer's up-cards of 4, 5, or 6. Basically, you are getting more of your money into action against dealer's hands that show signifi-cant weakness with these cards as the dealer's upcard. Your action is, therefore, again not only to expect to make a better hand than the dealer's final standing hand, but also to wager that the dealer will bust. As shown in the comments for the 2,2 hand, this is a favorable situation in which to make such a move.

YOUR HAND	DEALER'S UPCARD	YOUR DECISION
4,4	2, 3, 4, 5, 6, 7, 8, 9, 10, Ace	Hit

This is the worst of the pair hands. You simply can't make anything helpful out of splitting this hand. The best that can happen is that you draw an Ace for a soft 15, but then you have to hit again and most of the time you simply will wind up with bad hands and even bust. The better op-tion is to hit against *any* dealer's upcard. The best you can make with a hit is to get an Ace for a standing hand of a soft 19, or a 10 for a standing hand of a hard 18. In either situa-tion, these are the best hands you can make with just a one-card-draw. Of course, you can hit the 4,4 hand, get a 3 and have 11, and then hit the 10 and get a 21. If this happens, count yourself lucky. Situations like this do happen, and that's why you hit this hand rather than split it. You can increase the number of better hands that you can make out of this bad hand, by hitting, than you can ever make out of splitting, and without risking more of your money. This play is, therefore, more of a safety play than an aggressive offensive play. You want to get as good a hand as you can, and do so with as little risk as possible. Consequently, to split is to risk more for lesser gain, and for this reason it is not a good play.

The only time when this situation may be different is if you treat this as an 8, and use the double-down play against the dealer's upcard of 5, 6, or 7. However, you would have to be pretty sure that the deck is rich in 10-value cards, and even then you are not guaranteed a success the majority of times. If you do this, then the action belongs in the section for the hand of 8, and not here. Here we are discussing splits for pairs, and it is most definitely not a good situation for a split. You should not be so concerned about trying to exploit this mediocre hand for merely an extra few tenths of a possible percentage point in gain in the overall probability of a win. It's just not worth the trouble. If you get this hand, just hit the 4,4 and then deal with the total in accordance with the MBS chart. This will make your blackjack play not only simpler and enjoyable, but more profitable over your session or casino visit.

YOUR HAND	DEALER'S UPCARD	YOUR DECISION
5,5	2, 3, 4, 5, 6, 7, 8, 9	Double-down

Never, *ever*, under any circumstances split two 5s against *any* dealer's upcard! If you ever split the 5,5 hand, the best you can hope for is either a soft 16 or a hard 15, and then you have turned a powerful double-down opportunity into wasteful garbage. If you ever split this hand, I will find out about it and introduce you to some of my large friends from Las Vegas, and they will in turn introduce you to a rattlesnake at the bottom of a very conveniently located nearby mine shaft. Just kidding, of course—but the point is made. When you have a 5,5 hand, *always treat it as a 10*, and double-down in these situations against the dealer's upcard of 2, 3, 4, 5, 6, 7, 8, or 9. Period. End of story. No further discussion needed (I hope).

YOUR HAND	DEALER'S UPCARD	YOUR DECISION
5,5	10, Ace	Hit

Again, treat this as a 10, and *never split it.* Here your choice is to hit because the dealer is showing a power card. Hit the hand and you will risk less. When you gain a push or a win, be happy with it, because any 10 against any of these dealer's upcards is potentially in serious trouble. Just remember never to split these 5s, and that's all there is to say in this case.

YOUR HAND	DEALER'S UPCARD	YOUR DECISION
6,6	2, 3, 4, 5, 6	Split

Your 6,6 hand is a stiff, a hard 12 if counted together. It's a lousy hand. Your best option is to split against the dealer's upcard of 2, 3, 4, 5, or 6, because these are cards that show the dealer's weakness. Your play here is twofold: first, you hope to improve a very bad two-card hand by splitting it into two hands that may wind up better in their final total than you could have achieved had you hit it instead; and second, you are wagering as well that the dealer will bust. It is a more profitable play to split against any of these dealer's upcards because in these situations you take the potential bust away from your own hand and hand it instead to the dealer. When you win, you have turned what could easily have been a losing hand into two winners. You could also possibly wind up with an overall push in some situations. Basically, you are trying to exploit the dealer's weakness and get more value for your bet by splitting the 6,6 hand in these cases, while at the same time protecting yourself against an automatic loss if you treat this as a hard 12, then hit, and bust.

YOUR HAND	DEALER'S UPCARD	YOUR DECISION
6,6	7, 8, 9, 10, Ace	Hit

The situation gets worse with this hand against any of these dealer's upcards. Here you have no choice but to treat this as a hard 12, and work with it from there. Splitting the 6,6 against any of these dealer's upcards will cost you money very quickly, and is not a good play. The primary reason is that if you split this hand the best you can hope to get to any of the split 6s is an Ace for a soft 17, and then you still have to hit this hand against any of these dealer's upcards (except, possibly, the dealer's upcard of 7). In addition, of course, you are also likely to get a 10 to any of your two split 6s, and then you are stuck with a hard 16, the worst hand in blackjack. For these reasons, treat this as a hard 12 in *these* situations, and it will give you far more opportunities to make something out of this hand. More often than not, to risk more of your money by splitting the 6,6 hand against any of these dealer's upcards is to wind up with *two* really bad hands instead of just one.

YOUR HAND	DEALER'S UPCARD	YOUR DECISION
7,7	2, 3, 4, 5, 6, 7	Split

This hand against any of these dealer's upcards is about as bad as the 6,6 hand mentioned above. Here you have a hard 14, and this is pretty bad. It's a stiff, one of the series of really bad hands, which are any hard hands 12 through 16, and in our case in this section, the hard 12, hard 14, and hard 16. These three hard hands are the only hard-hand totals that can be made by the combinations of two cards of the same value on the initial deal, which are the 6,6, 7,7, and 8,8.

In the case of the 7,7 against any of these dealer's upcards, your best decision is to split and place more of your money into action in a situation that, as in the 6,6 hand described above, is the better opportunity against the dealer's potentially weak hands. Notice that here we have also added the 7 to the range of dealer's upcards against which we should split our 7,7 hand. This is because by splitting the 7,7 hand, we can make two soft 18s that beat the dealer's 17 if the dealer is showing a 7 and has a 10 in the hole, or we can make two hard 17s, in which case we push against the dealer's total of 17. (That's in most situations. However, in casinos where the dealer must hit soft 17, it is better *not* to split the 7,7 against the dealer's upcard of 7, but, instead, hit the hand. This results in fewer losses overall in these casinos and on these tables and, therefore, is the better play under those conditions.)

Because of these situations, where we can actually win with a soft 18, or not lose with a hard 17, this hand is also a candidate for a split against the dealer's upcard of 7, in addition to all the others listed here. The remainder of the reasons that this is a good play apply equally well from the discussions already described for the 6,6 hand, and the other applicable hands shown above.

YOUR HAND	DEALER'S UPCARD	YOUR DECISION
7,7	8, 9, 10, Ace	Hit

As with the 6,6 hand, here we are stuck with one of the worst of the bad situations. We have a hard 14, and the best we can hope to make out of this hand, if we split against any of these dealer's upcards, are two soft 18s, which we can't hit against the dealer's 8, and must hit against the dealer's upcards of 9, 10, or Ace. We simply have a bad situation getting worse, and therefore we are again facing a position where, if we split against any of these dealer's upcards, we are risking more of our money against the dealer's power cards and risk making two very bad hands out of just one.

YOUR HAND	DEALER'S UPCARD	YOUR DECISION
8,8	2, 3, 4, 5, 6, 7, 8, 9	Split

In many blackjack books, videos, training seminars, or newsletters, you will find the following statement: "Always split Aces and 8s." Often this statement is further expanded by adding, "Always split Aces and 8s against any dealer's upcard."

Well, I disagree. Yes, I recommend that the A,A hand always be split—but not the 8,8 hand. This hand is a hard 16, and this total is the worst of all hands in blackjack. For this reason, and primarily for this reason, the overall methodology and statistical frequency of derived odds indicate that a split against the dealer's upcard of 2, 3, 4, 5, 6, 7, or 8 produces *fewer losses* overall. This is mostly because, even in situations where we wind up with bad hands, one of our split hands may in fact win and the other lose, which will be a push when these two bets are added together, and therefore we have not lost. In other situations, both of our split hands may push, and in that case we have not lost either. Of course, our split hands may, in fact, win, even though rarely.

If we draw the perfect Ace to each of our split 8s, we will wind up with a soft 19, which will be a winner most of the time against the sequence of potential hands that the dealer can make with a 10 in the hole from the starting upcard of 2, 3, 4, 5, 6, 7, or 8. If we draw a 10 for a total of a hard 18, then we can tie against the dealer's upcard of 8 if he makes an 18, win if he makes a 17 from his upcard of 7, and lose if the dealer's total is 19 or more, or in those situations where the dealer draws multiple cards and stands on totals higher than ours. Further, we have a reasonable expectation of winning against the dealer's upcard of 2 through 6 because he may, in fact, bust. For these reasons, splitting the 8,8 hand against any of these dealer's upcards is the correct way to play, and results in overall better profitability.

The only contentious issue here may be the dealer's upcard of 9. Here the decision can go either way. Some experts say that you should split the 8,8 hand regardless, because the chances of the dealer having a 10 or an Ace in the hole are not that high, while your chances of busting on any one-card-draw on a hard 16 are far higher. Others say that you should only hit this hand, and they cite virtually the same reasons for that conclusion. The truth is that the differences in statistical probability are so minor in overall win expectation for any of your playing sessions or visits that, even under perfect laboratory conditions, you would not find a swing great enough to warrant a specifically more profound decision.

In my opinion, any time you can get more money into action under the *majority* of favorable circumstances, you should do so, and for that reason I recommend that you split the 8,8 hand even against the dealer's upcard of 9.

YOUR HAND	DEALER'S UPCARD	YOUR DECISION
8,8	10, Ace	Hit

However, against the dealer's upcard of 10 or Ace, I move to disagree with the majority of other authors and experts on blackjack. I think that against either of these dealer's upcards, the odds of your losing *both* of the split hands made from the original 8,8 are far higher than can be compensated by any number of wins in these split situations against these two dealer's power cards.

Any time you have a marginal situation like this, the

question you should ask yourself is: How many wins do I have to gain in order to compensate for the more frequent losses that can be suffered when splitting this hand against either of these two dealer's upcards? My answer is that you would have to gain wins in about a 4:1 ratio in order to compensate for the approximately 73 percent of the time you will lose split hands of 8,8 against any of these dealer's upcards. That means that you will have to make up losses of not just your original bet, but also the loss of the extra bet you will have to make to split these two 8s.

I think that the better play is to save money. Save not just *this* money, but save the next series of wins as well. Treat this as a hard 16 against these two dealer's power cards, hit the hand, and hope for the best. That's about all you can do. This way when you win, or push the hand, you will also save this bet, and maybe even gain an extra win. What's more important is that you will not have risked an extra bet in a bad situation. This means that later on you will have saved the extra wins that you would have had to gain in order to compensate for the loss of just one of these split hands against what can easily be a dealer's already pat winning hand.

I'm sure that some people will disagree with me here and will continue to assert that hitting the 8,8 hand, and therefore treating it as a hard 16, is a bad play. That no matter what, we should always split the 8s in the same way that we always split the Aces. Well, when we split the Aces, we have a chance to make two very good hands out of one very bad hand. When we split the two 8s we can make two very bad hands out of one bad hand. I think the difference is obvious, and the financial benefits to your blackjack play equally so. That's my opinion and I'm sticking to it.

YOUR HAND	DEALER'S UPCARD	YOUR DECISION
9,9	2, 3, 4, 5, 6, 7	Split

This is the fun part of the splits. On a 9,9 hand, you have one of the best chances in the game of blackjack to get more money into action under favorable conditions and with a greater win expectancy. Against any of these dealer's up-cards, your 9,9 hand is the perfect candidate for a split because it's only a hard 18 when counted together, while if you split it you can make two hands of 20, with the draw of an Ace to each 9, or two hands of 19 with the draw of any 10 to each of the split 9s. The point is, just as with the A,A hand, here you can make two good hands out of one hand that is mediocre at best. Against any of these dealer's up-cards, your split hands made from the original 9,9 hand are much more favorable to win than if you treated the hand as a hard 18 and merely stood pat. With hands made from 2, 3, 4, 5, or 6 the dealer's chances of busting are about 43 percent in combined totals. With the dealer's 7, if he has a hard 17 or even a soft 18, any number of cards drawn to each of your split 9s will make your hand a winner, while it might have only pushed, or even lost, if you had merely played it pat as a hard 18. For these reasons, the 9,9 hand against any of these dealer's upcards is among your better opportunities to make more money with an overall greater win expectation.

An argument can be made for standing on the 9,9 hand against the dealer's upcard of 7. Assuming that the dealer does indeed have a 10 in the hole, then his hard 17 will force him to stand, and, consequently, your 9,9 hand treated as a hard 18 will win. If the dealer has an Ace in the hole, his 7 up will make his hand a standing 18, and therefore your 9,9 hand played as a hard 18 will push, and not lose. Although these two situations do arise quite often, equally often your split of the 9,9 hand will result in either a win for both hands, providing a tidy profit, or an overall push, when one of your hands wins and the other loses. In the end, the situations are about equal. However, by splitting the 9,9 hand against the 7, those occasions when you win both hands will far outweigh the other situations; therefore, you will wind up with an overall marginal win by splitting. It's still not the best of the situations, and even though about 54 percent of the time the 9,9 split hands will not win unless the dealer busts, in those situations where they do win, the win value is greater in real money than the statistical loss or push that is the alternative.

YOUR HAND	DEALER'S UPCARD	YOUR DECISION
9,9	8, 9, 10, Ace	Stand

However, your 9,9 hand again turns sour when facing these dealer's upcards, with perhaps the only exception being the dealer's 8. If the dealer shows an 8, and in fact makes a hard 18, and you stand pat on your 9,9 hand, then you have pushed and not lost. *Not losing is as important in blackjack as winning.* With the other three alternative dealer's upcards of 9, 10, or Ace, your hard 18 is in trouble, but so would be any of the hands you could make out of splitting the 9s. Therefore, in these situations and against any of these dealer's upcards, expect that the dealer already has a pat hand, and don't risk more of your money unnecessarily. The bet you save here will mean fewer required wins at other times to compensate for the loss of the extra bets on the splits in these unfavorable situations.

YOUR HAND	DEALER'S UPCARD	YOUR DECISION
10,10	Any dealer cards	Stand!

Never, ever, split two 10s! *Ever.* Against *any* dealer cards. Like the 5,5 hand, splitting two 10s is the most bone-headed of all bonehead plays, and if you do it I'm just going to have to send those guys from Vegas out to teach you a lesson. Just kidding, again, of course—but the point is obvious. When you have 10,10, you have a total of 20, and this can be beaten only by 21. So you are a favorite to win. In fact, you are the second favorite to win, the first being blackjack or any 21. So don't be a fool. Be grateful for a great hand and keep it as it is. Yes, you will lose even on this hand sometimes—but by splitting these 10s you will go broke so fast that you will need a lifeline to the ATM wherever you go. Just don't do it—and that's truly very good advice.

The Real Game in the Casino

In this chapter we will discuss the following: the single-deck fallacy, surrender, insurance, deck penetration, multiple decks and the shoe game, and the infamous shuffling machines. Within all of these categories are imbedded some of the greatest problems facing blackjack players in the modern casinos of the twenty-first century. Often these problems are glossed over in texts that concentrate more on the theory of the game than on the real truth of the game as it is actually played in casinos.

No matter how well blackjack can be played according to the theory of the game, in the real world there is no casino anywhere—of which I am aware—that will allow you to play blackjack in that optimum manner. In the best of all possible worlds, blackjack would be a game dealt only from a single hand-held deck shuffled by a human dealer, all cards would be dealt first-card-to-last before any other shuffle took place, and there would never be any cut cards or random mid-game shuffles. Dream on. If this were so, even the players with the most rudimentary knowledge of Basic

Strategy could gain an edge over the casino, which would quickly wipe out not only the blackjack game itself but any casino that offered it. Therefore, when you read anything about blackjack, and you get to the section where the single-deck games are touted as "the best," remember the truth: It just ain't so in the real world, no matter what the book says. This is also the case for the other categories discussed in this chapter.

The "surrender" option is a good one for the player, especially "early surrender," but this is now almost extinct. Even if offered, most players simply don't know what it is or how to use it properly to *their* advantage. In the few casinos where surrender is still offered, where most likely only late surrender is the option, people will surrender the wrong hands in the wrong situations, and this further increases the house edge over the game and eats into the player's win expectations. It is fruitless to try to explain to players that their win expectation has just been lowered because of the wrong use of late surrender. Most people will simply not understand, or not care. However, you should care, and you should learn, because it is your money that you are throwing away.

Insurance and deck penetration are two other concepts in the game of blackjack that are often misunderstood by players. Insurance is often taken when it should not be, and this further erodes the player's ability to win money. Casinos tout insurance, even though by *refusing* to take insurance, it is actually the *player* who has the advantage overall. When you let the dealer talk you into taking insurance, you are handing more of your money to the casino and keeping less of your wins. Also, many players insure the wrong hands, which further adds to the casino's overall "hold" on the game. The simple fact that casinos not only offer insurance, but also *recommend* it to players should be enough of a warning to let you know that it is not a bet that helps you. Even though blackjack is basically a break-even game if players play at least Basic Strategy, casinos continue to "hold" anywhere from 6 percent up to 20 percent on blackjack games. This is so largely because players make silly mistakes and do the wrong things at the wrong time. Yet the truth is out there, and it can be shown and learned.

Deck penetration is something that is even less understood by most players. What is it? Well, that's where the cut card comes into play. It is used to separate the deck into two parts. The front part will be the cards in play for this round, and the back part will be cut out of play. How much of the deck is cut out of play directly affects your ability to win money. The more cards are cut out of play, the less you win, because this represents *fewer* opportunities for you to make winning hands. The more cards are left *in play*, the better it is for you. This becomes even more important when we discuss multiple decks and the shoe game.

In many casinos, most games are either the two-deck hand-held kind or the four-deck, six-deck, and even eight-deck shoe. The more decks you have to face the worse it gets for you, because now there are that many more cards to be dealt, making more combination variations that may not be in your favor. Although it is possible to get a decent shoe game, the truth is that the better games are the two-deck games. If you must play a shoe game, perhaps because there are no other games offered in the casino you are visiting, then look for the four-deck games. It is here where the deck penetration will have the most effect on your ability to win. If the casino cuts fully half the decks in the shoe, then you are facing a 50 percent penetration and this is really bad for you. What you want is at least 75 percent penetration, thus leaving two-thirds of the cards in play.

Finally, we have the shuffling machines. What a nightmare for the players! At least when you have a human being shuffling the cards, it actually still looks like a game between people. The truth is that blackjack as it is now dealt is largely a game more akin to a slot machine than a card game. This is even more so with the use of these shuffling machines. Plus, there are now even bigger machines called "continuous shufflers," which are multiple-deck shufflers that keep on shuffling the cards continuously, spitting out a few cards at a time, either as hands or as partial decks to be used in play. Recently, there have been even bigger machines installed at many blackjack games that are continuous shufflers, but with an added Machiavellian twist: These are now called "randomizers." This means that they not only continuously shuffle the cards, but now also exchange cards between decks and keep mixing them up at random. All this is designed to eliminate any kind of advantage to the player, particularly players who track cards or count cards. Neither tracking nor counting is possible against these shufflers.

Avoid games with these monsters like the proverbial plague. Don't *ever* play these games. No matter how good you are, you are not playing blackjack anymore, but merely playing a slot machine with really bad odds. If all you have in your casino are blackjack games using these machines, stay away and let the management know that you will no longer play at their casino as long as they use these machines. The use of these shuffling machines is the worst thing that ever happened to the game of blackjack. The sad fact that casinos are using them is a testimonial to the gross ignorance of the majority of blackjack players. Anyone who knows anything about blackjack would never, ever, play blackjack against these machines.

So this chapter is designed to show you how the real world of the actual casino is quite different from the theory of blackjack as you find it in just about every kind of book and text you can currently locate. It is a sad, sad fact that blackjack is being abused—by casinos who want to squeeze an even bigger edge from the game, and by players who are largely too ignorant to give a damn. This doesn't mean that blackjack should be avoided. Not so. There are still plenty of casinos where you can get a decent game. It is still a game that can be beaten, and still a game in which you can make very good money. However, you must know more than ever about the game—and not just the theory or the strategy, but also the details of what to look for, and how to handle it once you find it. That's why it's important not only to learn the good, but also the bad. Once you know both, then you will be able to make accurate judgments, and even if you have no choice but to play in a game whose majority rules and playing conditions may not be among the most favorable, at least you will know that and be able to react accordingly. This will give you the chance to save money, and saving money is still a part of your overall profits. Profits from blackjack are not just the wins, but also the losses saved.

THE SINGLE-DECK FALLACY

Theoretically, the single-deck game is the best one to play. Theoretically. In reality this is not so, because you will never actually be able to play it that way. Here's why the single-deck game is theoretically so good.

In a single deck there are fifty-two cards total. This means that there are four of everything. So now we know that there are four Aces, four Kings, four Queens, four Jacks, four 10s, and, well, you get the picture. Therefore, even if we don't know how to count cards, we need only a very tiny amount of mental effort to realize how many cards have been dealt, and what they are. If we observe five hands played, for example, we now know that at least ten cards have been dealt (two starting cards for each of the five hands, such as when four players are at the table, plus the dealer, who also gets two cards). So, immediately, we know that there are now only forty-two cards left in the deck. At this time we can also take a quick look at the cards that have been exposed during these five hands.

We don't even need to look for the *kind* of cards they are, but just their *values*. For instance, it's not necessary to look for, say, the Kings, Queens, and 10s. We just look for all the 10-*value* cards, and that saves the mental effort. So, perhaps in our five-hand example, there were seven cards dealt whose value in blackjack was 10. Therefore, we now know that out of the entire deck, which contained the maximum possible number of sixteen 10-value cards (four 10s, four Jacks, four Queens, and four Kings = sixteen), seven have been dealt, and therefore there are only nine such cards left. We may also have noticed that two Aces have appeared during these five hands. Now we also know that there are only two Aces left. What about the other cards? If we are just a tad clever, we would have looked also for the 5s, in addition to the 10-value cards and the Aces. This is what is often called "tracking the deck," or deck-tracking. What we are actually doing here is applying one of the earliest forms of blackjack strategies, which called for the tracking of 10s, 5s, and Aces.

Okay, we are able to do all this and it isn't that hard. What does that do for us? Well, based on the above scenario, we know that on the next deal we can expect *fewer* 10-value cards, because there are only nine left in the whole deck. We also know that there are only two blackjack possibilities left, because only two Aces remain. Plus, we have not seen any 5s; therefore, we know that the deck is rich in 5s. Overall, we have determined that the deck is "negative," which is a card-counting term describing a poor player deck, namely an *unfavorable* situation. So we make a small bet, the smallest bet allowed by the table minimum. We do this because we expect that the next hand will contain small cards, perhaps 5s in combination with 10s, which will result in stiffs, or a series of small cards requiring dangerous hits.

The converse is also true. What if in our example we saw all the 5s out and only three 10-value cards in those five hands, and no Aces played? Well, then we would know that all the 5s are gone out of the remaining deck, that there still are thirteen 10-value cards left and all of the Aces. We now have a "positive" deck, meaning that all four possible blackjack hands are still available, the remaining deck has most of the 10-value cards still left to be played, and all of the small danger cards are out. How does this benefit us? It's obvious. We can anticipate that the next hand is likely to contain high-value hands, such as 10,10, or even blackjacks (A,10), or, at the very least, decent standing hands and very few stiffs. So we make a big bet, the biggest we can.

That's why single-deck games are theoretically the best to play, because even with just common sense you can fairly easily determine what kind of cards are left to play and bet accordingly. In our examples, we would make the smallest wager possible when the deck is *against* us (i.e., favors the casino), and make very big wagers when the deck *favors* us. The outcome, in the long term as well as the short term, is obvious. The players would win big bets in situations when the deck favors them, while the casino would win only small bets in situations when the deck favors the casino. It's simply bad business to let this happen, and that's why single-deck blackjack games are never offered with even the most rudimentary of any kind of favorable rules for the player.

Today, many casinos are touting single-deck blackjack games—but when you go to play there you soon find out that on a full table a dealer will average a mere two hands per deck before shuffling. Even if you get a one-on-one game, difficult to find but usually available around 3 A.M., you will soon discover that casino rules will force the cut card to be placed about halfway through the deck. This means only half the cards will be dealt before a shuffle (a mere 50 percent deck penetration). Even with a one-on-one game between you and the dealer, you can expect at best three or four hands. In addition, many casinos will simply have the dealer shuffle the deck after each hand, or after each two hands, if they so much as suspect that you are making "knowledgeable" bets. The point is this: A single-deck blackjack game is theoretically the best to play, but in reality no casino will give you an opportunity to play it using all available player advantages.

I always get a chuckle when I read books that tell their readers to play only single-deck games. Why? Where will you find such a game that will actually be a good game to play? I have played single-deck games in Las Vegas casinos and I can tell you from direct experience that the single-deck game you find in the real world is nothing like the single-deck games touted as the best to play. In fact, because of the reasons embodied in the theory of the single deck, there is no game available in any major casino with a single deck where you can gain even the slightest advantage as those professed in the texts teaching single-deck strategies. What kind of an advantage can you possibly gain when you are dealt one hand from a freshly shuffled single-deck game, and then the deck is shuffled immediately again before the next hand is dealt and so on for each hand played? None. Each such deal is an *independent* event, instead of a *dependent* event as it should be when we are dealing subsequent hands. You might as well play a machine for all the good this kind of game does you.

The same also applies to all the other tricks used by the casinos to entirely eliminate any of the player advantages of a single-deck game. One such trick is placing the cut card halfway into the deck or, even worse, only one-third into the deck, thus cutting off half or even two-thirds of the cards from play. Will you gain an advantage in this game when you are dealt two hands from a freshly shuffled deck? How about three hands? Four hands? Five? If you are dealt five hands from the single deck, and there is only you and the dealer, on average there have been about fourteen cards dealt thus far (initial two cards for each of you and the dealer times five for the five hands dealt, plus a conservative estimate of an additional four cards between both of you for hits during these five hands). So, out of the deck of fifty-two cards, fourteen cards are now gone. Take a single deck of cards and cut off fourteen cards and see how far into the deck you have penetrated. Then mark this on your deck, and next time you go to a casino where a single-deck game is offered, put your deck in your pocket and go to that casino and observe where the dealer places the cut card, or how deep into the deck he will go for five hands dealt before he will shuffle. What you will find in most instances is that your experiment is a far more generous treatment of single-deck blackjack than you will actually find in the casino.

What your experiment actually shows is a 25 percent penetration into the deck, meaning that about one-quarter of the cards were actually put into play heads-up between you and the dealer. This will almost never happen in a one-on-one game between you and the dealer. If this does happen, then it will probably mean that there are more players at this table, and if you can get to see five hands with three or more people you will be very fortunate indeed. Even that will not give you an edge because you will never get an opportunity to exploit whatever favorable situation may arise. By the time you get these five hands out, and determine from observation, card tracking, or card counting that you have a favorable situation, the deck will be shuffled again. What if you get that chance and make that big bet? As soon as the dealer sees this, he will immediately shuffle and he will never deal you that hand. That's what the dealers are taught in single-deck games where more than one or two hands are dealt consecutively. Plus, now you will get the heat from the pit boss, and if you pull your big bet back when you see the dealer shuffle up, you will most likely be tagged as a counter and asked to leave. So what have you gained in this single-deck game? Nothing—and that's the truth.

SURRENDER

Again, this is a concept theoretically favorable to the player, but in reality almost impossible to find or practice to the player's advantage. What is it? "Surrender" is your option (as the player) to relinquish (or "give up") half your bet instead of playing out the hand. This option is available to you *only on the first two cards dealt.* This means that if you are dealt, say, a 10 and a 5, for a stiff hand of a hard 15, and the dealer is showing, say, a 10-value card (and does not have a blackjack in late surrender), you may choose to give up half your wager instead of risking losing it all, since you can easily bust your hand with the necessary draw, while the dealer may already have a standing pat hand. Having the option of giving up half your bet and thus saving the other half without risking all of your wager is a very good option for the player, if used correctly.

There are two kinds of surrender: "early surrender" and "late surrender." Early surrender is your option to give up half of your wager *before* the dealer checks for blackjack. For this reason, early surrender is by far the better of the two options for surrender. Late surrender is your option to give up half of your wager, but only *after* the dealer checks for blackjack. Therefore, in late surrender, you still risk losing your entire wager if the dealer does, in fact, have a blackjack. For this reason, late surrender is not as favorable an option as early surrender. Here's how these two options can affect you.

In early surrender, you may be dealt a hard 15 or a hard 16, which are two of the best candidates for surrender. Either of these hands is about as bad as hands in blackjack can get. If early surrender is offered, you would always surrender these two hands against the dealer's upcard of any 10-value card or any Ace. In fact, you would also surrender this hand against the dealer's upcard of 7, 8, or 9 as well, but for the sake of this example these additional early surrender decisions are moot. In this example, the reason early surrender is so advantageous for you is that now you can immediately surrender your hard 15 or hard 16, and do so *before* the dealer checks for his potential blackjack. In most casinos, dealers will automatically check their hole cards for a possible blackjack when they have an upcard of any Ace. In many casinos, but not necessarily all, dealers will also check for a potential blackjack hand if they have an upcard of any 10-value card. This depends on the house rules, but the truth is that in most casinos today the dealer will check his hole card whenever he has any 10-value card or any Ace as his upcard.

So, in early surrender, you can immediately relinquish half your wager *before* the dealer checks for his potential blackjack hand. Thus you are able to save half your money without risking the entire wager. In this situation, you simply say, "Surrender," and the dealer will take half your bet *before* he checks his hole card. If he then checks and does have a blackjack hand, you have saved yourself half your money in a situation where you would have automatically lost the entire bet. In the event that the dealer checks his hole card but does not have a blackjack hand, you still can rest comfortably, knowing that no matter what the dealer's final hand may be, your chances of winning any hand of hard 15 or hard 16, or indeed any of the hard stiffs, are low, and therefore your goal for profits from the game of black-jack, in this case, are in the realm of bets saved. Remember that in blackjack your overall profits are not only from wagers won, but also from wagers saved. For these reasons, early surrender offers you one of the most powerful tools for *saving* money.

However, it is also because of this hugely player-friendly situation that you will almost never find this option available on any blackjack game in any casino. Yes, it can be found in some places, but there this otherwise player-advantageous option is usually countered by a series of other not-so-player-friendly rules. Consequently, any advantage thus derived from the availability of early surrender is, in these cases, usually completely invalidated by other rule alterations and restrictions. Such other rule restrictions or alterations, or both, may include double-down only on 10s and 11s, no resplit, no double-down after splits, dealer hits a soft 17, and very poor deck penetration. These are the most common rule alterations that may be employed in casinos that offer surrender, particularly in the very rare situations where early surrender may be offered.

What about late surrender? How is this different from early surrender? Using the example above, let us continue to assume that you have been dealt either a hard 15 or a hard 16, two of the prime hands that are candidates for surrender, early or late. Now we are using these hands as our examples in a situation where *late* surrender is offered, and the dealer's upcard against either of these stiffs is the infamous 10-value card or the Ace. In early surrender, you are able to choose to surrender these hands against any of these dealer's upcards *before* the dealer takes any action to check his hole card for the possible blackjack hand. The difference *now* is that you can no longer do this. You must now wait for your surrender option until *after* the dealer checks his hole card to determine whether he does or does not have a blackjack. How does this affect you?

It affects you very profoundly. If the dealer does indeed have that blackjack hand, then you have automatically lost your entire wager and have never even gotten the chance to use the surrender option. That's the big difference between early surrender and late surrender. Further, if the dealer does *not* have a blackjack hand, now you have to face the decision of whether to continue with the hand and hit the stiff, and risk a potential bust card in which case you will lose the entire wager, or to surrender your hand now knowing that the dealer does not have a blackjack. A whole range of assumptions must now be considered by you in the process of making your late surrender decision. Does the dealer have a pat hand? Will he have to draw? Are your chances of busting your stiff just too great? Would the dealer bust? Well, that's about the shape you're in. Late surrender is, therefore, not nearly as valuable to you as a tool to win at blackjack as early surrender indeed can be.

The decisions you are facing in late surrender situations are much more dependent on what kinds of cards are left in the portion of the deck remaining in play. It is in these situations, as well as in other equally valuable situations such as on double-downs and splits, that some techniques, including card-counting, provide most of their added value to you as the player. If you knew, for example, from counting cards that the remaining deck was rich in small cards, then perhaps you might not take the option of late surrender and would hit your stiff instead. In this situation you would also know that the chances of the dealer having a blackjack hand were low and that, likewise, the chances of his hand being a stiff, or a low-total standing hand, were quite high. Conversely, if the count were positive, namely that you knew that the remaining deck had a lot of 10-value cards left in it, then you would probably not hesitate and indeed would take the late surrender option and save half your money in a situation where your chances of being beaten were very high. All of these situations are refinements to your blackjack game. In truth, you will most likely never face a situation of either of these examples in any casino you may visit. The vast majority of modern twenty-first-century casinos do not offer surrender at all. Of those that do, virtually none will offer early surrender.

The only casino of which I know that does offer early surrender is the Las Vegas Club in downtown Las Vegas on their designated special six-deck shoe game. This game in this casino also has other rules, such as players being able to double-down on the first two *or* three cards, unlimited splits and resplits and double-down after splits and resplits, automatic winner for six-card-under-21, and other rules often described as player-friendly. The trouble is that this is available only on a specially designated six-deck shoe game, with a 50 percent penetration, meaning that only half of the shoe is ever dealt, plus the shoe is now shuffled by a machine. All of these other changes and methods of dealing this game in that casino completely invalidate any advantage that any of these so-called player-friendly rules may provide. In reality, these games are mostly a promotional gimmick, because the rest of the rules, conditions, and playing methodology entirely eliminate any potential advantage. Therefore, what you are actually playing is a game whose advantage to you is really lower than other comparable blackjack games without all these gimmicks and options. Again, you are left with a game whose rule alterations and methods of dealing mean that any perceived player advantage is overcome by other means. As a result, none of this is actually to your benefit.

If you do run across a casino that offers surrender, it will probably be only late surrender, and available only on a shoe game, probably six decks or more, and most likely the rules of that game will be very strict and not very good over-all. Therefore, even if you do find a game where such late surrender will be offered, chances are that the game itself will be a bad bet for you. Consequently you will be far better off playing a different blackjack game, either on a different table in that casino, or in a different casino. Don't just auto-matically sit in a blackjack game because you see a promo-tional tout that offers "surrender" there. If you do see such a table, first ask whether it is late or early surrender. Most of the time the answer will be that it is only late surrender. Then ask about the rules of play. In many situations when you ask these questions, you will soon find out that the rest of the rules of play on this table that offers late surrender are quite different and very restrictive as compared to the other blackjack games in that casino or the casinos nearby. It is not worth it for you to give up other player-friendly options to play at a table where late surrender is offered, mostly because any advantage you may gain from late sur-render is only marginal, even if it is used correctly at all times. The only time you may find this to your advantage (and a very small advantage to be sure) is if you are a very good player, or a card-counter, and can, therefore, exploit even late surrender for a few tenths of a percentage gain overall.

For most players, the simple truth is that surrender is just not worth the effort. Particularly late surrender, since this is the kind that is mostly offered in those casinos that still offer surrender at all. You are largely wasting your time if you are overly concerned about it. The best you can do is just remember that you should surrender a hard 14, a hard 15, and a hard 16 against the dealer's upcard of any 10-value card and any Ace. This is simple to remember. Therefore, if you do find yourself in this situation, then that is what you should do. This will add a little bit of extra edge to your overall game. Little and tiny, that is all, that's why it's not that important, and that's the real truth.

INSURANCE

If you ran this kind of an insurance scam in the world at large, you would most likely be doing hard time in some very uncomfortable prison. This description is being kind to the insurance option, or bet, offered in blackjack games. What is it?

Insurance is a side bet offered in virtually all blackjack games. This option is marked on the table, usually just above your designated betting circle, or area. This is so marked with a double stripe inside of which most commonly are printed words that say, "Insurance pays 2 to 1." It is in this area in which you would place your insurance wager, in the event that you wish to purchase such insurance.

This side bet of "insurance" is offered in situations where the dealer's upcard is any Ace. The idea behind this bet is that you wager an additional amount, equal to one-half of your original wager, that the dealer will indeed have a blackjack. This wager is offered by the dealer before he checks his hole card. Normally, the dealer will announce, "Insurance?" and then also often check with all players who have active wagers in play, either verbally, or through eye contact or, which is more common, by motioning with his free hand across all betting areas that show active wagers for that hand. If you wish to take this insurance option, you place half the value of your original bet in the area above your betting circle marked as indicated, the line that says "insurance." Once this is done, the dealer then checks his hole card. If he does have a blackjack, he immediately turns it over, and all players who did not wager on the insurance option automatically lose their bets. If you did take the insurance option in this example, the dealer will then collect your original wager, because that lost automatically to his blackjack hand, but then he will also pay you your insurance wager at 2:1.

For example, if you wagered $10, and decided to take insurance, you would bet an additional $5 chip in the "insurance" area. Now, when the dealer checked his hole card and did in fact have a blackjack hand, your original $10 wager was lost, but your insurance wager of $5 wins at 2:1; therefore you get $10. In effect, you broke even. You saved your bet, and that's why it's called insurance. Often the dealers will just move your original wager to the insurance wager rather than first collecting the losing bet from your original bet and then reaching back into the chip tray and paying the insurance wager. This is done just to save time, because the purpose of insurance is to save your bet, and therefore the hand is a wash, a break-even, in the situation where the dealer does indeed have that blackjack. If he does *not* have the blackjack, then your insurance wager is automatically lost, and you then must proceed with the hand thereafter as you would normally play it.

Overall, insurance is a sucker bet. For anyone playing merely Basic Strategy, and particularly for those of you who will now be playing my MBS, you will be losing more money each time you make this wager over your playing sessions or casino visit. Your first indication of why this is a really bad bet is the fact that the casinos offer it at all. Do you honestly think that the casinos would offer you something that was a really good bet, and then actively solicit the bets as they do with insurance? If this were so, then the casinos would also offer early surrender, and announce it as an option for each occasion when the players have a stiff against a dealer's upcard of a 10 or Ace. Also, they would deal only single-deck games first-card-to-last. Well, we already talked about that, and it ain't gonna happen in the real world, so let's deal with it, live in reality, and move on.

The point is that the insurance option is of use only to those players who are experienced, or perhaps are card-counters, and who can therefore anticipate that the hands which were dealt are likely to consist of 10-value and high cards because they have counted a positive deck. Even then, this option at best provides only a minuscule addition to the player's edge over the house, and it is still a touchy proposition even among very skilled players and expert card-counters. If you are playing in a game in which the decks are shuffled by shuffling machines, then forget this altogether. No card-counter can ever hope to count any decks that are continuously shuffled by these machines.

In the actual world of the twenty-first-century casino, this option to wager more money on insurance is a bet designed to cost you money and eat into your potential wins.

If you have a really bad hand, such as any stiff, why would you insure it? You would be risking your insurance wager as well as your original bet because you stand to lose both. If you have a very good hand, such as 10,10, why would you give up half of your expected win by wagering an additional amount on the insurance for the one long shot that the dealer will actually have a blackjack?

What if *you* have a blackjack? Well, there is another way of asking for insurance, and that applies only to this situation. Let us assume, for this example, that you have a blackjack and the dealer's upcard is an Ace. Now the dealer will ask everyone for insurance. When it's your turn, instead of placing half your original wager in the insurance bet area, you can now verbally tell the dealer, "Even money, please." This simply expedites the process, and tells the dealer that you are willing to settle for a 1:1 payoff on your hand, thus giving up the extra 50 percent you would have gained on a 3:2 payoff, to which you are entitled on any blackjack against any dealer's hand that is not also a blackjack. By doing this, you have accepted an immediate payoff, and the dealer will pay you right away and take your cards, and all this is done before he checks his hole card.

If he *does* have a blackjack, and you did *not* take the insurance option, either by making the requisite wager in the appropriate area or by asking for "even money," then your blackjack hand will be a push, a tie. You lose nothing, but you win nothing. If, on the other hand, the dealer did *not* have a blackjack, and you *did* take insurance on your blackjack, then you have accepted a lower payoff than you would have otherwise been entitled to receive. It is also for these reasons, and particularly on the player's blackjack hands, that the casinos push the insurance wager, because in these situations the casinos will save themselves the extra money they would have had to pay you had you had a blackjack and the dealer did not.

There are actually two sides to the debate about insurance on a blackjack hand against the dealer's upcard of an Ace, the only situation to which these discussions apply. One side of the argument says that it is better to gain a 1:1 payoff by asking for "even money" rather than risk a no-win push in the event that the dealer does indeed have that blackjack. The other side of the argument says that it is a bad idea to take insurance at any time, particularly so in case you have a blackjack against the dealer's upcard of an Ace, because in these situations you are actually risking nothing, but are in the running to win at 3:2, which constitutes the majority of your expected profits in blackjack play.

I tend to agree with the latter position. To my mind, I risk nothing in this situation. Therefore, I wish to gain as much money for my great blackjack hand as I am entitled to receive. I wish to force the casino to either tie my great hand or pay me the full amount that is my due. For all other hands, insurance is a bad bet largely because of the situations already discussed.

Of all the hands that are possible in blackjack, the dealer has the exact same chances for receiving a blackjack hand as you do. This will happen about 21 percent of the time. Twenty-one times out of each one hundred hands, on the average, there will be a blackjack hand dealt. (The actual real-world percentages vary depending on the number of decks used, as well as the placement of the cut card. Theoretically, the hand of blackjack will occur about this many times out of a hundred hands dealt, for *all* players, and not necessarily only for the dealer.)

You and the dealer have the exact same chances of receiving such a blackjack. The illusion that blackjack hands seem to favor the dealer is just that: an illusion. It is only because we, as human beings, tend to remember the situations that hurt us in some way much more than those that helped us, that we seem to think that dealers have blackjack hands more often. It simply isn't so.

It may also seem as if blackjacks come in bunches. This may, in fact, be so, but that is more a short-term slice of overall probability that will equate over time. In the situations where blackjacks seem to appear with greater regularity than can be theoretically expected, it is not true that the dealer will have more of them than the players. All persons in action at that blackjack game have exactly the same chances of receiving a blackjack hand, and this includes the dealer. Therefore, in the situation where the dealer does have an Ace as his upcard, your wager of insurance means that you are betting extra money in a very unfavorable situation. Only about twenty-one times out of a hundred hands can you reasonably expect that there will be a blackjack hand on the table, and then not necessarily there for the dealer. So you have to take into account other variables, such as how many blackjacks have been dealt so far, how many players there are at the table, how many hands have been dealt so far, how far into the deck the game has progressed, what was the deck penetration, how many decks are still in play, how many decks the game started with, and so on. Once you add all this together, you will soon discover that taking the insurance option is to place your money at risk on a very rare occurrence, indeed.

If the dealer does have that rare blackjack hand and you lose your wager, or push with your own blackjack hand, then that's part of the game. Don't habitually risk more of your money on the insurance bet just because you want to protect your hand on these infrequent occasions, or settle for less money than you are entitled to receive when you have that blackjack. If you do, you will keep losing not just that insurance bet most of the time, but also many times your original wager as well. What if your hand is an 18 or a 19? What if the dealer does not have a blackjack and you did insure these standing hands? Well, he can have a 9 under that Ace, and now he has a 20, and your 18 and 19 hands are toast. You have lost not only your money on these wagers but also the extra money on the insurance bet. Now you will have to make up three losses instead of just one in order to get back to even with your money.

Simply put, the insurance wager is a really, really bad bet under any circumstances and therefore you should never, ever, take it. Period. That's the real truth in the real world of the actual game as it is played in the casinos you will visit.

DECK PENETRATION

This is yet another of those little things of which you should be aware, but that will in reality not have an overwhelming impact on your game in most situations. Where deck penetration is important is primarily in single-deck and two-deck games. Since we already talked about the fallacy of the single-deck game, the deck penetration situation discussed here will concentrate on the two-deck hand-held game, and then, of course, the shoe games.

Many casinos play the two-deck hand-held game. This is actually one of the best playing options for you. In most casinos, these decks are still shuffled by the dealers, and therefore machines are not used in the majority of these two-deck games. This is also good because in a two-deck game there are now eight of everything (double the number of cards in the single deck). Therefore, we can still fairly accurately determine the kinds of cards that have been played and the kinds of cards that are still left to play. That's where the importance of deck penetration factors as a potentially good or bad situation for you, the player. What is deck penetration?

Deck penetration is, simply, the depth of the deck where the dealer places the cut card. This is the point where the next shuffle will take place. The deeper into the deck the cut card is placed, the more cards will be played before the next shuffle, and therefore this is good for the players. This is called "deep penetration." On the other hand, when the cut card is placed only halfway into the deck, or even only one-third of the way into the deck, this means that very few cards will actually be put into play before the next shuffle and this is, therefore, *not* good for the players. This is called "shallow penetration." Simply put, in order to be easily remembered, the farther into the deck that the cut card is placed by the dealer, the more cards will be played during that round, and this is therefore the better game.

The same also applies to the shoe games. When you are playing in a game that uses four decks, six decks, or eight decks, the deeper the penetration the better it will be. There are several reasons, but mostly, any time you can get a game where the majority of cards from that shuffle are put into play *before* the next shuffle takes place, the better it is. In shoe games, deep penetration will allow you to better exploit some of the trends, or clumps, of cards (more on this immediately below in the section on the shoe games). Conversely, the shallower the penetration, the fewer cards will be dealt before the next shuffle; therefore, you will have fewer opportunities to exploit potentially favorable situations.

Of course, none of this matters in the games that are shuffled by machines, since these games continuously shuffle the decks. In those games where the machines are used to shuffle one or two decks at a time, which are then picked up by the dealer and cut, the level of penetration still applies because then we can still preserve, somewhat, the deck integrity because the deck is not continually shuffled by the machines. Overall, whenever you are approaching any game where a shuffling machine is used, keep on walking. Find another game, or go elsewhere. In regular games, without shuffling machines, look for games where the dealer will allow deep penetration. Even encourage it if you can, either by conversation or by an extra toke. Sometimes it may work. Overall, just remember that the deeper the penetration, the more hands you will get to see and play before the next shuffle. This will always be a better game for you than those games where the penetration is shallow.

MULTIPLE DECKS AND THE SHOE GAME

In most casinos that offer the two-deck games, the cut card will be placed about two-thirds of the way into the two decks, which is deep penetration, and so you will be able to see many more cards dealt than in the way the single-deck games are now mostly played. In a two-deck game, there are eight of everything, double the single-deck number of cards. This is probably the best game to play if you have any inclination to practice some card-tracking, or perhaps card-counting. It is also the better game for all of the MBS decisions I show in Figure 1.

A six-deck shoe will use six standard decks of cards, all shuffled together. Different casinos will place the cut card at different depths. Most will do this halfway, so you will see only three decks dealt, but some will cut off only one and a half decks from the bottom (deep penetration), so you will see many more cards because now you will have four and a half decks in play before the next shuffle. The advantage to you in a six-deck shoe (with deep penetration) is that cards tend to "group" (known as "clumping"); therefore, it is possible to hit winning streaks more often than with two-deck or single-deck games—conversely, frequent long losing streaks can happen as well.

In a six-deck shoe there are six times as many of each card—twenty-four Aces, Queens, Kings, and so on. This makes for many possibilities in winning and losing combinations, and makes it almost impossible to practice card counting. Current casino rules of shuffling, cut card placements, number of burn cards discarded prior to play, hitting soft 17, and, lately, using shuffling machines instead of dealers to shuffle cards, all make the game so much more difficult to beat that most of the popularized strategies, and even card-counting systems, are rendered almost worthless. Almost, but not quite.

This does not mean that if you are a casual player, you should not play blackjack in these games. No matter how difficult the casinos try to make the game by subtle rule alterations, dealing and shuffling techniques, and so on, blackjack is still a game that not only offers substantial enjoyment, but can be played for profit.

Six-deck shoe games are not as bad as they appear. When playing a six-deck shoe game, you are well advised to play in accordance with the MBS as I have shown it. You can also combine this with a practiced ability to spot short-term trends and possible "clumping" of high-value cards in a sequence. All these skills will benefit you in the short term, particularly a player-favorable "clumping" of cards—if you learn to spot this and bet into such "runs" correctly. In this manner, a six-deck shoe can offer you a long winning run, indeed. Conversely, you will be able to avoid betting into runs of low-value cards, which tend to benefit the casino.

That's why the information in this book is so important, even if you play blackjack only every now and then, or on your vacation to a casino destination. By understanding the information I provide here, you will be way ahead of many thousands of other people who think they know how to play blackjack, but in reality are making some of the most serious mistakes possible in this game. You don't have to be one of them.

The Two-Deck Game

Now let's discuss the multiple-deck games a little more closely. Personally, I think that any time you can find a two-deck hand-held game where the decks are shuffled by human dealers and where there is deep penetration, this is the best game to play. There are several reasons that this is so. First, unlike a single-deck game, in a two-deck game you will see far more hands before the next shuffle. Although the two-deck game is only marginally worse, theoretically, than the single-deck game, casinos treat the two-deck game largely in the same way as they treat the multiple-deck games of four, six, and eight decks. This means that they don't pay nearly as much attention to the possibility of good play by the players as they do in a single-deck game. In a single-deck game, there are at best only three to five hands dealt, on average, before the next shuffle. Often there are only one or two hands dealt before the next shuffle. Also, if the pit boss or the dealer thinks you are making some "knowledgeable" wagers, they may even shuffle up on you after each hand dealt. This is not so in the two-deck game.

If you can find a two-deck game where the cut card is placed deep into the deck, say one and two-thirds decks, then you have found a game where the deep penetration is about 75 percent. This means that slightly more than one and a half decks of the two decks in play will actually be played before the next shuffle. This is about as good as it gets among blackjack games as they are played in today's casinos. Surprisingly, there are quite a few of these games available in many casinos in Las Vegas, in tribal casinos, and even on some riverboats. The rules of play may, however, vary. On some of these tables you may be permitted to double-down only on 10 and 11. You may also not be able to resplit cards, and also may not be able to double-down after splitting. This is not, however, necessarily so. There are still several casinos where you can play this game with most of these options in effect, particularly the ability to double-down on any two cards and split and resplit Aces. If you can find a game where you can take advantage of at least some of these options, then this is one among the several better blackjack games that are available. However, if you find a two-deck game where none of these options are available, and where the cut card is shallow, leaving most of the decks out of play, then this is not a good game even though it may be so promoted. Therefore, in such situations where the majority of these player-favorable options are *not* allowed, you should not play there.

In the two-deck games where the majority of the favorable rules *are* in effect, and where there is deep penetration, your chances of winning are much greater. Here's how some very simple methods of observation can help enhance your skills with the MBS on this two-deck game.

In a two-deck game, there are eight of everything. This

means that there are thirty-two 10-value cards and, naturally, eight Aces. This also means that you have a total of eight possible blackjack hands, combining the eight Aces with eight of the 10-value cards. (Actually, 128 different blackjack two-card hand combinations are possible, sixty-four such hands per single deck. At least according to the mathematics. However, in the real world of actual in-casino play, all you have to remember here is that eight Aces make possible eight blackjack 21 hands, and that's it. For an interesting discussion of the mathematical probabilities, please refer to the section "Too Many Blackjacks" in chapter 15.)

If all of these eight blackjack hands are so played, then there will be twenty-four 10-value cards left. Out of these cards you can expect the best possible combination of twelve hands whose two-card values are 20. Overall, your best set of expectations are the eight possible blackjacks, plus a total of sixteen possible two-card hands of 20 (without any blackjacks hit), or a lesser number when blackjacks are hit (minus one for each blackjack hand seen). Therefore, there are a total of forty cards in the two-deck game that have the most effect on your best possible hands (the thirty-two 10-value cards plus the eight Aces).

If you have a two-deck game with deep penetration, the majority of the cards from these freshly shuffled decks will be placed into play. If this is so, you can fairly safely assume that one-quarter (25 percent) of the cards will *not* be played. By extrapolating this to the 10-value cards and the Aces, you can now make an educated estimate that the cards that *will* be played therefore have 25 percent *fewer* of the 10-value cards and Aces. This means that instead of expecting the full thirty-two 10-value cards and the eight Aces to be dealt, you can now expect that only twenty-four 10-value cards remain among the cards that will be played, and only six of the Aces. Although this will not always be so perfectly balanced, on average you can safely make this assumption based on the placement of the cut card into the two decks. This will allow you to make a reasonable estimate of the number of cards that will actually be played, the number of cards cut off from play, and, therefore, the educated estimate of how many of each of the most *valuable* cards are left among the cards that will be dealt during this round of play.

Now, as the cards are dealt, you can quickly scan the hands as they are exposed and keep a quick mental tally of how many of the 10-value cards and Aces have been dealt. You are not necessarily looking for the blackjack hands, or the hands totaling a two-card 20. You are simply tracking the decks for 10s and Aces. This is the simplest and most rudimentary system of card-counting.

As the hands continue during this round of play, it does not require great mental abilities or a photographic memory to simply recognize how many of the possible remaining 10-value cards and Aces have been dealt out so far, as each hand is played. Remember that you have estimated that there are approximately twenty-four 10-value cards that will be in play this round, and six of the Aces. Therefore, for each Ace that you see, you now know that there is one *less* Ace left. The more Aces that are dealt, the *lower* the chances of hitting a blackjack hand, or drawing an Ace when such may be needed. Likewise, the more 10-value cards that you see dealt, the *fewer* of these remain in the cards still left to be played in this round. So, if you know that there are about twenty-four 10-value cards among the cards that will be played this round, and you have seen ten of them dealt in the first two hands, then you know that there are only fourteen such 10-value cards still left among the cards still to be played this round. Combine this with the number of Aces that you have seen dealt, and you can make a very reasonable series of assumptions as to the potential value of the subsequent hands that may be dealt. In the situation where you have seen most of the 10-value cards dealt, and some of the Aces, you now know that the remaining cards have more of the low-value cards left, and this is, therefore, a poor deck for you. So you make small bets. Conversely, if you have seen several hands played, and have seen no Aces, or only one, or very few 10-value cards, then you know that the cards that are still left to be played contain an unusually high concentration of the high-value cards. This then means that this is a good deck for you and, therefore, you will make bigger bets.

These are the simplest principles of card tracking and card counting, and the best game in which to employ them is the two-deck game as described here. There are enough of these games available in the casinos you will visit to make learning this method worth your while. It's not that hard to do, and you don't have to be a genius or a mathematical wizard or have a great memory. It's really just a form of practiced common sense. Yes, it will require you to practice so that you can teach yourself to spot these cards quickly and make mental notes of them. However, this will take only a few times, maybe a couple of hours or so, depending on your commitment and abilities. Once you learn this, and do it in the actual casino, it will become even easier. What this will do for you is enhance your play beyond just the methods of the MBS, which teach you what to do with the cards you get and the totals you achieve. With card tracking of 10s and Aces, you will enhance your play performance by also knowing when to make larger wagers, and why. You will not win them all, but then that's the game. However, you will win more often, and win more money by doing this. Therefore, over the run of your session or visit, it will improve your end-result performance. Plus, it's more fun. You'll feel like you know more than the other players, and you will actually be quite correct.

Four-Deck Games

Although not nearly as favorable, the shoe-dealt games can still offer some good opportunities for blackjack profits. It should be obvious that if the only choices that are available in the casino where you happen to be visiting are shoe-dealt games, then the *fewer* decks the better. Among the shoe games, the four-deck game is best, simply because it has the fewest total cards. In fact, if you think about it, you can treat the four-deck shoe almost exactly the same as the two-deck game, which we talked about immediately above. In the four-deck game there are now four times the number of cards in the single deck, or twice the number in the two-deck game. If you have learned the two-deck game, then it should not be that hard to multiply everything by two and come up with the series of decisions that can make the four-deck game almost as good as the two-deck game.

Although they are very rare in Las Vegas, and Nevada in general, there are enough of the four-deck games found in Atlantic City, the East Coast, Midwest, tribal, and riverboat casinos that the game is worth a short analysis here. Provided that most of the player-favorable options are actually available in the four-deck game, it can be treated almost exactly like the two-deck game. In order for this game to be as good as the two-deck game, and better than the six-deck or eight-deck shoes, then the four-deck game must include at least most of the following:

1. It must allow deep penetration to at least 70 percent, thus leaving a minimum of three of the four decks in play for each round.
2. The game must not be shuffled by a machine, particularly by the continuous shufflers and/or randomizers.
3. Players must be allowed to double-down on any first two cards.
4. Players must be allowed to split and resplit Aces.

5. Players must be allowed to split and resplit any pairs.
6. Players must be allowed to double-down after splits and resplits.

All these options should be available to you in the four-deck game. If they are, then the game is worth playing and can be played almost identically to the two-deck game, and can often be better under these conditions. If these options are not available, then don't play this four-deck game. You will actually be better off playing the six-deck shoe, where usually all of these options are available. However, if you find a four-deck game where at the very least there is deep penetration, where you can double-down on any first two cards, and where you can split and resplit Aces and any pairs, then this is not that bad. On the other hand, it isn't the best, so you may not wish to play it, at least not as your staple diet of blackjack play.

In a four-deck game, there are sixty-four total 10-value cards, and sixteen Aces. In a game where there is deep penetration, we can therefore use the same formula as described in the two-deck game, and make the educated estimate that we will see approximately forty-eight total 10-value cards, and about twelve Aces. Now we can keep track of the cards as they are dealt, and keep our mental total of what value cards have been played and, therefore, what kind of cards are still left.

Although this method becomes more difficult as the number of decks increases, it is still a valuable tool in the four-deck game because only a little more effort is needed to keep a reasonably accurate running total of the kinds of cards that have been played. If you are able to do this on this game, then you can use it to your advantage in the same manner as you would for the two-deck game. Your overall results should be about the same, depending on the rules of the four-deck game, and which of the favorable player options are in effect, which are prohibited, the level of deck penetration (and, of course, your abilities to keep track of the 10s and Aces), and your potential error rate in doing so.

You can determine all of this for yourself once you start to practice. Begin with the two-deck game, and after you have mastered the tracking of the 10s and Aces for that game, try it with the four decks and see how you do. Most of the time, if you have done a good job of teaching yourself to do this for the two-deck game, you will have no problems being able to do this also for the four-deck shoe, and this will therefore open up more opportunities for you in more casinos.

Six-Deck and Eight-Deck Games

The six-deck and eight-deck shoe games are another matter altogether. Most of the time, avoid all eight-deck games. Period. If all you can find in that casino is an eight-deck game, just don't play. With eight decks, you are basically playing nothing more than a slot machine, since the various rules of play and the way the game is dealt will erode any kind of abilities that you may bring to the table. Just stay away from any game that uses more than six decks, and that's all I'll say about it here. Therefore, I will now discuss only the six-deck shoe game, as the natural progression from the two-deck and four-deck discussions above.

In a six-deck shoe, there are ninety-six 10-value cards and twenty-four Aces. It now becomes almost impossible to simply keep track of the 10s and Aces. Even if you find a game with deep penetration, in this game even penetration of 70 percent to 75 percent means that more than two decks will be cut out of play. Plus, in many casinos, the cut card is placed only 50 percent into the deck, thereby cutting off three full decks from play. Even the best educated estimates for tracking the 10s and Aces, which worked so well for the two-deck game and almost as well for the four-deck game, are now practically worthless. It is simply not possible to predict with any degree of knowledgeable certainty, or mathematical probability, just where the majority of the 10s and Aces are. The majority of them could easily have clumped in the three decks that have been cut out of play. Even if the Aces were all clumped in the three decks that are going to be played, what good is that? Not much, since most of the 10-value cards are out of play in this example. The point I am making is that in the case of the six-deck shoe, the principles used in tracking cards are so inaccurate and generally unreliable that it is simply not worth the effort. That's why other methods were developed.

The best method for estimating what kind of cards are left in the decks is what is called "card counting." This we will explore in more detail in the next chapter. For now, simply put, card counting is a system similar to the tracking of 10s and Aces that is used by knowledgeable players to keep a running estimate of the potential positive or negative values of the decks, as play continues. Blackjack is a statistically *dependent* game, as opposed to a game such as roulette. Results in roulette, and other similar games where each event is independent of previous events, are completely detached from previously obtained results. What happened in the past has no bearing on what may happen next time. In blackjack, however, the odds change as the game continues through the shoe (or decks dealt). What this means is that as the cards are dealt out to each player, hand after hand, the expected values of the kinds of cards left in the deck still to be played (and thus the relative potential values of the kinds of hands that these cards would make possible to be obtained) also change. As more small-value cards are dealt, this means that more of the large-value cards are left in the remaining deck, or decks. The fewer Aces, for example, that have been dealt, likewise means that the more

Aces are left in the cards still to be dealt (or those that remain cut out of play). Therefore, blackjack, and games like blackjack, are games of *dependent* events. What happened on the previous hands has a direct bearing on what the value of the next hand, and subsequent hands, may be.

By following a strict guideline for assigning positive and negative values to each kind of card as it is dealt, card counting blackjack players can make continuous adjustments to the expected probability of certain types and values of hands that may be dealt. Therefore, when this system indicates that the remaining decks to be played contain an unusually high concentration of large-value cards, such as 10s, then such a player will make a bigger wager. Conversely, when the opposite is indicated, the player will make a smaller wager.

This is by no means an exact science. As in any other dependent situation, indefinable or unknown variables continue to erode the absolute certainty of whatever events are anticipated. Therefore, this method of keeping track of the cards is merely inductive in nature, rather than deductive. This does not diminish its overall applicability to the game of blackjack, or the financial successes that may result when this system is practiced as nearly perfectly as possible and under the most favorable of circumstances. The most powerful help that this system provides is the ability to make educated assumptions as to the likelihood of winning hands occurring. Of course, this also means that such hands will occur during the next event, or the next series of events, and will do so for all the players at the table, including the dealer, and not necessarily only for the player who is able to make such educated estimates. For this reason, even the most skilled card counters do not always win, nor do they always experience the success they are due under these favorable conditions. All that these methods can do is to enhance what we have previously established as the tracking of cards.

In our examples for the two-deck and four-deck games, we used the simple systems of tracking just the 10s and Aces. More skilled players may even wish to add the 5s to their tracking situations. Actual card counting takes this further, and specifically assigns values to each card in the deck, and this is then added and subtracted continually in the mind of the player who practices this as the hands are dealt. This is a far more precise formula for tracking the cards, and thus anticipating the kinds of hands that may be obtained, than the mere tracking of 10s and Aces, even with the 5s thrown in. This is especially so in the six-deck game. Although very hard to do, counting cards in a six-deck game is about the only reasonably surefire accurate method of anticipating the kinds of hands that the player may obtain on the next hand, or series of hands. It is, however, very, very hard to do; only a few players can do it well, and continue to do it for a long-term profit. It is also not always very accurate, or useful, as we will shortly discover.

Most of us would have a very hard time trying to keep a running count in a six-deck game. Although not impossible, it is a system that requires a lot of practice and learning, as you will shortly find out in the following chapter on counting cards. Back in the mid-1980s I became enamored with blackjack as a game from which to make a living. I discovered systems of counting cards that made abundant sense to me. Since, at that time, blackjack games were still able to be found in single-deck and two-deck games, and even six-deck shoe games with very favorable rules, it was not that hard to think of playing blackjack for a living—and I did. For a while. I practiced every day for at least three to four hours, for a whole year. I became very good at this and was able to count a six-deck shoe with absolute accuracy 99 percent of the time. I also practiced the side counts of Aces and

5s and included that in my repertoire. The reasons that I selected the six-deck shoe were twofold: first, the six-deck shoe game in Las Vegas at the time offered all of the favorable options, and the penetration was 80 percent or better on many tables; second, I simply wanted to know if I could do it (I had previously successfully learned to count the single- and double-deck games).

So I drove from Los Angeles, where I was living at the time, to Las Vegas. This was a simple trip for me since I drove up at least once a week, usually for the weekend. Traffic wasn't nearly so bad at that time, not on the highway and certainly not in Las Vegas. It was a nice trip then. I arrived at the Las Vegas Hilton, which at that time had one of the best six-deck blackjack games in town. After relaxing for a while, I sat down at a $25 blackjack table at 2:30 A.M., and bought in for an initial $300 (with the rest of my bankroll for that game easily accessible to my hand in my pocket). Although this buy-in was undercapitalized for this kind of game, and I recommend against buying in for so little in a "green" game, I had my reasons for doing so at the time (one of which was not to draw attention to myself immediately with a large buy-in).

I was lucky to find an empty table and for the rest of this session had a one-on-one game with the dealer. This was the best of all possible worlds for that game at that time. I played for three hours in this real casino game, and under all of the real casino conditions and distractions. I counted the decks perfectly. After three hours I walked away with over $3,000 in chips. I went to my room and slept for the next twenty-four hours. I was *that* exhausted by this process.

From that time on I played only the two-deck games when counting cards. My ability to count cards did not diminish, but I was simply unable to physically handle the strenuous effort required to do this for the six-deck shoe. I

proved my point—I could do it—but I also proved that
doing it for a living was not an option, because of the wear
and tear on the mind and body. Counting the six-deck shoe
accurately is *that* hard. Make no mistake about it. If you do
it perfectly, you will have to be physically and mentally an
athlete of the highest caliber. Otherwise, you will fail.

Thereafter, I chose to concentrate on the easy games: the
two-deck games that were plentiful. This was a breeze compared to the six-deck shoe. I never regretted what I had
done, because this formed the very strong foundation that
later enabled me to make a success of my career in gaming
on a multitude of fronts. Had it not been for that experience,
and others like it over those years, this book might not have
been written. Suffice it to say that in this discussion of the
six-deck shoe game, even perfect card counting may not be
viable for the majority of players. There are, however, other
methods for gaining an advantage in the six-deck game that
are much easier to do.

Card Clumping

One of these methods is called "tracking the clumps." Card
"clumping" occurs when the decks are shuffled by human
dealers. No human shuffle is ever perfect or ever completely
random. After a while, certain groups of cards tend to clump
together, forming streaks and runs of like-value cards. These
clumps may be composed of a series of high cards, such as
a series of 10s, or of low cards, such as a series of cards 2
through 6. Of course, mixed runs of cards are likewise possible, but these are statistically meaningless for these purposes because here we are only concerned with learning to
spot clumps of either high cards or small cards.

It is also important to mention here that in any six-deck
shoe game that uses the mechanical shuffling machines,
tracking of clumps is not possible. These machines often

additionally randomize the cards, and this renders the vast majority of the deck completely without any recognizable pattern, be it clumps or counting of cards. Further, in games that use continuous shuffling machines, no principles of blackjack skill can be used. For these, and many of the other reasons already mentioned and yet to be mentioned, the best you can do for yourself in playing blackjack is to completely avoid any and all blackjack games where any kind of shuffling machine is used. (There is only one way that I have found in which the game of blackjack can still yield a continuous profit even against machine-shuffled games, including continuous shufflers and randomizers. This is a very specific and highly detailed program of how to wager and what to look for, and is detailed in my book on Advanced Strategies. However, even then I still recommend that you simply stay away from any blackjack game that uses these shuffling machines. It's just not worth it.)

Well, now that this has been made clear, we can continue with the discussion of clumping. This is possible in situations where human dealers shuffle the cards; therefore, if you must play a six-deck shoe game, always look for one that is shuffled by a human dealer and not a machine. Then look for the majority of the player-favorable rules and conditions, and when you have found this, then you have the kind of six-deck shoe game that can be played with the following suggestions.

In some casinos that use the six-deck shoe game shuffled by a human dealer, after the shuffle they burn a series of cards. These may be from only one to four, up to six or more. Normally, about six cards are so burned from the freshly shuffled six-deck shoe. In most casinos these burn cards are set aside face down—but not always. In some casinos they are shown face up. Admittedly, this is *very rare*, but if you do find a casino that does this it will give you an immediate advantage in starting your tracking of clumps. If you see that the six burn cards are mostly high-value cards, such as 10s, then you know that the beginning of that shoe may actually contain a clump of high-value cards. Conversely, if you see that these initial burn cards are low-value cards, then this may indicate that the first part of the shoe contains small-value cards. Of course, if these initial burn cards are a mixed bag, then it means little, other than that these initial cards contain a random mix. Naturally, all these suggestions apply only in the case where you can see the first series of burn cards face up. Mostly, you will not.

If the first series of burn cards are not shown face up, then you need to evaluate the potential clumps in this shoe as the game progresses. You can only begin to gain an understanding of how the cards are clumped once you start seeing the cards dealt. Since the six-deck shoe game is mostly dealt with all cards face up, you will be able to clearly see how they come out of the shoe. Here *seat selection* is also important. Try to sit in the *third-base* position, the "anchor" spot on the table. This will give you a clear view of the entire table and all the player's hands before you. It will also give you time to spot the cards as they are dealt out of the shoe. The second important thing to do is to look for the *order* of the cards as they are dealt out of the shoe. Remember that the cards will be dealt around the table, one card at a time to each player spot and then the dealer, one after the other, and not two at a time. This means that in order for every player, including the dealer, to receive two cards, the dealer will have to make two sweeps of the table dealing the cards. Depending on the number of players in the game at any given time, the total number of cards that are so dealt sequentially will vary.

Let us assume for the sake of this discussion, and example, that you are sitting in the third-base seat and that there are four other players in the game with you, making a total of five players plus the dealer. This means that a total of twelve consecutive cards will be dealt out of the shoe for each hand played (two cards to each of the five players, plus the dealer, dealt one after the other for two sweeps, one card at a time; thus the cards come out of the shoe *consecutively*). By watching for the *sequence* of consecutive cards, you can begin to make educated assumptions as to the nature of the order of the cards in this shoe. What you are looking for are *patterns* of like-value cards. For example, you are looking for a series where the majority of the consecutive cards are all small-value cards (2 through 6), or, conversely, a pattern of consecutive high-value cards (10-value). Any such pattern of a series of consecutive cards of the same, or similar, value indicates a potential clump of cards in this shoe. What you need to determine then is whether the clump will favor you or the casino.

If the sequence is composed of high-value cards, this may indicate a clump of big cards, and therefore suggests that you will be more likely to receive a standing pat hand on the initial deal. It is therefore at this time that your wagers should be increased to take advantage of this clump. On the other hand, if the clump shows a run of small cards, then the advantage lies with the casino because your hand will likely consist of cards whose total value will require one or more hits; therefore, your likelihood of busting, or being forced to stand on a mediocre hand, is much higher. In this situation you want to bet small, and save your money.

You should be aware, however, that this suggested method of tracking clumps of cards, and the recommendation of when to increase the wager, is *almost directly opposite* to the teachings of the card-counting running count. Here the suggestion is that when you spot a trend of high-value cards, you are seeing a clump of cards that will favor you for this short-term clump. In card-counting, the very same sequence of high cards would produce a negative count, thus suggesting the exact opposite wagering strategy. The point is that neither system is 100 percent accurate, and it cannot be so accurate because of the conditions of the real-world actual in-casino play, with all the various rules and restrictions.

In tracking clumps of cards, you are looking to make wagers when the group of cards will favor you for that very short sequence of the high-value card clump. In card counting, you are seeking out more consistent wagering opportunities, so the method is quite different.

These two systems are not necessarily in conflict with each other. One can support the other in assessments of the potential value of the remaining cards to be dealt. A clump of high cards may be exploited even when the card-counting running count may indicate a negative value. These are judgment calls that only you can make after becoming an expert at all of these methods. Therefore, my suggestion here is not to allow yourself to be confused by these options. The simplest form of tracking cards is the clump recognition. Once you have mastered this, then you can decide for yourself if the skills of the running count may be more to your liking. More on the running count, and the difficulties faced while trying to practice it, in the next chapter.

Spotting trends in clumps is by no means a perfect way to track cards in a six-deck shoe. It is no substitute for skilled card counting, which can be far more accurate over longer periods. Spotting trends in clumps relies heavily not only on your ability to play perfect MBS at all times, but also on your ability to make accurate, or at least reasonably accurate, observational judgments on the possible value of upcoming cards. Since this is only an *observational* evaluation, and not one based on actually *knowing* the composition of the remaining cards, such as may be obtained from an accurate running count or the true count, then the accuracy will be somewhat diminished. Nevertheless, for the casual player who has mastered the MBS, but does not wish to learn the complex methods of counting cards for the six-deck shoe, trend spotting card clumps is a much easier and less stressful way to enhance your blackjack profits.

These systems and suggestions for the improvement of your blackjack game are not intended to replace the MBS. On the contrary, your ability to track clumps is *directly dependent* on your skill in learning the MBS. All of these discussions of various forms of tracking and counting cards are directly dependent on the fact that you first must know the MBS *completely*. Without this, not even a perfect ability to count cards, or spot trends of clumps, will help you win. That's why the MBS is so crucial, and must be learned before any of these other methods can be used.

Whether or not you take any of these suggestions for the enhancement of your blackjack profits to heart will largely depend on whether you wish to help yourself or not. You can't help yourself or your game if you won't learn the MBS. Without it, you will always be the perennial victim, the casino fodder of which there are millions. That's why casinos win so much money—because even smart people become complete babies when it comes to gambling. The allure of the experience completely dulls their senses and abilities to think—but you can help yourself by learning this *before* you go to the casino. Enough said. Let us assume here that you are interested in helping yourself and your game and that you will indeed learn the MBS, and we will move on with our discussion of trends and clumps.

What the tracking of clumps will do for you is provide you with basically a no-brainer method of anticipating the kind of hands that you are likely to receive on subsequent deals from this six-deck shoe. It will provide you with an indicator of the likelihood of high- or low-value cards being grouped together in this portion of the shoe. How far this clump may extend is the other decision you are facing. Will this be a large clump, or one with only a few cards? Well, in the above example, you will see twelve consecutive cards dealt out each time. This is a pretty good indictor of the kinds of clumps that may, or may not, be present in the shoe at that moment. By sitting in the third-base seat, you will get a chance to see all these cards and be able to have enough time to give yourself some basic calculation opportunities as to the possible makeup of the remaining cards in that shoe. You may even wish to add the principle of the tracking of 10s and Aces to your observation of trends in clumps, and this may provide you with an even better framework for your wagering decisions.

The point of all of this is to provide you with an easy-to-use system of spotting better betting opportunities so that you can increase the size of your wager in favorable situations, and lower the size of your wager in unfavorable situations. That is all that these principles are designed to do. To make profits from blackjack, you must be able to vary the size of your bets. These systems show you ways in which you can do this, and do so in situations that are calculated by you, based upon *knowledge*, as being among the favorable opportunities to so increase your bets. The only alternative is to guess. If that's how you plan to play, close this book right now and go and lose your money, because that's exactly what will happen to you. Then you can come back and read this book again from the start, and maybe then you will understand what is offered here. Even the most rudimentary method of tracking card clumps is designed to give you the necessary indicators as to when you should increase your wagers, instead of having to rely on pure luck or "gut instinct." Playing on "gut feelings" or on "instinct" is financial suicide in any gambling game, and particularly so for blackjack. Therefore, when you learn the MBS, and then must play a six-deck shoe, knowing trends and spotting clumps will help you make profits.

Trend Spotting

Trend spotting is another application of the "clump" system. In a six-deck shoe, there will be several occasions when the players will win far more hands than they are statistically "due" to win. At other times, the dealer will make far more winning hands than is statistically indicated over the long haul. These trends may go contrary to the observed clumping, and it is therefore advisable that you recognize the difference. Spotting clumping will provide you with the opportunity to anticipate the kind of value of hands that you may be receiving from the subsequent deals of hands from this shoe from that point on, for as long as that clump may last. How long that will be is directly dependent on the size of that clump, as well as your ability to keep track of it and knowing when it turns, or ends.

Trends, on the other hand, may happen even when the clumps indicate that the order of the upcoming cards may be contrary to the trend that is being exhibited. For example, the clumps may show that low cards are grouped for the next series of hands. Normally, this would indicate that you make small wagers, because the chances of your making good hands are lower, and the chances of the dealer's drawing better hands are greater. However, there may have developed a trend, whereby the dealer suddenly can do nothing right and keeps making hands whose standing totals are lower than the players' hands, or keeps drawing cards that bust the dealer's hand. In such a situation, you have spotted a *positive trend*, because here the dealer has turned what is usually described as "cold," while the players have gotten "hot." These are examples of counterstatistical anomalies. Simply put, against all expected statistical or mathematical expected values, the contrary is happening. This is, therefore, one of the extremes, and such extremes happen very regularly and that's why trend spotting is a very useful tool, particularly for a six-deck shoe.

Statistical anomalies, which such trends actually are, happen on both sides of the spectrum. There will be times when, for example, the players are getting all the great cards, such as all the high-value cards, and make standing hands of 19s and 20s, while the dealer makes stiffs and still wins. In this converse trend, the dealer will continue to defy the probabilities by continually drawing cards and making 20s and 21s against the players' hands of 19s and 20s, quite against any order of reasonable expectation. This is also an extreme, the direct opposite to the player-friendly extreme discussed above. In such situations, no matter what you do as a player, you can't beat such a hot trend for the dealer. If this happens, and you are able to spot this trend early, sit out the series of hands, or simply leave the table. Don't play on a table where you get good hands, but they get beaten by a dealer who is running "hot." On the other hand, when you sit at a table where you may be getting lousy cards, but they win because the dealer is "cold" and the trend is decidedly with the players, then you should stay and press your bets even on cards whose lousy values you may not ever have even considered playing. Trend spotting is, therefore, a very valuable tool for the knowledgeable player.

However, you must keep in mind that such trends may be very short and that knowing *when* they end is hard to do with any degree of accuracy. Therefore, trend spotting, similar to the tracking of clumps, is not an exact method of keeping track of the cards, or the potential value of winning hands for you. It is very important that you remember this and not allow yourself to be swayed by the rush of luck in a positive trend when you spot one and are lucky enough to exploit it at that moment. Even your ability to spot such trends will not be absolutely accurate at all times, and often you may actually misidentify the trend and make a serious error. Don't worry too much about it. As long as you know the MBS, overall you will make a profit from blackjack because now you know that any of these systems of tracking or spotting trends are merely designed to enhance your overall abilities, and are not in themselves the only certain methods of winning.

All of this is part of a greater picture, and as long as you keep that in mind, you will not hurt your ability to make profits, even if you do make a mistake and erroneously identify a trend or clump that turns out to be wrong. It will happen—but if you are using the MBS and are only using trend spotting or clump identification as an enhancement, you will be more successful than all of the players who merely use hunch plays, or bet the same amount on each hand. Of course, the most professional approach to gaining the most edge from your blackjack play is to learn to count cards, and that is the subject of the next chapter.

SHUFFLING MACHINES

At this point it becomes relevant to mention something more about shuffling machines. Although I refer to them throughout this book, I think it is important for you to know exactly what they are, how they work, and what they are designed to do. Briefly, a shuffling machine is a mechanical piece of equipment that has been invented and designed to shuffle playing cards used in casino pit games. Games such as blackjack, Pai Gow, Let It Ride, and Caribbean Stud use these machines. The shuffling machines were actually invented by a truck driver who wanted to solve a problem he read about in the newspaper.

The story behind this is the perfect stuff for a Hollywood movie. As the myth goes, this tale of success began one rainy day at a truck stop somewhere on the long-haul truck routes in the midwestern U.S.A. A trucker from Minnesota by the name of John Breeding was mulling over an article he'd read in the *Wall Street Journal*. This particular article was about the problems many Atlantic City casinos were having at their blackjack tables with card-counters. The card counters to whom that article referred were professional blackjack players who had mastered a system of tracking the cards, and thus were able to beat the game in Atlantic City casinos. Although counting cards is *not* illegal, casinos don't like card counters because they think they win too much. This is also a myth, as we will learn in the next chapter, "Card-Counting."

This fateful truck stop and cogitation took place in 1982. John became convinced that he could invent a machine that would shuffle cards. Such a machine, he thought, would provide more random shuffles and eliminate "clumping," dealer cheating, and other such "human" situations. Therefore, he thought, such a machine would be very desirable for the casinos. Having made this determination, he set out to invent one. It took him ten years, but by 1992 he had succeeded, and his company, Shuffle Master, Inc., launched its first series of card-shuffling machines. At that stage, these machines could shuffle only one deck at a time. This wasn't very useful for most of the casinos, since by that time casino blackjack games—for which this shuffling machine was originally designed—were played mostly with two decks, or multiple-deck shoes. So John had to do a little more thinking, and invented Let It Ride.

Let It Ride is sort of a cross between blackjack and poker. The betting arrangement is like blackjack but the hands are poker hands. Each player at the table makes three bets of equal amounts before the hand is dealt. To each player the dealer deals three cards, and in the center of the table he deals two community cards face down. After they look at their hole cards, the players may take back one of their bets or let the bet ride. The dealer turns over one of the community cards and the players again have the option to pull a bet back or to let the bet ride. The dealer then turns over the last community card and the players are paid odds on their bet according to the rank of their hand from a royal flush to a pair of 10s.

Let It Ride is a game that is ideally suited to the single-deck shuffling machine, and by inventing it, John Breeding also invented the market for the shuffling machine. Not only did he now have a new game that he could sell, but one that was designed to use his shuffling machine. And so the legend was born. By 1993, the Let It Ride game was launched, quickly became a huge hit, and the rest—as they say—is history.

Well, that's the story behind the shuffling machines. Although John Breeding first thought that the machines would be applicable to blackjack, it turned out that he had to invent a whole new game before anyone would actually try his shuffling machines. The game of Let It Ride turned out to be hugely popular, even though it is a really bad game, odds wise, for the player. However, the players loved it, and since the casinos could often hold upward of a 20 percent house edge on this game, it proved a veritable table-game gold mine. This is how the shuffling machine innocuously sneaked into the casino, and now we're stuck with it.

Although initially conceived as something that would speed up the game, as well as combat card counters, the truth is that the machines slow the game down to a crawl. This is especially true of games where the machines spit out presequenced clumps of cards. Players and dealers are forever waiting for the stupid thing to finish shuffling. There are constant jams and misshuffles that cause the game to stop while someone attracts the attention of the pit boss so that the shuffling monster can be fixed.

In recent years, newer versions of these clunkers have been forced upon the unsuspecting public. These machines are called "continuous shufflers," and they are able to shuffle multiple decks of cards, such as those used in shoe games. Not only do they shuffle multiple decks all at once, but they continue to shuffle the cards constantly, even as the dealing goes on. So there is never any cut card, and never any beginning or end to the "shoe." Each time the hand is finished, the dealer scoops up the played cards and places them in the mouth of this mechanical monster, which then devours these cards and immediately adds them back to the other cards that are being continuously shuffled, even as the dealer takes out the next round of cards. So, theoretically, you can get back exactly the same lousy cards you had on the hand before—and so on and on. This never ends, even when there are no players. The shuffling goes on and on as long as the power keeps flowing, and the noise from it is terrible. The only time this stops is when the decks are changed, or when the table breaks down and is closed.

Such continuous shuffling machines mean that there is absolutely no way in which any card counter can practice that system. This also means that even the Basic Strategy player will be largely defeated, because the machine keeps on shuffling the same cards constantly, without any beginning or ending to the shuffle point. If you play with these machines, you are playing merely a slot machine with cards, and are not playing blackjack. You might as well burn your money. At least that will give you some warmth. Playing blackjack with these machines means that you are wasting your time, your money, and your efforts.

On top of all this, there are now also other machines, which are called "randomizers," further refinements of these already terrible machines. These randomizers not only continuously shuffle the cards, but they also switch the cards from deck to deck as well! This means that no matter what portion of the several decks in use are going to be dealt out by the dealer, all these cards are not just continuously shuffled, but are also being exchanged between the various decks. So it is possible for all the "good" cards to be shuffled away from you. This machine further erodes anything that could even be called "skill" in blackjack. Games using these randomizer machines are even worse than the slot machines. At least on the slot machines, the worst you can get on a $5 machine, or even a $1 machine, is about a 2 percent house edge, and in some casinos, only a 1 percent edge. On blackjack games using these randomizer multiple-deck continuous shuffling machines, the house can expect anywhere from a 6 percent to a 20 percent edge. The truth is that if you play blackjack with these machines, you are being exploited. There's no "nice" way to put it.

I've said this earlier, but I'll say it again: My very serious advice is *never*, ever, under any circumstances, play any blackjack table that uses any kind of a shuffling machine. If you do, you are throwing your money away, and doing it needlessly because there are plenty of other blackjack games that do not use these machines and are a lot better. If all you have in your casino are blackjack games that use these machines, don't play them and don't go there again. Write to the executives and tell them that you will go elsewhere because you aren't interested in wasting your money on these horrid games. Even if you have to buy a plane or train ticket, or drive three hundred miles somewhere else, it will still be cheaper for you than to spend even just an hour on a table with these shuffling machine monsters. I can't put this any plainer, so enough said.

Card Counting

A single deck of fifty-two cards (no Joker or wild cards) was commonly used in blackjack games until the 1970s. Smart players quickly developed several card-counting strategies, and this allowed them a big edge over the house. Since casinos were not in the business of losing money, they found ways of combating this.

Counting cards is not very difficult with a single deck. In a single deck there are four of everything. Four Aces, four Kings, four Queens, and so on. As the cards are dealt, it is quite easy to remember how many Aces have been dealt, how many 10-value cards, how many 5-value cards, and so on. Therefore, skilled players would know which cards were left in the deck and bet accordingly—but the casinos quickly caught on and put a stop to this by altering the rules.

Incidentally, counting cards is *not* illegal. Casinos simply don't like card counters because they think card counters will win too much. Over the years, however, various changes in the rules of casino play have made blackjack a hard game to beat, even for a very skilled card-counting player. Hard to beat—but not impossible.

One of the first changes that casinos made to the rules of blackjack was to stop dealing single decks from top to bottom. They then began using the "burn" and "cut" cards to reduce the number of available cards that would be played. Thus the card counter would not see all the cards, and would, therefore, have to make a certain set of assumptions to modify his applied game theory. As card-counting and betting systems improved (chief among which were the invention of the "plus-minus" counting system, "true count" and later derivatives such as a "side count of Aces" and— often in combination with the Aces count—a "side count of 5s"), casinos simply went to more decks, from one deck to two, to four, to six, and even to eight decks in some casinos. This makes it exceedingly difficult for card counters to get an accurate, or "true," count.

The by-product of this, however, was that blackjack became not nearly as popular as before, and with the advent of video poker and more sophisticated slot machines, modern casinos soon began to feel the pinch. Therefore, in recent years, casinos have again started to reduce the number of decks and somewhat liberalize the rules. We have already discussed the various ways that the number of decks and the rules of the game can affect your ability to make profits from blackjack. In this chapter, we will concentrate on discussing the systems of card counting, which have been developed over the decades by many dedicated blackjack analysts, mathematicians, theoreticians, authors, and professional players.

Blackjack card-counting systems can be divided into the following groups:

1. Tracking
2. The "Ten-Count"

3. The "running count"
4. The "true count"

We have already discussed the tracking of cards. Basically, this is the simplest form of card counting, and centers more on observational rather than actual figures in determining the value of the remaining cards to be dealt. Wagers made according to these tracking principles are still more profitable than simple hunch play, but are not very accurate. In the tracking of cards, much depends on the player's ability to do this, make accurate estimates of what kinds of cards are left, and then wager accordingly.

THE TEN-COUNT

The Ten-Count is more accurate than tracking. The Ten-Count was the principle of card counting introduced by Ed Thorp in his book *Beat the Dealer,* which became a best seller in the early 1960s. This was the first mathematically sound method of counting cards in the real world of actual in-casino play. Simply put, this Ten-Count centered on the player's ability to keep a running total of how many of the 10-value cards had been dealt thus far. Since at that time almost all blackjack games were dealt from a single deck, and none of the player-unfriendly rules and methods of dealing that are now common were in use, this method of counting cards was quite successful. After all, in a single deck it was not that hard to count the sixteen 10-value cards in the deck.

Later, this system of counting the 10-value cards was further enhanced by the addition of the side count of Aces and 5s, which were by then determined also as cards that had an effect on the player's ability to beat the game. It seems obvious to us, in the twenty-first century, that 10s, Aces, and 5s are the key cards to our profits from blackjack, but all

those decades ago these discoveries were considered profoundly new. They may not truly have been so new, because
many gamblers probably would have already applied somewhat similar strategies for blackjack, although such were
never before so enumerated, quantified, and analyzed in
such precise and mathematically accurate formats.

What the Ten-Count, along with the side counts of Aces
and 5s, enabled players to do was to make quite accurate
judgments in a single-deck game as to the makeup of the
remaining cards in the deck. If, for example, two-thirds of
the deck had been dealt and the player practicing the Ten-
Count, with the side count of Aces and 5s, counted only five
10s out, one Ace out, and three 5s out, then he knew for an
absolute certainty that the remaining one-third of the deck
of cards that was still left to be played contained eleven 10-
value cards, three Aces, and only one 5. This made his ability to wager large sums an easy decision because he was no
longer victim to an indefinable "luck," but he knew, really
and actually *knew*, that the remaining cards would provide
him with a powerful edge over the casino.

It is for this reason that the Ten-Count was such a powerful revelation at that time. Of course, today it is impossible
to practice the Ten-Count with any such degree of accuracy.
Today single decks cannot be exploited in the same manner
as they could be in the days when the Ten-Count was so
revolutionary. Even in the early 1960s, casinos soon learned
how they were exposed to smart blackjack players, and
started to change the way the game was played. First came
the introduction of the cut cards and the burn cards so that
counters playing the Ten-Count could no longer rely on the
total accuracy of their count, because they no longer were
able to see all of the cards. Then came the multiple decks.
However, before the game was changed to the game we now
know in today's casinos, there came the development of the
running count.

THE PM COUNT

The running count, often also called the "Plus-Minus" or the "High-Low" count (or system), was developed as the result of efforts by many people. Their contributions are already widely acknowledged in many texts, and I have also listed some of them earlier in this book. All of us who write about blackjack owe a debt of gratitude to the people who, for many decades, dedicated themselves to developing these systems and methods. Although there are many, many versions of the running count system, with ever-escalating complexities, it is the plus-minus counting system that is by far the simplest and easiest to learn. For the sake of brevity, I will hereafter concentrate only on this system of counting cards, and I will call it the PM count, short for "Plus-Minus." For those of you who have read other books that have touched upon this system of counting cards, this is the same system as that known as the "High-Low" count.

The PM count is so simple because it divides all of the available cards in the fifty-two-card deck into three groups. All of the small cards, the cards 2 through 6, are assigned a "plus" value of "1." Therefore, whenever any such card is seen, the player assigns to it the value of "plus 1." The cards 7, 8, and 9 are assigned the value of "0" (zero), and thus treated as neutral. All of the 10-value cards and the Ace are assigned the negative value of "minus 1." Here's how it breaks down:

The PM Count

Cards:	2, 3, 4, 5, 6	each = +1
Cards:	7, 8, 9	each = 0
Cards:	Aces, Kings, Queens, Jacks, 10s	each = −1

The reason this is called the Plus-Minus count is that you keep assigning either the "plus" or the "minus" value to each card as you see them dealt. The reason it is called a "running" count is that the count continues throughout the shoe, or the decks being dealt for the current series of hands, until the next shuffle. Therefore, you are "running your total" all the way through all the cards being dealt until you reach the next shuffle point, where the process begins all over again. The way this is done is as follows.

Suppose you have seen this sequence of cards dealt:

5, 7, 10, 3, 6, Queen, Ace, 4, 2, 9, 3, 6

This is not an unusual sampling, because this many cards can easily be dealt for six players, or five players plus the dealer. This is a sequence of twelve cards, and is similar to the examples we have used earlier when we discussed the much simpler methods of tracking cards. Here, however, we are discussing a very precise method of actually knowing which cards have been dealt and, therefore, which kinds of cards are more likely to remain in the deck, or decks, still to be dealt. Consequently, this exercise provides us with far more accurate information.

The way the above sequence of cards would be counted is like this:

+1, 0, −1, +1, +1, −1, −1, +1, +1, 0, +1, +1
Plus 1, Zero, Minus 1, Plus 1, Plus 1, Minus 1, Minus 1,
Plus 1, Plus 1, Zero, Plus 1, Plus 1

This provides the final running count for this sequence as the running total of +4 (plus 4). This is because of the assigned plus-minus value to each of the cards we have seen. Those values are shown in the table on the next page.

Although what the table shows may look confusing, it is actually quite simple. All you have to remember is that we have here merely added the progressively different running totals of the values assigned to each card as we have seen it dealt.

CARD VALUES		COUNT	RUNNING COUNT
The 5	=	+1	+1
The 7	=	0	+1
The 10	=	−1	0
The 3	=	+1	+1
The 6	=	+1	+2
The Queen	=	−1	+1
The Ace	=	−1	0
The 4	=	+1	+1
The 2	=	+1	+2
The 9	=	0	+2
The 3	=	+1	+3
The 6	=	+1	+4

Add this up with me here:

+1 add 0	=	+1
Add −1	=	0
Add +1	=	+1
Add +1	=	+2
Add −1	=	+1
Add −1	=	0
Add +1	=	+1
Add +1	=	+2
Add 0	=	+2
Add +1	=	+3
Add +1	=	+4

Again, here is our series of cards:

5, 7, 10, 3, 6, Queen, Ace, 4, 2, 9, 3, 6

When we saw the 5 dealt, we assigned this the value of +1, and since this was the first card we saw, our running count at that point was +1. Then we saw the next card and it was the 7; to that we assigned the value of 0 (zero); therefore, when we added the +1 for the 5 card to the 0 for the 7 card, we had a running count of +1 (add the +1 to the 0 and it equals +1). Then we saw the 10 card, and we assigned this the value of –1 (minus 1). When the –1 is added to the +1, then we have the running count total of 0. Then we saw the 3 card, and to this we gave the value of +1. Since our running count prior to seeing the 3 card was at 0, we now add the 0 to the +1, and we have a running count of +1. Then we saw the next card, and it was the 6; to that we applied the value of +1, and added this to our running total, which was now +2—and so on.

This system of valuing the cards allows for a quick and fairly easy way of determining the composition of the remaining deck, or decks, still left to be played. What this PM count does is to allow you to make a very educated series of estimates as to the expected composition of the remaining cards. Specifically, the PM count allows you to numerically identify the kinds of cards that *have* been dealt out so far, giving you a clear indication of which kinds of cards have as yet *not* been dealt out. For example, if we have a "plus" count as our running count, this means that more of the low-value cards—the 2 through 6 cards—have been dealt out, leaving more of the 10-value cards in the deck. Having a deck, or decks, rich in 10-value cards is good for us, and bad for the casino. This means that more blackjack hands are possible, and more standing hands of 19s and 20s. The higher the positive running count, the higher the "plus" number gets, the better this is for us because we now know that the remainder of the deck has many more big cards than little cards. So we can now safely make larger bets because the odds are in our favor.

It is for these reasons that the PM count can be such a powerful tool for the skilled blackjack player. It is useful not only because it shows when to make the large wagers, such as when the running count is $+6$ and higher, but also when *not* to make large wagers, or no wagers at all, such as when the running count is either at 0 (zero), or, worse, at minus-any-number. If you are counting cards using this simple PM method, and your running count is at "minus" overall, then this is the time to either make the smallest wagers possible or, better still, leave the table. Using the PM count properly can give you a decided advantage in short-term, as well as long-term, profitability of your blackjack play. Correctly using this system means always to make the large bets when the running PM count is high (very positive), and make the smallest wagers when the running PM count is at zero or at negative. Preferably, using this system correctly will mean that whenever your running count is below zero, and has entered minus territory of -3 or more, you will leave this game. Or, at least, sit out the next series of hands, if the casino will permit this, until the count gets back to positive territory. You can then resume play at that table, or, preferably, you would have left the table, pretended to wander around, and then perhaps selected another table or came back to this table seemingly out of whim. As a card counter, disguising yourself is also very important, because you can get barred. (Most casinos are considered private clubs, and therefore are able to refuse service, or bar anyone they choose, without explanation. If you are spotted as a good card counter, you may be asked to leave, or be barred permanently from playing blackjack in that casino, even though card counting is not illegal. So card counters often use disguises. However, current advances in surveillance technology, including face-recognition software, will soon make any kind of a disguise all but worthless.)

For right now, remember that although the PM count is a simple system, actually doing it correctly under real-world in-casino conditions is not nearly so easy. You will have to be able to count these cards very quickly and keep an accurate running count in your head while doing all the other things, such as making your correct wagers, particularly if you are also using a betting progression (which is highly advisable), chatting with other customers, being joyful like any other tourist, getting your drinks (nonalcoholic, I certainly hope), and generally looking as though you are having a great time and have no clue whatsoever about anything going on at the blackjack table. This is very, very hard to do while still keeping an accurate count.

If you want to make card-counting part of your blackjack repertoire, then you must practice—and practice and practice and then practice some more. It will not be easy. It will be hard, and you must be able to get it down to a skill that is 99 percent accurate at all times, for any game, and under all conditions. It's not impossible to learn. Here's how you can start your learning process, and your practice, with a few easy-to-do hints.

Get several decks of cards, and some plastic cut cards. You can buy these in any gaming supply store, such as the Gambler's General Store on Main Street in Las Vegas, or at most gaming equipment suppliers. If you can't get the right ones where you live, then you can always order them over the Internet or by mail order. Get the right kind of cards and equipment, however, because the closer you can get to the actual situations you will find in the casino, the better you will be at your eventual skill level.

If you have the financial means to actually purchase a real blackjack table and all of the equipment and place this in your home, this is the best you can do in your preparation for being a real card counter. However, many of us do not have such means, or simply do not wish to make such an investment. In that case, all we actually need are the real cards—the kinds of cards that are used in the casinos. Once you get these cards, and the cut cards, make a blackjack table layout. You can do this on your kitchen table, in the living room, or anywhere. It doesn't matter where or how you do this, as long as it is as close to your vision of the blackjack table as you can make it. Then take the decks and start to practice.

First, take two decks. This is a common game in the casinos, and as I have stated earlier, is among the better games you can encounter. Shuffle both decks together, and cut them (don't use the cut card yet). Start dealing the cards face up one after the other (don't try to deal actual hands as yet). For now, just keep turning the cards face up from these two decks, one after the other, until all the cards are dealt. As you are dealing each card, add the "positive" value to each card to which such value should be assigned by the PM count system, and subtract the "negative" value for each card whose value should be so designated, and add the "0" (zero) value for each of the 7, 8, and 9 cards you see. At the end of both decks, when you have dealt all the cards one after the other and kept a running total of the values, your count should be at zero ("0"). This is because all of the cards are divided into two equal groups of "plus" value cards and "minus" value cards, while the third group contains the "0" (zero) value cards. Therefore, when all cards are counted from the entire decks, the final tally should be "0." If, that is, you have done this correctly.

If you have counted correctly, then your count started with a zero and ended with a zero. This is good. All decks that are dealt from first card to last should start with the count of zero and end with the count of zero. This shows not only that the decks are true and correct, but that you have also counted the cards correctly. This is very important, because if you have ended the count with anything other than zero, then you have made a mistake (or the decks do not contain the correct number of fifty-two cards, which is unlikely). Normally, if you have counted down both decks from the first card to the last, you should be at the count of zero. If not, you need more practice—and you *will* need more practice, believe me. It will not be easy to do. Even if you count the cards for the first time, after having learned the PM count from the information I have shown here above, and actually get the final count to zero, which means you have done the count correctly, this may only have been luck the first time around. Try it again, and again—and again. You will need to practice this system of counting cards until you can count all the cards in both decks like this, one after the other, in under ninety seconds and always be correct in the final tally. You are allowed only one mistake out of a hundred tries. Even that is one too many. This kind of speed and expertise is absolutely necessary because you must achieve at least a 99 percent accuracy all the time. Impossible? No. Hard? Yes! Valuable? Most definitely.

Why is this so important? Because in the real casino you will be facing numerous distractions. You will not only have to also keep track of your bets and consider the interruptions from other people—players, dealers, pit bosses, chip fills, currency exchanges, cocktail servers, announcements, promotions, slot machine noises, and so on—but you will also have to keep a sharp eye for the values of cards in other players' hands! In the real casino, you will not see the cards dealt so nicely and neatly as in this practice example. There you will see the cards handled by other players, who will not always be so accommodating by showing them plainly and easily. Remember that two-deck games are usually dealt face down, which means that to get the values of other players' cards, you will have to count the exposed cards first, then go back to each player's hand as they take action, and then as the dealer turns their hands over. This further complicates your ability to be able to get an accurate running count. For these reasons, and many of the other ancillary and companion reasons that are part of this system, you absolutely must have the running count learned to that level of accuracy. Always, at all times, no matter what the distractions.

Therefore, once you have achieved the ability to count the two decks accurately as described, and do so to 99 percent accuracy over each hundred times you have so practiced, and do this in under ninety seconds, then you are ready to practice the real-world in-casino situations. Although when you are at home you can only approximate the casino conditions, you can, nonetheless, make your practice sessions closely resemble the kinds of situations you will encounter in the real casino. Start this aspect of your counting practice by dealing several hands to "players," and one hand to the dealer. For example, deal out five hands to five "players," and then the dealer's hand, just as it would be dealt in the casino. You take the seat of one of the players. All cards are dealt face down, as will be the case in the real casino in the two-deck game. Only one of the dealer's two cards will be dealt face up. Now assume your position as the player (whichever seat you wish to choose).

Now look at your hand, and count it; then count the dealer's upcard. So far, these are the only cards you can see, therefore the only cards you can count. Now start to play the other "players'" hands, as they would be playing them in the real casino, in that order. If the player requires a hit, then hit that hand from the deck just as the dealer would do. However, remember to count only those cards that are *exposed*, such as the cards that the player hitting the hand will receive from the dealer. These are the only other cards you will see until either the player busts his hand, or the dealer turns the hand over after he has completed his hand. Count the card, or cards, that were received and dealt face up to that hand. If the hand is now a standing hand, stand, by leaving the player's hand cards face down just as they would in the real casino. If the player's hand busts, then toss the cards face up as the player would do in the real casino. At that point the dealer would scoop them up, place them in the discard tray, and move on to the next player. In your practice scenario, you should do the same. If such a bust hand is exposed by that player, count the cards as they are exposed. Repeat this process for all hands, including your hand and finally the dealer's hand, and count all the cards that you will see and that will be so exposed during the process of these hands. Then, for those hands that players still hold and that have not busted, count those cards as the dealer turns them over, including any of the dealer's draw cards as well as his down card. When all this is done, scoop up all the cards so dealt, and place them into a discard tray (or, if you don't have one for your home training, simply set them aside).

Now, before you continue with your training, go back to all the cards that were dealt in this first round of your example. Remember what you think the running count should have been after the conclusion of this round of hands. Then take all the cards from the discard tray in your home training example, and count them again, slowly, one by one. If your count is the same as the one that you achieved during the course of playing the actual hands, then you are doing very, very well. Many times, however, you will find out that you did not count the real-world example as well as you think you did. The point I am making is that counting cards in theory is far from the same thing as the reality, or the actual doing of it. By now you should have been very good at counting the cards one by one from the entire decks of cards, and be able to do this quickly. However, you are now suddenly faced with the example of having to do this in a far less perfect situation, one full of problems and distractions. Although this is nowhere near the kind of reality that you will find in the real casino, it is as close as you can get without actually going to the casino and facing the issues there.

You can further increase your confidence in this method

of practicing the PM count by trying to repeat this process in a more distracting environment. After you have practiced on your own, and are now able to get an accurate count most of the time, even with all of this incomplete information, try doing it in front of the TV. Or in the family room, or at your friend's party, or with the TV, radio, and stereo playing all different programs. Turn one TV on to the news, another to a game show, turn the radio to a talk program, tell your spouse or friend to tell you about their day, and while all this is going on, try to practice the PM count as described above. See how closely you can get to the actual reality of the running count with all these distractions, and how fast you can do this. This kind of a situation is about the closest you will get to the one you will have to face in the real casino.

The real world of casino card counting is nothing like the nice, clean, theory. The real world is full of ways and means that are in conflict with your ability to keep an accurate count. If you are to succeed, you must keep an accurate count at all times, no matter what the distractions. You will need to keep your betting structure in mind as well. It's a lot to do, to remember, and to do well and accurately without ever making any mistakes. If you do make a mistake, this will eat into your ability to generate the positive swing of the odds in your favor. The more mistakes you make, the less accurate the method will be and the fewer wins you will have. Don't kid yourself. The real truth of card counting is that it is very hard. Very hard to do accurately, consistently, all the time, every time, no matter what happens.

Here's a hint. You may use what can be called the "nullification principle" to help in your counting of cards. This is a method of helping you to count *fewer* cards in your running total in the PM counting method. What this means is that whenever you see two cards whose values are the direct opposite of each other, cancel them out.

For example, when you see a 10-value card and a 3-value card, the running count would normally be, first −1, and then +1, which equals 0. However, by applying the "nullification principle" to your PM running count, you can simply "zero-out" these two values, in effect canceling both cards out, because when counted *together* as a group of two cards their *combined* value is "0" (zero). This will help you a lot, since it will save you mental energy in keeping the PM running count individually for each card seen. By grouping opposite-value cards into groups that nullify each other's value, you will speed up your ability to count cards in the real world of the actual casino, and be able to maintain a more accurate running count.

As another example, let us use the series of cards we have adopted in the examples shown earlier, which were the following sequence of cards:

5, 7, 10, 3, 6, Queen, Ace, 4, 2, 9, 3, 6

Now we can count the 10 and the 3 in that series as a *combined* 0, the 6 and the Queen likewise as a combined 0, and the Ace and the 4 also as a combined 0 (zero). The 7 and the 9 are also counted as a zero each (because that's what the PM count dictates for neutral cards). Therefore our running count will be easier to maintain, because here we are counting the series as +1, 0, 0, 0, 0, +1, 0, +1, +1 = +4, which is the actual running count, as we have seen from the examples listed above. Don't be confused by this—it's quite simple. The table on page 210 shows how it comes out.

Adding the nullification principle to your PM running count, as a method to enhance and speed up your count, will enable you to better handle the fast-paced and distraction-filled environment of the actual casino. You can try to practice these methods at home, by using the examples generated here. The more you practice, the better you will get.

The 5	=	+1	
The 7	=	0	as is the case with all the neutral cards
The 10 and 3	=	0	now combined together in the nullification principle
The 6 and Queen	=	0	because they also zero-out (cancel each other)
The Ace and 4	=	0	because they also zero-out
The 2	=	+1	
The 9	=	0	as is the case with all the neutral cards
The 3	=	+1	
The 6	=	+1	

As you can see, the final running count is +4.

COUNTING THE SHOE GAME

I began this series of practice examples by using the two-deck game. This is, actually, the more difficult game to master for the PM count, largely because in the real casino you will not see all the cards face up, and when you do you will not see them for a long period of time. You will see many cards for only a fraction of a second. You will, therefore, have to be able to read them, assign them their count value, zero them out if you apply the nullification principle to your method of counting, and then add the count to your progressive running count, very quickly and accurately. All this is very hard to do, especially for games whose hands are dealt face down. That's why I started with this example, because I first wanted you to become aware of the difficulties in doing this. Now we can focus on the shoe-dealt games, where all the cards are dealt face up.

Although the six-deck shoe (and other shoe-deck games)

have all their cards dealt face up, other than the dealer's down card, these games are mathematically not as good for your blackjack profits as the two-deck games. However, when you are counting cards as we have described in this chapter, being able to *see* the cards *as they are dealt* is a distinct advantage. It will allow you more time, and that, in turn, will allow you greater accuracy. However, the advantage gained from being able to see the cards as they are dealt does not equal the deficit that multiple-deck shoes have on your overall percentage. With each deck added to a shoe, the casino's general advantage over the Basic Strategy player rises by about 0.3 percent. In a six-deck shoe, the casino's advantage over the Basic Strategy player is about 0.6 percent to 1 percent, depending on the various other rules of the game as dealt from the six-deck shoe in the casino where you happen to be playing. If you are playing the MBS as indicated in this book, the casino's advantage over you, in a six-deck shoe game whose rules of play include the majority of the player-friendly rules that we discussed earlier, is about 0.1 percent. For all intents and purposes, this is statistically even. By adding your ability to count cards perfectly with the PM method, and also by enhancing this with your ability to use the nullification principle to speed up your count and overall accuracy, you will have about 0.5 percent edge over the casino in this shoe, under those rules and conditions of dealing. Later, by applying "true count," you can increase that again (more on true count below).

The real truth is that even applying a card-counting system to the six-deck shoe, you can gain at best only a marginal advantage over the casino, in general long-term percentages. By using a true-count method, you will increase this percentage slightly, but it still means little over the mostly short-term slices of your exposure to blackjack, either on your visit, trip, or vacation. Over the years as you play, these small bits will add up. Basically, you will lose less and less, and then start to win a little more and more. By continually applying your skills over longer periods of time, and continuing multiple visits to the casino, your long-term results will show a remarkable improvement. Such improvements are measured not only by the amounts and frequency of your overall wins, but also by the reduced frequency, and amounts, of your cumulative losses. Therefore, even small increments of advantage you can gain from learning the count systems will have an impact, although this impact may largely not be visible in the short term. It will be visible in the long term, if, that is, you wish to seriously commit yourself to improving your blackjack game with these methods and systems.

In a six-deck shoe, you lose considerable advantage in your PM counting system. This is somewhat compensated by the fact that on most six-deck shoe games you will be allowed more of the player-favorable rules than you may get in the two-deck games. Nevertheless, by simply applying a perfect PM count, you will only slightly increase your advantage, and it will be very hard to do. And it will be very hard to maintain this kind of effort for any length of time. If you do want to apply the PM count to a six-deck shoe, here are some advantages and hints.

Sit Where You Can See All the Cards

If you can, always sit in the third-base, or "anchor," seat at the table. This is the seat to the far right of the dealer (the far left from the player's perspective). This seat will receive the last hand, and be last to act on every hand, just before the dealer takes action on his hand. There are several distinct advantages to sitting in this position.

First, you will be able to clearly see all the cards as they are dealt. As I have mentioned earlier, most six-deck shoe games are dealt face up, which means you will see each card for each player immediately as it is dealt out from the shoe by the dealer. This also means that you will be able to see all these cards dealt out of the shoe *consecutively*, which will enable you to make a very accurate running count.

Second, you will be able to see every player's action before you have to consider your hand. This means that you don't need to pay any attention to your hand, other than to count the cards as they are dealt out from the shoe at the beginning of the hand in progress, along with all the other cards dealt to all the players seated in this game, until it is your turn to act. By having this extra time, you can therefore concentrate on accurately counting all the cards as the dealer deals them to all the other players as they are making their decisions.

As each hand is played, you will continue the running count for each card dealt out for each hit each player gets, and so on, until it is your turn to act. Then, and only then, do you need to pay attention to your hand. By the time you get to be this good at blackjack, you should already know what your decision will be and make that decision quickly and automatically. There should be little for you to think about. If you need to take hits, do so and then count each card as it is dealt. When you have finished with your hand, whatever the outcome, count the dealer's card as he turns it over, and then add to the progressive running count any cards that the dealer may be required to draw. Once you have done all this, the hand is over. The dealer will pay winning hands and collect losing bets from those players still in the hand at that time, and then will take all the played cards and put them in the discard tray face down. However, by then you have already seen all these cards; therefore, you should now have a reasonably accurate count.

All of these actions by the players, and the dealer, give you added time to make an accurate count, and for this reason sitting in the third-base seat is the most advantageous to you in these situations where you are counting cards from a six-deck shoe dealt face up.

Add a Side Count of Aces and 5s

You can enhance your profitability by adding a side count of Aces and 5s to your running PM count. What this means is that you will also keep count of how many of the Aces and 5s have been dealt out, in addition to keeping the running PM count. Of course the more stuff you add to your system, the more information you will have to keep in your mind, and juggle it accordingly. It gets harder the more information you keep adding, and accuracy can therefore suffer—but it can be done.

By keeping this side count in addition to your running PM count, you will be able to make more accurate judgments as to the exact composition of the remaining decks yet to be played. If, for example, you count that sixteen of the twenty-four possible Aces and seven of the possible twenty-four 5s have been dealt out early in the shoe, with most of the decks remaining in play, you will now know that the rest of the cards have very few blackjack possibilities, while containing a higher number of cards that can improve the dealer's bad hands. Therefore, even if your running count suggests better betting opportunities, you may wish to modify your normal wagering strategy for this situation, because now you know that many of your profitable hand opportunities are already gone.

It is for reasons such as these that the PM count, and any refinements to it, are so important to the serious blackjack player. By knowing this information you can alter your Basic Strategy and wagering decisions accordingly. You will pick up a few tenths of a percent in added value, but not very much. Still, this can be profitable in a variety of situations.

Add the Streak Count or Trend-Tracking

The streak count is virtually identical to what I have earlier described as the tracking of clumps. Either positive or negative clumps produce streaks. Positive clumps can produce streaks favoring the players, while negative clumps produce streaks favoring the casino. By using the PM count, you should overcome the reliance on merely the observations of clumps and streaks. In fact the PM count should indicate in which of the streaks you happen to be. A very high positive PM count should indicate a favorable streak, while a significantly negative PM count should indicate the opposite. However, this may not always be so. Many times your skills in observation may indeed pick up on something earlier than the running PM count could indicate. Remember that the PM count becomes effective only after a series of cards have been dealt. Therefore to obtain verification that a positive streak is occurring, the PM count will indicate it only *after* the shoe is well into the favorable streak, or clump. However, early observation of the trend can allow you to complement the PM count, and thus exploit a streak, or clump, of favorable betting situations.

This also applies to trend-tracking. As mentioned earlier, trends are short-term slices of overall probability extremes. Such trends may show up as sequences of events where players win and the dealer is "cold," while at other times the players may be getting great cards but lose because the dealer is "hot." Learning to spot such trends, as well as clumps, can give your PM count an added edge.

Add the Side Count of 10s

You can use Thorp's Ten-Count system in addition to your running PM count. In fact this is the best use of the Ten-

Count under the current conditions of dealing blackjack in virtually all modern twenty-first-century casinos. Using the Ten-Count alone will no longer produce the kind of results for which it was originally developed. However, by adding this to your running PM count you can take advantage of significant improvements in your overall wagering and strategy decision making. I have already mentioned that you can add the side count of 10s and 5s, but that was not necessarily in accordance with the tracking principles provided for in the Ten-Count itself, as presented by Thorp. In reality, they are very similar because both rely on your ability to keep count of additional cards. However, the side count of 10s and 5s, because of its complexity, is a little harder to do than just employing the principles of the actual Ten-Count itself, as defined by Thorp, in addition to the PM count.

All of the above suggestions for the refinement of your PM count for the six-deck shoe game require additional skills. Particularly, they require considerable mental abilities as well as accuracy. What this means is that you will have to master the ability to keep a running accuracy over several items. If you employ everything, you will require expertise in the following:

1. A thorough mastery of the MBS, played perfectly without error at any time.
2. Absolute accuracy in the running PM count, as defined.
3. The mastery of trend-tracking, clump-tracking, and streak counts.
4. The ability to keep a side count of Aces and 5s.
5. The ability to keep a side count of 10s and 5s.
6. The ability to add the Ten-Count as your side-count companion to the PM count.

All of these disciplines put together, if done perfectly, can yield an advantage in your favor over the casino in a six-deck shoe game, with favorable playing rules, of about 0.6 percent to 1.3 percent over the long haul. Unfortunately, unless you are a superman (or woman), or a charter member of Mensa, the plain truth is that all of this is practically impossible to do in the real world, with any degree of consistency and accuracy.

But does this mean you should never learn any of this and simply play blindly, without any knowledge or discipline? Absolutely not. Even though all of these systems of counting cards are very hard to do, the information and skills you acquire by learning them is very valuable in all your gaming, and all your blackjack games, even if you don't practice all of this at all times and don't always play perfectly. Every bit of information about blackjack you gain that sticks in your mind will help you play a better game—and a more profitable game. None of this information, or the skills you acquire as a result of practicing these skills, are ever lost. They all have an impact everywhere on your gaming, as you will find out once you start to go to casinos and seek to better yourself by playing with these principles.

Soon you will start to look at your blackjack game with different eyes. You will start to see small things, such as trends, unfavorable rules (such as when the dealer must hit soft 17), the placement of the cut card (and become aware of the level of deck penetration), the kinds of cards that are being dealt, and so on and on. Soon you will automatically start to alter your game, even subconsciously, and start making better and more informed decisions. All of this will be the result of learning this information. It will be valuable to your play even though the truth is that all of it put together is nearly impossible to actually do.

The benefit to you is not that all of these disciplines put together may be hard, but that all of them put together can be learned and practiced. Once learned and practiced, they will combine to strengthen what is already your natural game—and that's where the benefit truly lies, for you and everyone like you—and me. We all benefit by this cumulative knowledge and practice.

THE TRUE COUNT

At this point I should again remind you that the previous section was concerned with the six-deck shoe game, and that these principles of counting cards, and all of their added side counts, are far more plausible to do in the two-deck games. Even a four-deck shoe will be easier to count in this manner. As I have said earlier, the two-deck game is probably the best overall, and in this game you can easily add all of the above principles of counting and tracking cards, in combination with each other, and be able to actually do it. The simple truth is that the two-deck game is just easier to count and track. Even though the game itself may not always have all of the favorable playing rules that can usually be found in the six-deck shoe game, even then the two-deck game can be better, particularly when you employ the PM count along with the other side counts mentioned above. When you are able to do that, your two-deck game will yield a much better overall advantage. If the playing rules consist of the majority of the player-friendly options (which we have listed earlier), and you use the PM count along with the side counts as shown, then you can gain an. edge over the casino of somewhere between 0.6 percent and 1.8 percent. This is a very significant improvement, and is actually not that hard to achieve—with practice, of course.

Also, by further refining your game with the ability to calculate the true count, your abilities will also additionally enhance your profits. By using the two-deck example here, applying the true count as a refinement of the PM count, in addition to the other factors required, you can actually gain an advantage over the casino of about 1 percent to 2.3 percent. This is a huge swing in your favor, and is absolutely dependent on your ability to become a perfect card counter who uses all of the available methods and keeps them accurately in his mind at all times, wagering accordingly, and playing the two-deck game with the *majority* of the player-favorable rules. These games are available and can be found. There are several Las Vegas casinos where you can play this game exactly this way, although I should mention that these games may no longer be available in all gaming centers, with all of the player-friendly rules.

As I write this, in the summer of 2002, Las Vegas casinos using the two-deck games are already altering their rules of play, trying to limit players' success. Nevertheless, largely owing to competition, there will always be some casinos in Las Vegas that will offer this two-deck game with the majority of the player-favorable rules. For this reason, my comments and recommendations for the two-deck game stand. Increasingly, though, depending on your geographic location, or your ability to travel to Las Vegas, you may wish to consider learning more of these systems as they apply to the four- and six-deck shoes. These will be the games you will find most often in all of the casinos around the U.S.A., and elsewhere in the world.

For the six-deck shoe, the advantage of the true count also improves performance, but in this case it is easier, and better, to limit yourself to using the PM count with the true-count refinement, and not try to add the other side counts. This would make the process too difficult in the real world of the actual casino, and your accuracy could suffer significantly. Remember that the advantage of the PM count, and now certainly the advantage of the refined true count, are useful to you only if you do this *accurately*. Without your ability to perform these counts accurately, your decisions will be wrong more often, and this means that your profits will erode faster. This is more so for the six-deck shoe because here the financial volatility of your wagers and bankroll will fluctuate with much greater swings than in the two-deck game.

In the two-deck game you can usually play more conservatively, not only because most of these games will not have the wider variety of playing options—such as being able to split and resplit and double-down on any two cards and split and resplit Aces and double-down on all splits and resplits—but also because the two-deck game has fewer options for volatile swings in wagering ranges. In the six-deck shoe game, you will encounter many more situations where the wagering strategy calls for splits, double-downs, double-downs after splits, resplits, and so on. All of these will contribute to a wider range of wagering possibilities and significantly more widely ranging fluctuations in your financial fortunes. For these reasons, use of the true count in the six-deck shoe game is a much more desirable addition to the PM count, since this will tend to diminish such financial volatility and give you a more accurate gauge for the true composition of the remaining decks still to be played.

What Is the True Count?

The "true count" is a method used to more accurately determine the composition of the remaining deck, or decks, of cards still to be dealt in any round of dealing of blackjack hands. It is a *refinement* to the PM count, *not* a substitute or replacement. The true count allows skilled players to reach a more accurate prediction of the true value of the remaining cards in the decks that are still to be played in that round of dealing, hence the term "true" count.

By being able to make these predictions, skilled players, who accurately use the PM count and are then able to accurately refine this using the true count, will therefore be able to make certain significant alterations to the strategy of their play as well as their wagering decisions. For example, if the player using the true count knows that the remaining cards are mostly 10-value cards, and he is dealt a hard 15 against the dealer's 8 upcard, he may choose to stand instead of hitting the hand as would be indicated when using the Basic Strategy only. This is done by such a player in such a situation because he knows that the likelihood of his drawing a 10-value card to his hard stiff is very possible; therefore, he can choose to alter his strategy and stand, since this gives him an advantage in two ways. First, he will not bust his hand by drawing that 10-value card that he expects to be drawn from the remaining deck rich in such value cards, and second, he will therefore protect himself against a sure loss by placing the onus of decision upon the dealer. Since this player knows that the deck is rich in 10-value cards, therefore if the dealer does not have a 10-value card or a 9 in the hole (which would give him the standing hands of either 18 or 17), then the dealer may have to draw. In this case, the player with the foreknowledge of the high concentration of 10-value cards in the remaining decks actually has turned a really bad hand into one whose percentage value over the dealer is now very high, since if the dealer must so draw, the odds now are that he will draw a bust card and make the player's stiff into a winner, while it would have been virtually an assured loser had he not been able to so accurately use the true count and thus alter his playing decision in this instance. Of course, such a player's other option may have been to surrender the hand, if the surrender option was available.

All of these above examples are made possible by a player who can accurately use the PM count and then refine it by using the true count. I caution you here, however, that deviations from the MBS are possible only for players who are *experts* at the PM and true-count systems. Only then can these players make such decisions deviating from the MBS and form their own wagering strategy decisions depending on what the situations may be. This is very hard to achieve, and this level of professionalism is practiced consistently by less than 1 percent of all the tens of millions of blackjack players who visit the casinos on a daily basis. This caution is important here, because I am in no way advocating that you rely on the true count and the PM count as your *only* resources in blackjack. In fact I caution you *against* trying to use the true count and PM count *unless* you become very, very good at mastering the MBS completely, and then mastering the PM count absolutely accurately, and then, and only then, refining your skills with the true count. For all of us who do not wish to immerse ourselves in blackjack strategies, it is not necessary to become so embroiled. Blackjack can be played enjoyably, with fun, and for profit even without the use of these hard-to-actually-do systems—but for educational purposes, they are quite interesting and helpful to know.

HOW TO CALCULATE THE TRUE COUNT

Calculating the true count is actually quite easy, but it is not foolproof. It requires that you be able to estimate the number of decks that still remain to be played. The formula for calculating the true count is as follows:

$$\frac{PM\ count}{Number\ of\ decks\ remaining}$$

This is a division exercise. The PM count divided by the number of remaining decks of cards still left to be played in that round of dealing equals the true count. For example, if the PM running count is at $+4$, and there are two decks left to play, then the division is as follows:

$$\frac{+4}{2} = +2$$

In words, this is the running PM count of $+4$ divided by the number of remaining decks, which is 2, and this equals the true count of $+2$.

The value of the true count is that it more accurately predicts the actual composition of the remaining cards *in the decks that are still left*. The way you do this is to first find out how many decks are being used in the game you are playing. This is common sense, and you should always know how many decks are in play before you sit down. If you can't figure that out just by looking at the cards on the table, then ask the dealer. Generally, single-deck and two-deck games will be hand-held. Shoe games of four decks, six decks, and eight decks will be played from a shoe. It should not be that hard to find out how many decks are being used in that particular game.

Once you know how many decks are being used, then simply look into the discard tray, and see how many cards have been played. From your practiced knowledge of being able to gauge the size of a deck of fifty-two cards, you then estimate the number of decks that have already been played. You do this by observation, and you will need some practice in order to achieve a reasonable degree of accuracy. Once you have mastered the ability to gauge the number of decks by looking at the discard tray, you will be able to determine the number of decks already played, and the number of decks still left.

For example, if you can see that two decks have been played, and this is a six-deck shoe game, then you know that four decks are still left to be played. Therefore, when you know the running PM count you simply divide that count by the number of decks still left to be played, and this gives you the true count. The reason you count the remaining decks, which also include the decks that have been cut out of play by the use of the cut card (deck penetration), is that you don't know which cards are in which parts of the remaining decks. You cannot, therefore, assume that the cards upon which your PM count is based are in the decks which are still to be played, those which are in front of the cut card (the shuffle point). So, to correctly calculate your true count, you must use the PM count number and divide that by the *total* number of remaining decks, including those decks, or parts of decks, which are cut off from further play (behind the shuffle point). If you do not do this, and instead use only the number of decks that are before the shuffle point, those that contain the cards that will actually be put into play before the next shuffle takes place, then you are merely guessing. You have no way of being certain whether your PM count, into which you are dividing the remaining decks, indicated that the cards left are in those parts of the decks that are before, or after, the shuffle point. For this reason, you always use the *discard tray* to gauge the number of decks played, and then divide the PM count with the number of total decks remaining. Otherwise, you would invalidate the PM count, and would use an incorrect figure for the division to arrive at the true count. This would invalidate the entire process and render a vastly inaccurate result.

Using the true count, particularly in games with fewer decks, such as the two-deck game, will allow you to make better wagering decisions, as well as enable you to more closely alter the MBS to fit the specific situation (once you become an expert at these methods). The main advantage of the PM count and true count when used together is the ability to increase the bets in very favorable situations, and decrease the bets in unfavorable situations. While the PM count alone will provide you with an estimate of the possible makeup of the remaining decks, the true count will bring your estimations closer to the actual reality. Therefore, if your running PM count indicates, for example, a positive number of +6 in a six-deck shoe game, but there have already been three decks played, then the true count will be only +2 (6 divided by 3 = 2). This is, therefore, not nearly as favorable as the PM count alone would have indicated. That's where the value of the true count lies, because it allows you to gauge more accurately the reality of the actual cards in the remaining decks.

On the other hand, the true count may in fact be higher than the running PM count. If we use the same example as above, and we have a running PM count of +6, but this is very late in the shoe and only half of one deck remains, then the true count is actually +12. When you divide +6 by 0.5, the result is 12. This means that the true count indicates a truly favorable wagering opportunity because here it was possible for you to calculate that the cards left in the decks to be played are in fact better than indicated by the PM count alone. However, please understand that this was only an example. In casino six-deck shoe games, there will virtually never be any situations where the penetration is so deep that there would actually be only half a deck remaining. The illustration, however, serves its purpose, because often, in fractions, the true count will, in fact, be higher than the running count.

Both of the above examples show how the true count can be used to refine your game, and refine the value of the running count. In the first example, the favorable running count of +6 was actually not nearly as favorable because the true count showed that the real situation was actually a true count of only +2. Still good, but not as good as that indicated by the running PM count. In the second example, where it was even later in the shoe, the true count indicated that the actual composition of the remaining decks was much better than that indicated only by the running PM count. Both counts showed a favorable betting opportunity, but the true count indicated more accurately just how good it really was.

PROBLEMS WITH COUNTING CARDS

There are several issues that will have an impact on your ability to properly benefit from counting cards. First, let's detail some of the problems with the true count.

Problems with the True Count

When you are trying to use the true count, the main problem is that you have to *estimate* the number of decks that are still left to be played. "Estimate" means to only approximate, which is, by its very definition, not accurate. Therefore, whatever true-count number you will eventually come up with will be only as accurate as your estimate of the remaining decks to be played. Therefore, the description of this system of counting as a "true count" is somewhat of a misnomer. In reality, this should be called the "approximation estimate." Unless you can actually count the exact number of cards that have been played, and be able to actually know the exact number of cards still left to be played, and then are able to actually fractionalize this to make up the absolute number of decks and the fraction of decks remaining, anything else will only be your guess. Only if you are able to so completely know the exact number of cards and the exact number of decks remaining will you be able to accurately calculate the true count, based on the true-count calculation formula.

However, here is the second problem. In order to calculate the true count, you must first be able to keep an *exact* running PM count. Not just an approximate PM count, but the actual, accurate count. This, of course, is not possible in the real world. Although you can practice at home until you are 100 percent perfect in the counting of any number of decks, in the real world of the casino you will never be able to do this. First, there will be burn cards discarded before the start of the freshly shuffled deck. You won't see those cards and will have to begin your running count already at a disadvantage. Second, there is the cut card (the penetration). This will cut off more cards, and you won't see those either. Therefore, your running count is based only on imprecise observation, because you begin with a deficit by not knowing the cards that have been burned, and then won't see all of the rest of the cards because the cut card will cut off anywhere from 25 percent to 50 percent of the cards. So, at best, your running count is based only on the count of the cards that you will see, and this will be at best only 75 percent of the decks and at worst only 50 percent of the decks, minus the burn cards. Your accuracy in the true count is therefore already compromised by your inability to have anything even approaching a reasonably accurate running count.

The third major problem with the true count is that not all of the decks will be played. Therefore, even if you are able to get a good running PM count, and are able to accurately estimate the number of decks still left to be played, what exactly did that do for you? Well, theoretically it tells you the most likely combination of the cards in the decks remaining to be played. However, not all of the decks still remaining will actually be played. Here the cut card comes into play again in the depth of the penetration. Suppose the true count indicates that you have a very positive expectation of the remaining decks being rich in 10-value cards, which by the rules of the true count would indicate a very favorable wagering opportunity. For the sake of this example, let us say that the true count late in a six-deck shoe game may show a +10, or higher. Remember that the formula for calculating this is to take the running PM count and divide it by the number of decks left.

In this example, to get this figure in an actual casino game late in a six-deck shoe, the running count would have to be +20, and the remaining decks only two. This will yield the true count of +10. What this means is that there have already been four of the six decks played so far, with only two decks remaining—but where is the cut card? Well, in this casino we perhaps have a very favorable penetration policy and so here they cut only 20 percent off the decks, leaving a penetration of 80 percent. Very nice, but hardly available in many casinos anywhere. Yes, there are some casinos where this may be found, but penetration this deep in a six-deck shoe game is very rare. So, to continue with our example, you now have a very lucrative betting opportunity —but wait—if your running count and your true count are correct, then *this is the shuffle point*! So you have reached the cut card and you will never be able to make the next wager. Well, what if you are only off in your estimate by one card? If this is so, then the actual cut card is just behind the next card to be dealt, and this means the dealer will have to deal another round before the next shuffle. Okay. Now you think you're sitting pretty, and you make a large wager. That's good—but what if the high concentration of 10-value cards was in fact located in the *last* of the two decks still left? What if the cards that will actually be dealt out for this last hand from that shoe are all low-value cards? Now you have made a larger wager, and are a great underdog to win, because the low cards are coming out instead of the high cards you expected. This is not nearly as farfetched as you may think. Situations like this happen all the time, and herein lies the greatest fallacy of the true count: There is simply no way to allow for these occurrences by using the true count. No matter what, even the true count is inexact and largely false in the information it provides.

The truth is that the true count is all but useless for gaining any kind of advantage because it still relies on variables that cannot be quantified. It is impossible to gain any accuracy from the true count because:

1. You must first rely on the accuracy of the running PM count, which is impossible to actually get.
2. You must rely on accurate estimates of the number of decks remaining, which is impractical to do and largely not possible.
3. You must be able to have *all* the cards from the remaining decks *dealt*, in order for the true count to mean anything, which is impossible in the real-world casino.

Therefore, the true count cannot be useful because it is, at best, only a vague estimate based on incomplete information and total guesswork on your part as the player. You are consequently not gaining anything by using it, and are making your blackjack game much harder and very much less pleasant as a gaming experience.

Is there anything good to be said about using the true count? Well, yes, there is. Learning it is good because it helps your mental game. As I mentioned earlier, any part of blackjack knowledge that you can gain will help you with your overall ability to make profits from blackjack. Just because using the true count in the real world will not be anything like the theory that is touted by those who still insist that card counting can be done with accuracy and for profit, the discipline that you will acquire as the result of learning this system will help you in other aspects of the game. For this reason alone, it is worth at least knowing about it and how to do it. Be aware, however, that although this system is discussed in all the blackjack books, the original application of the running PM count and the refinement of the true count were intended only for the single-deck game, which was still dealt all the way through the deck, first-card-to-last, as the game used to be in the early part of the second half of the twentieth century. Now, in the twenty-first century, none of this is actually possible; therefore, using these systems is no longer plausibly applicable. It just will not help nearly as much as it is touted to do.

Problems with the Running PM Count

Now let's briefly discuss the problems with the running PM count. Because the running PM count has always been acknowledged as imprecise, it does not inherently possess as many of the intrinsic difficulties as the true count, although both are interconnected. The running PM count always depends on three factors:

1. The number of burn cards burned face down, which the player never sees.
2. The deck penetration, and hence the number of decks (and cards) that will never be in play and, therefore, that the player also will not see.
3. The player's ability to accurately count with the PM counting system.

Because of both the facts of #1 and #2 in this immediate example, the player will never be able to have a completely accurate running count at any time.

First, there will be the burn cards dealt out, face down. Now, whatever the number of these cards, from this point on the player using the running PM count is automatically at a disadvantage. These burn cards are now out of play, and the player has never seen them. So the player starts with the "0" (zero) count, but in reality the count could have been as many cards positive as have been burned, or as many cards negative as have been burned, or, indeed, completely neutral, or any positive or negative beginning combination made possible by whatever the number of burn cards may have been. So, even though the player here starts with a neutral count, he is in fact starting with a guess, and not a fact.

Second, once the cards are being dealt out, the player can only begin the count at that point. After several of the cards and hands have been dealt out, it only then becomes possible for him to make even a rudimentary estimate of what the count may be. Since the running PM count is intended to give the player the advantage in wagering and strategy opportunities, the player is now forced to make further guesses based upon this progressively changing information, even though all of this information has already been seriously flawed by the fact that several unknown, and hence uncounted, cards have already been taken out of play. This simply means that the count is already compromised, and as the count continues these initial errors are compounded and propagated further.

Third, as the game progresses throughout that round, or shoe, the player counting with the PM method is making more and more decisions as cards continue to be dealt. However, he is making these decisions based on the additional assumption that the remaining cards will be dealt, even though he already knows that this isn't so. Only the cards *before* the cut card will be dealt, and those cards *behind* the cut cards will *never* be dealt during this round. Consequently, it doesn't matter what the running PM count indicates, because whatever it indicates may in fact not be anywhere near the real truth. If, for example, the running count indicates a hugely rich deck of 10-value cards toward the end of this round when approaching the cut-card shuffle point, which is an indication of a large wagering opportunity, or an applicable strategy modification, or both, the fact may actually be that all those nice fat cards are grouped among the cards that will *never be played*, those cards and parts of decks that are behind the cut card, and thus cut out of play entirely.

Consequently, in the real world, the actual truth behind card counting is that it can't work to anything like the degree of success and accuracy that is often shown in many of the blackjack books, texts, and videos.

Can card-counting actually work? In theory, yes, absolutely. In practice, in the casinos of the twenty-first century, as the game is being played and dealt today, it mostly will not work. I will grant, however, that there still are enough games available, such as some of the more liberal two-deck games, where very accurate card counting can, and still does, work. This is what I call the "workability" of the system. This "workability" simply represents the situations where even imprecise information is better than no information at all, and, therefore, this can be useful in the kinds of situations and applications for which this system was designed. Simply put, it can be put to use, even though we already know that it is inherently flawed and unreliable— but it can be "workable."

However, when it does work, it can work only imperfectly, because none of the principles that make it work so well in theory can actually be used in the real world of casino play. No matter how good you get as a card counter, and no matter how good a two-deck game you may find, in no casino today—of which I am aware as of the time of this writing—can you play blackjack and be able to count perfectly with all of the information you need to be so perfect. All such games use the cut cards and cut off parts of the decks. All such games use burn cards. These two facts alone mean that no card-counting systems can ever be accurate. It doesn't matter what the books say, or what the charts say, or what the mathematics shows, it's all wrong.

Any card-counting system that depends on counting cards like, or similar to, the PM running count and the true count, are all *guesses* vested in incomplete and highly corrupted information.

It simply cannot be otherwise. Any system that relies on incomplete and imprecise information is not a *method* that can have any kind of reliable success. Certainly not nearly the kind of success that many books, texts, and videos on blackjack claim. It's simply not possible, and that's the real truth.

In addition, there is still one more problem, and this is a big one—the shuffling machines. Any game that uses shuffling machines cannot be beaten consistently even by the best card counter. Anyone who says he is a card counter and can beat machine-shuffled games using any of the standard card-counting methods is a liar. Particularly so for machines that are continuous shufflers, and even more so for those that are randomizers as well. There is simply no way to beat a blackjack game that is being shuffled by these machines if you use any of the established card-counting systems, or any of their derivatives. Whenever you are playing any blackjack game that is shuffled by a machine, you are completely a victim of blind luck.

Depressed? Don't be. Blackjack still yields good profits, and can still be exploited for all the good things, such as the good rules and games that I have described earlier. Also, there are still many methods, other than these card-counting systems, that can be used to better effect, particularly under the present conditions of dealing blackjack in major casinos. We will discuss some of these methods, as well as wagering opportunities, in chapter 11, "The Big Secret." For now, it's okay to learn and practice the card-counting systems described in this chapter. It will help your discipline, as well as your overall game. Just remember not to rely on them alone. There is a lot more to blackjack than just these old "systems."

9

Keys to Winning

For most of the second half of the twentieth century, black-jack writers and experts have singled out several principles for steady success for beating the game. Among these, the following have found their way into the majority of the books and texts on blackjack, and are mostly universally accepted by blackjack experts as those tried and true principles upon which to base your success as a blackjack player. These have been shown as follows:

1. Knowledge of the game
2. Card counting
3. Sufficient bankroll
4. Money management
5. Discipline

By all means, these are several of the key ingredients that any player of blackjack should acquire in order to assure, at the very least, a reasonable success in the game. Unfortunately, there are some major problems with two of these suggestions. They are vested in items #2 and #4, as shown above.

As we have seen in the previous chapter, counting cards is not as good and useful as it is touted to be, particularly in the real world of twenty-first-century casinos. Therefore, any reliance on these systems as the cornerstone of your blackjack success is inherently flawed even before you start. Basing your reliance for blackjack success in these systems is precisely what most of these books and texts on blackjack have been suggesting for decades—that learning and practicing these card-counting systems is the only way to assure your success as a consistently winning blackjack player. This is simply not so. All this will do for you is enable you to make slightly better *guesses* as to what the cards in the remaining decks *might be*. However, it won't tell you where these cards are, and it won't even tell you how you should treat your next hand by means of what kind of wager or what kind of strategy modification. These systems also suggest that you perform a series of additional guesses, based upon what the possibilities in this situation may be. Unfortunately, these remedies for the potential possibilities are in themselves dependent on highly inaccurate assumptions in the first place. Consequently, learning card-counting systems is useful only in two ways:

1. As an exercise in blackjack knowledge.
2. As a means of acquiring additional skills in situations where even such imprecise information is better than none at all.

The second major problem I see with the above time-honored principles of blackjack success is over-reliance on what has vacuously been called "money management." Well, what exactly is this? Many authors of various books on blackjack, and various other texts, have written about money management. Some hold this to be the holy grail of blackjack success. It's basically a whole bunch of hot air.

Money management is nothing more than some common

sense along with a dash of self-discipline. In a nutshell, all this means is, "Don't blow your whole wad when you first walk into the casino." It can also mean, "Don't give back your winnings." Because of this admonishment, many blackjack writers will expand and exalt money management as some kind of a heroic, almost Homeric, quest. It just means that you should try to hold on to your money and make it last for your entire visit, instead of dumping it all at once. What if you do dump it all at once? Walk in, plunk the money down on the nearest blackjack table, play one hand, and lose. Now all your bring-in money is gone. Why did you do that? Well, probably because that's what you wanted to do, right? Why not? You came to play, and play you did. That was your choice and your desire. You wanted to get this off your shoulders, you wanted to play crazy, and you did it. Why should you feel like a schmuck because of it? You shouldn't. Herein lies the other problem with "money management": the grind.

Many writers suggest to you that you should always treat blackjack as a job. As work. As a grind. A daily grind, day in and day out, squeezing out the little percentages, the little tenths of a percent and even a hundredth of a percent in added advantage to you—and do this for the "long haul." That's another favorite expression. Even I have used it. It's a good way to indicate that the small bits of profits add up over time. However, these proponents of money management as the holy grail of blackjack success all seem to teach that you should make blackjack your job, or at least treat it as a job when you go to the casino.

Why? I did this as a job. I played blackjack as a job. I don't want to do this as a job. Do you have ten years of your life to dedicate to becoming a professional blackjack player? If you don't, why would you want to treat blackjack as a job? Why would you want to go to a casino on your vacation, on your weekend trip, or a visit for whatever reason, and then sit there hour after hour and grind it out bit by bit and treat the game as your other job? You already have a job, right? If you treated blackjack in this way, you would be going from one job to the other. That's no fun.

By asking you to treat blackjack as a job, these books often try to qualify their authors' insistence on money management as a means to blackjack profits—but that's not the real truth, and that's not the reality. Most people who wish to play blackjack do not want to do this as their job—or even think of it in those terms. Most people just want to have fun—and win money. Have fun doing it, have a good time, and have a relaxing time. There's no reason that this cannot be so. You can play blackjack successfully, and you do not have to treat it as a job. (For those of you who actually *do* want to make playing blackjack your job, as a means of making a living, it is possible. However, your entire approach to the game must be substantially altered from the perceptions that you now hold. Money management will then become part of your business discipline. This will be your business investment, and you can treat it in that same manner. Also, this still has little to do with what is being touted as money management in much of the blackjack literature. If you are such a serious player, and do want to learn how to play blackjack as a job, then I refer you to my book on Advanced Strategies.)

I cringe each time I read something about blackjack and I see whole sections, chapters, and even the majority of the books, all about money management. It makes me tired just looking at it. Playing blackjack like that is exhausting. It's work. Yes, of course I don't want to waste my bankroll, and neither should you. Even I have written in previous books about the importance of money management. Well, I was also wrong. Whatever the words "money management" may mean to you, to me this is simply part of the section that I call "Discipline." The words "money management" do not need to represent something "extra," or something inherently supervaluable. Therefore, I think that the expression "money management" is intrinsically inaccurate, or perhaps entirely wrong. Playing blackjack is not your job, not your business, it is your *entertainment*. Because this form of entertainment can be done for profit, some very simple principles of discipline should be employed. This does not mean you have to be a hawk and watch your pennies like some accountant whose life depends on not making a "money management" error.

Your success in blackjack, and your profits from blackjack, will not depend on how well you learn any of those "money management" techniques, but simply on what you do with the money you bring with you, and the money you win. That's *discipline*. Even that has nothing to do with treating blackjack as a job. What discipline or money management will mean to you is entirely dependent on what the value of your money is to you at that moment. Money management, as it is mostly written about, is nothing more than an accounting version of self-discipline designed to keep you from squandering your winnings, provided you treat blackjack as a job. If you don't treat blackjack as a job, then money management means nothing to you and all of that information that was so carefully crafted by those authors is wasted on you.

Instead, the help that is being offered to you should focus on how you can better avoid becoming a victim to the distractions in the casinos. That is what I have called the "Discipline" part of my recommended "keys to winning." Here, then, are my five categories for winning and making profits playing blackjack:

1. Knowledge of the game
2. Patience
3. Bankroll

4. Persistence
5. Discipline

What do these mean? How do you apply them? Well, like this:

KNOWLEDGE OF THE GAME

This means knowing the game of blackjack. Knowing the rules, how it is played, what the various rule changes may be from casino to casino and perhaps even from table to table. This means knowing the Basic Strategy and, in this book, what I have called the Modified Basic Strategy (MBS). It also means knowing how to bet, when to bet, when to do what is required during the course of the game, and how to do it. All of this is absolutely essential information. All of it can be found in this book. Learn it, practice it, and become familiar with it. This is the foundation stone of the house you will build, which will be called "Your House of Blackjack Profits."

Knowledge of the game also means never having to guess. All the strategies, rules, and actions that you will face in the game of casino blackjack should be firmly planted in your memory. Your decisions should be automatic. There should never be a single moment when you don't know what to do. Once you learn the rules of the game and the MBS, there are no decisions to be made.

How can you apply this? By playing the game automatically, always like that, and this means you will be playing just like the casino. The casino has no "thinking" involved in the game of blackjack. They have hard-and-fast rules to follow, and that's how they play. Always, all the time, with no decisions to be made. It's automatic. You will also be able to play this way. In addition, you have your knowledge of the MBS to guide you, and this provides for more flexibility than the house rules allow for their dealers. Plus, you will be able to do something that the casino cannot—you will be able to double-down, to split, resplit, and to double-down after splits. You will be able to get 3:2 on your blackjacks and refuse insurance. What this means is that you will be able to play the same game as the casino, but be able to take advantage of the rules that allow you to do something that the casino cannot do. Therefore, you will be playing blackjack for *profit*!

Did you have to do any mental gymnastics to achieve this? Well, no. After you first learn the rules of the game, which you cannot do without because otherwise you could not play, and after you learn the MBS, from that point on you will be armed with the most powerful ammunition that you can get in the game of blackjack as it is now played in the casinos of the twenty-first century. With this armament, you will gain an edge over the game by employing the arsenal of tools that are being offered to you by the availability of the majority of the player-favorable rules and options, which only you, as the player, can exploit.

You will now be able to play blackjack enjoyably, have fun, be relaxed, and have a great time. You will be able to take advantage of all the favorable options that the casino will offer you, while never giving up anything or ever being caught in any disadvantage. You will simply and plainly have the best of all worlds. Your blackjack playing experience will be rewarding, easy, and comfortable. What's most important, it will *never* be anything like a job.

PATIENCE

This means not getting frustrated when the cards seem to go against you. It also means not getting hotheaded when something that should work out, doesn't. Patience means just that—to remain calm and in the game without altering your method of playing. Nothing will always be perfect, not in life and not in blackjack. There will be times when you will lose. Be patient. It will turn around. Converse statistics are merely a trend to the negative extreme, and the opposite will also occur. Being patient in blackjack simply means that you will not let your emotions destroy your capacity to keep playing your best game, and that you will also remind yourself that any streak against you will eventually be followed by a like extreme in your favor. Patience also means that you will not allow others to influence you and talk you into bad decisions. Most of all, patience means that you will always remember that your knowledge of the game allows you to play the best that the game can be played.

How can you apply this? Many strategy experts indicate that you should walk away from any table where you lose three to four hands in a row. They say that this is an indication of a "hot" dealer, or streaky cards favoring the house. This is wrong! Three or four of anything is not nearly an indicative sample. Even in the most rudimentary statistics, samplings of events this few in number render any decisions based upon such meager results as statistically useless. If you did this, and got up from every table where you lost three or four hands in a row, you would be spending most of your vacation or casino visit jumping from table to table. You would get dizzy. In all of your playing sessions, streaks of several-in-a-row, either as winners or as losers, will occur about 20 percent of the time. What does this mean? Well, first it means that such losing streaks of several hands in a row will happen only about two times out of each ten times you sit at a table. Therefore, it is not enough of a frequent occurrence to warrant you to jump up and leave each time it happens. Second, it means that a statistical anomaly has occurred, and that the converse will also happen eventually. Only three or four losing hands are, however, not enough of an indication that this is an extended trend that can result in financial damage to you.

If such a situation does occur, the best you can do is to sit out a few hands if the casino will permit this. Usually they will, for a hand or two, if you remain seated at the table. You can always grumble something like, "I need to change my cards," or some other similarly innocuous statement that will indicate that you are merely a "hunch" player, rather than the smart player you really are. The best way to take a rest for a few hands is to get up and go to the rest room. If you think you are in the middle of a situation where the trends are distinctly against you, just ask the dealer where the nearest rest room is and take a walk. Even if you know where the rest room happens to be, or don't actually have to go, the act of asking the dealer will reinforce the impression that you know nothing, but simply wish to take a break for personal relief. It's just a ploy for you to take a break from this run of negative cards. It doesn't mean anything intrinsically profound, other than the realization that losing more than four hands in a row could indicate a larger statistical anomaly. This does not mean that you should get up and immediately leave the table for good. Take that walk, and come back. Before you sit back down, as you are walking up, see a few hands. If the dealer is still making hands, such as drawing several cards to a better hand than the players, or consistently turning up hands of 19, 20, and blackjack, then you can make the rational decision to seek better action elsewhere.

Patience also means that you do not let these minor trends or setbacks alter your playing style or playing decisions. Often what may seem like a "cold" table, and hence a "hot" dealer, will turn just as quickly into a very favorable game indeed. Dealers change. Usually, dealers work forty minutes, and then take a twenty-minute break. Relief dealers come in at that time. The relief dealer may be entirely "cold," and turn what was a bad table into one that simply showers the players with winners. Also, the dealer who was "hot" for that sequence of three or four hands may just as quickly turn "cold." Not even card counting can help you here, because such statistical anomalies are part of the reality of the world of the game. By remaining patient throughout these series of a few bad hands, and betting the minimum, you can outlast these anomalies and often wind up with a very large win when the situation turns around. Patience, therefore, is able to be applied to a wide variety of your blackjack decisions.

BANKROLL

This is one part where I agree with every book and text that has ever been written about blackjack. If you want to play blackjack in a casino, you must have money. Otherwise, you can't play. It doesn't matter if this money is in the form of cash, a marker, or casino credit. However you slice it, money talks, and in casino blackjack you must have it in order to play. "Bankroll," however, is something a little different from just having money. "Bankroll" is the designation that is given to a specified amount of money that you have dedicated to your gambling. More specifically, as it applies to blackjack, bankroll is the amount of money that you have strictly dedicated to playing casino blackjack.

How much money should be in your dedicated blackjack bankroll? Well, that depends. It depends on how much you are willing to dedicate to such a blackjack playing bankroll. Usually, a good rule to follow is to have a bankroll of no less than a hundred times your minimum expected wager. Therefore, if you intend to play blackjack at the $5 table, with minimum bets of $5 per hand, you should have a blackjack playing bankroll of a minimum of $500. This does not mean you have to buy in for $500 each time at every table at which you may sit. All it means is that you have selected a certain amount that you are willing to risk, namely the $5 per hand bet. Therefore, in order to protect yourself against the inevitable losing streaks, you have also given yourself an adequate supply of money so that your skills and abilities in the game can yield the profits to which you are entitled.

Being undercapitalized is a prescription for total disaster. If you cannot bring a bankroll of at least a hundred times the minimum bet, then don't play. By playing without an adequate bankroll, you will become scared in situations where you should make certain decisions, such as when you should split, resplit, resplit again, and double-down on all splits and resplits. If you are wagering $5 per hand, and have four such hands where you split, resplit, and doubled-down on all, then you suddenly have $40 in action on what was initially only a $5 wager. If all you have for your trip is a $100 or $200 bankroll, you now stand to lose 40 percent of it in one hand (for the $100 bankroll), or 20 percent (in the case of the $200 bankroll). What if you lose? Well, then you feel lousy, and the rest of your game will suffer because you will now play even more scared. Scared to risk more money lest you lose it and have to spend the rest of your trip with nothing. Also, what if you were playing so scared that you didn't split, resplit, and double-down? What if you only split once and then hit instead, when you should have done the above? Now, you may lose the $10 that you bet, instead of the $40 that you should have bet. If you do, you "saved" the $30 you did not risk. However, what if you had won instead? Well, now your short bankroll caused you to give up a win of $40. Instead, you wound up with $10.

Scared money flies away quickly. This is a gambler's proverb—and it is very true indeed. If you cannot afford a decent bankroll, stay away from the blackjack tables until you get the bankroll that you should have. Why a hundred times the minimum bet? Because that's the safest gauge by which you ride out the bad streaks, and still come out ahead in the end. I would actually prefer to recommend two hundred times the minimum bet, but this might get a little out of line with what most people will bring to the game, or are willing to allocate to a blackjack experience.

Whether the one-hundred-times bankroll will be sufficient for you is also largely dependent on several factors. First, your ability to play blackjack well, in accordance with your knowledge of the game and your mastery of the MBS. Second, your ability to overcome problems, which you will inevitably encounter, and distractions, which we will discuss in the "Discipline" section. Third, this also depends on what the value of your money means to you at that moment. If you are a millionaire, and $500 is barely lunch money, then this bankroll advice won't mean much to you. If you are wealthy, you will probably be betting at $5,000 per hand, or even $50,000 per hand, or more. Nevertheless, the same principle applies. Bring at least a hundred times the amount of your minimum bet. Otherwise, you will most likely lose all of it, will play badly as a result of losing it, and most likely will go and get more—and lose that as well. If you are a millionaire and money doesn't mean anything to you, and you insist on playing badly, then mail me the money instead. I'll be sure to make better use of it than the casino to which you will lose it. Ahh, well, wishful thinking.

The point here is well made for all of us who wish to play blackjack as well as it possibly can be played, and to make profits. To make truly powerful profits from blackjack, you will require mastery of, and adherence to, all of the five items that I have listed here as my "Keys to Winning." It doesn't matter how wealthy you are. All that matters in regard to the bankroll is that you bring enough along to allow yourself the best possible series of circumstances available that will provide for a more rewarding, and certainly more profitable, gaming experience. Whatever the level at which you are willing to gamble, be it $3, $5, $10, $25, $50, $100, or more per hand as your minimum bet, unless you have the most reliably structured bankroll, you will not be able to play blackjack with the ammunition you need to make all of your playing opportunities pay off. That's why bankroll is so important. An adequate bankroll will allow you to play at your best.

PERSISTENCE

Persistence and patience are the two Ps in the pod (pardon the pun). Together, they make you a stronger, more relaxed, and more reliable player. What is persistence? As it applies to blackjack, it simply means not to give up when the going gets tough. Since you are now playing blackjack in the same manner as the casino (but with the advantage of the MBS, plus the ability to make wagering and strategy decisions accordingly), you must also have the longevity necessary to be able to achieve the winning events. While many people will be frightened when the cards turn bad, you should not be. If you are rational about this, you recognize that this will inevitably happen. You will recognize that the opposite will also happen. Putting all the keys to winning into your pocket of skills will enable you not to be frightened by the adverse situations you will encounter.

While other people will act like scared chickens, you will have the knowledge and rationale that enables you to make the proper decisions. Applying persistence to your repertoire of skills will allow you not to give up when situations are adverse. This does not mean that you should blindly throw good money after bad. If you follow all of the principles that I have outlined in this book, this should never be of concern to you. Persistence means that you will not give up on your skills, on your knowledge, or on your ability to play blackjack confidently and with an adequate bankroll. Persistence means that you will be able to stick to your game plan and to remain confident in the knowledge that you are doing everything you can to maximize the profit potential of the game. Not giving up—that's what the issue is here. Bad things will happen, inevitably. How you handle these situations is what is going to separate you from the losers.

DISCIPLINE

This is the hardest, but most important aspect of your blackjack play. As this applies to casino blackjack, there are two main categories that have the greatest effect on your success: first, handling the money; and second, handling the distractions.

The money—well, that's the part that many authors write about under the banner "money management." However, I think that the mantra of "money management" is misplaced as a section of its own. What to do with one's money is part of discipline, and, in particular, part of self-discipline. The single most important fact that is missing from many of the texts on blackjack that describe the principles behind money management is *the fact of the value of your money to you at the moment*. This is all relative, and the value will be different for each and every person. Perhaps you are an average casino visitor, one of the millions of people who earn an average annual income of $40,000, go to a casino destination an average of twice a year, and stay for the average three days and four nights each visit. I'm not suggesting that this is actually you. These are general statistics derived from millions of interviews with people who come to Las Vegas, and used here only for the sake of this example.

Such statistically "average" persons will gamble about six hours per day, of which about two hours will be spent on table games. So, over the course of that average visit, such persons may gamble about eight hours at a table game. Much of this will be at a blackjack table. Most of these people will bring an average gambling bankroll of around $1,600. This tends to fluctuate considerably by season and by general economic conditions. In some reports, this figure is shown as an average of around $800 per person per visit, while in others it can be around $3,200 per person per visit. I take the average of the average, and so the $1,600 figure is to me more appealing as the more realistic median. If this is so, then the average blackjack player will devote about one-third of his total trip bankroll to table games. Blackjack will be the table game of choice for about 86 percent of all these players, so for the sake of brevity here we will assume that all of these statistically average players will play blackjack as their table game of choice. One-third of the $1,600 will be about $533.00. That's for the entire trip. At this level this person can gamble at best only at the $5 table. Unfortunately, this is not always so. Most of these people gamble at stakes far higher, completely oblivious to any notion of any kind of monetary discipline. The result is that most of them will access additional funds and will, in fact, spend about five times as much in the end as they had initially thought would be necessary for their bankroll at the start.

Simply put, what this shows is that these people should have brought their entire bankroll with them in the beginning. Instead of just the mere $533 allocated to blackjack, and then having to access five times more for a total of $3,000 as a blackjack playing bankroll that will by the time it is accessed in bits and pieces also be mostly lost in like bits and pieces, these players should have brought their $3,000 with them as their starting blackjack bankroll in the first place. This would have provided them with a range of play from the $5 table all the way up to a maximum of a $30 minimum bet. This $3,000 blackjack bankroll would have provided them with a safe haven, and would have assured that they would be able to play blackjack with the best possible chance for success. Instead, these people went broke, and kept running to the ATM machines for more cash, to the credit card machines, cashing checks, or signing markers— and losing it all in the end. It is here where the value of your money to you in the moment comes into focus.

If you are not concerned about the loss of $3,000, or more, and you simply don't care, then what good is any kind of advice about money management? What good is any kind of knowledge to you, or any kind of advice whatsoever? I'd say little to none. If your goal is to go on your casino trip and blow your money recklessly, then that's what you want to do and no amount of writing about how to protect your money will mean anything to you. Of course, if you are very rich and $3,000 is pocket change, then disciplinary advice will mean something to you only when the numbers are increased proportionately to your specific playing bankroll.

The point I am trying to make is that any advice about self-discipline as it applies to the handling of your money will be valuable to you only when it reaches the point where you become scared of the accumulated loss that your lack of such discipline could inflict upon you. This is the point of fear (and fear of consequences). It is this fear factor that spans all frontiers between the average and the wealthy. No matter what the value of your money may be to you in the moment, when you reach the point where the loss of it, or any substantial part of it, will cause you to fear the consequences, then and only then will advice on money discipline be of value to you. Now you will listen, and learn. I hope.

I call this "money discipline." This is part of the overall

ability to control yourself, which is usually described as self-discipline. What I call "money discipline" is different from what others call "money management." To my mind, money discipline means more. It means knowing the value of the money, whatever amount it may be for you, before going to the blackjack table. It means knowing the consequences of the catastrophic loss of more than the allocated funds, or even the major portion of the allocated bankroll. It means knowing the value of the money won, relative to the output of work that was required to acquire it in the first place. If you earn your money at the average rate of $20 per hour, which comes to about $41,600 per year in total income, and you play blackjack at a level where your expected win is at $30 per hour, and you are *unhappy* with that "small" amount, then you have a problem with money discipline. Likewise, if you play badly and are undercapitalized, and you are willing to risk your money at the hourly *loss* of $100 or more (which is very common among the vast majority of the average players), then you are crazy. Of course, if you are a very wealthy player, then simply increase these amounts to the levels at which you play, and then this will make sense to you as well.

The two major problems that virtually all casino players experience in regard to handling their money are:

1. Not being satisfied with what they perceive as wins that are "too small."
2. Risking high hourly losses in "chasing the big win," while using an inadequate bankroll to warrant such expectations.

For most people, the casino experience will be liberating. Here is an environment where everything is possible, all sorts of challenges are being offered, and vast rewards can be achieved. Well, the bigger the reward, the bigger the risk, or the longer the odds against it. That's the part that most of these people fail to understand or, what is more accurate, choose to ignore. To win a million dollars on a slot machine means you will be investing large sums of your money for what often are extended playing periods with odds against you in the range of several hundred million to one. You stand a better chance, odds wise, of being bitten by a jelly-fish in the middle of the desert. However, it does happen, and that's the allure of small wagers with big win potential. The problem is that often such wagers are *cumulatively far from small.*

In table games, and in blackjack in particular, if you want to win a million dollars you will have to wager very large sums of money for long periods of time and play very well. Plus, you must be able to practice all the skills that have been outlined in this book, as well as master the art of money discipline. Yes, I called it an "art." Because that's what it is. To be able to handle your gambling money in a way that will retain the reality of it for you is truly an art. How do you do this?

Again, it depends. Mostly on you and your individual personality. Some of you may want to stash away little bits and pieces of your wins along the way, and thus split your money into smaller stacks, with some of these stacks hidden away and never touched. This will always assure you of having some money left, even if you lost all the rest of it. It's a good and safe way to assure yourself that you will never go home absolutely broke, but it is very hard to do in the spirit of the game and in the casino environment. Others may wish to allocate only parts of their overall bankroll to their blackjack sessions and play at levels lower than those at which their bankrolls would indicate they can play. Many players may want to limit their playing sessions to specific financial goals, both winning and losing. For example, at a $5 table you may wish to play only until you win $40, or lose no more than $20. Or you may wish to play for an hourly win of $60, and a loss of no more than $30. When any of these levels is reached, you stop playing and leave. Then you can stash some of your winnings, start another session, and do this all over again.

Any of these methods can be useful. Which one is better for you will depend on what you wish to achieve. If your primary goal is to be entertained in the casino, then your money discipline is relative only to limiting your exposure to large losses. If your goal is primarily to win money at the blackjack tables, then your money discipline will take on added importance. You will find for yourself a method that will allow you to keep more of your bring-in money and keep most of your wins. The way you safeguard your bring-in bankroll is by learning the game and playing it perfectly in accordance with the MBS, as well as all the other keys to winning that I have shown you. The way you safeguard your wins is both by continuing to play the game perfectly, and by allocating only a portion of your accumulated wins to any further sessions. As you win, you can add a portion of your wins to your starting bankroll. This will increase that bankroll. As that bankroll increases, you can rise to higher levels. There you will be achieving higher wins. Following this practice you will continually be increasing both the stash of money that you have won, and the amount of your playing bankroll. If you ever have a losing session, then you can simply lower your win expectation and go back to the lower level of play. When you have recovered from that loss, you will again be able to rise to the higher levels—and so on. In this way you will always assure yourself of the following:

1. Protecting your starting bankroll.
2. Protecting your wins.
3. Accumulating your wins and bankroll so that you can reach higher levels of play and higher profits.

It becomes a self-propagating process, and it is all directly relative to your perception of the value of the money to you during the moment, hence, your ability to master money discipline as part of your overall personal self-discipline as specifically applied to the casino environment.

This brings me to the second of the two major problems for most people, and that is handling the distractions. There are many. All sorts of things are happening around you in the casino. Noises, people yelling, walking, drinking, smoking, laughing, music blaring, dealers dealing, people talking, pit bosses and pit staff offering comps or offering to track your play, cocktail servers asking for drinks and bringing drinks, overhead PA announcements, promotional announcements, smells, colors, slot machine sounds, jackpots ringing, coins falling into trays, cold air—all sorts of things.

All of these will have an impact on your ability to maintain self-discipline and to practice money discipline. Everything around you is designed to liberate you from your rational thinking and comfortably settle you into mindless, thoughtless wagering. Everything in the casino environment is designed to distract you, to keep your head and mind spinning with so much input and so much excitement that the adrenaline takes over and all reason goes out the window. It is at this point that you will lose all of your discipline and therefore become immediately one of the crowd. That's precisely what makes the casino so much fun, and that's also precisely what the casinos are designed to be and to do. You aren't supposed to be able to think. You're just supposed to spend money.

All of us are susceptible to this influence. None of us are perfect. We all succumb to this allure and wind up in a daze doing things with our money that we would never even think of doing outside of the casino or in our regular daily lives. That's also what's so liberating about the casino environment and atmosphere. That's also what's so much fun— but it can be deadly, and these distractions can easily lead you down the path of financial destruction. If, that is, you let them. By practicing money discipline, you will never be in this position. No matter what the distractions may be, you will be able to enjoy them and to experience that liberating thrill and adrenaline rush, but you will do so with the foreknowledge that you are able to keep a hold on your money. How well you do at this only you can answer. You won't succeed all the time. Even the best of us will fall into this trap and lose our place at one time or another. The point of discipline, however, is to limit the times when we fall off the wagon, and to instill in ourselves the principles of "value": the value of the money, the value of the wins, the value of the lowered losses, the value of the experiences and entertainment gained—and the value of the entire trip, when we can go back home and still have our money with us. Or, at least, some of it left. Perhaps most of it, all of it, or *even more* of it. That's what money discipline, and discipline in general, will do for us in gambling.

Playing blackjack means that you are already playing one of the better casino games. Playing blackjack with the MBS and these "keys to winning," as well as all of the other information learned here, will mean that you are playing for profit, and you *know* you will make such a profit eventually. Plus, you know that you are doing all that is possible to limit your losses. This means that you have the full intention of not losing it all: bankroll or wins.

Gambling is the only form of entertainment where you can pay for this entertainment and after being so thoroughly entertained still go home with the money you brought, and even with more money than you started with. No other form of entertainment will allow you to do this. Therefore, when you choose blackjack as your gaming entertainment, you are choosing one of the best games you can for actual profits.

Discipline, therefore, does not have to mean "limiting yourself to unappetizing and boring drudgery." Instead, it should mean "allowing myself the freedom to win."

That is all that can ever be hoped for in anything: in blackjack or in life in general. Acquiring your money discipline (and blackjack discipline) is not a limiting experience. These are not chains that bind you. Rather, they are the ammunition for your success, the bridges for you to cross the wide chasms of trouble, the boats that sail you over the oceans of fear, and the rivers that give life.

Together, these "keys to winning" unlock the opportunities that are in you. The opportunity to take the best that you possess and turn it even further into your advantage.

10

A Matter of Perspective: How We Think vs. How They Think

Since this book is all about blackjack and how to play it for profit, this chapter may seem superfluous. However, it is actually quite important. There is a profound difference between how players think and how casinos think. Still more, there is yet an additional difference between how the management thinks and how employees think. All of this has a direct impact on your ability to make profits from blackjack. These are aspects of three fields of science:

1. The psychology of the owner, operator, or top-echelon executives
2. The psychology of the employee
3. The psychology of the customer

Each of these groups looks at the same thing very differently. Although this book is about only blackjack, the perspectives that can be explored from the mind-set of the three groups listed above apply to all casino gaming in general. Some of the insights that can be assessed from exploring these perspectives actually have a direct impact upon blackjack, and how you can make the most of the game.

Many people will understand the joke about the pessimist and the optimist. The optimist always sees the glass as half-full, while the pessimist always sees the glass as half-empty. I'm pretty sure you have heard this expression. Although this example is mostly used humorously, it does show a deep underlying difference between people, and how they may look at the very same thing, yet see entirely different facts. In law, this becomes very profound indeed, particularly when trial lawyers have to deal with so-called eyewitnesses. The problem there is that even though an eyewitness may have been at the scene at the time the crime was committed, that eyewitness may not have seen the events exactly as they actually happened. This goes back to the humorous example of the optimist and the pessimist and the glass of water. Even though this eyewitness has seen the crime, what exactly was it that this person saw? It is for this reason that lawyers often call several eyewitnesses, if available, or use other evidence in order to establish the actual truth of the case.

In casino gaming the situations that we are discussing here are nowhere nearly as profound as the cases that may be tackled by trial lawyers in criminal courts. Here we are discussing the differences in perspective as they affect our ability to maximize our skills in making a profit from playing blackjack. The example of the trial lawyers and their eyewitnesses is meaningful in that it further illustrates that just because we all go to the same casino, and we all play what is essentially the same game of blackjack, this does not mean that we all see, or treat, the game the same way.

Even among the three groups that I identified above, there are further differences. For example, if the person from group #1 is the actual owner of the casino, then he will think and react quite differently from the operator or top executive. As an owner, he will be far more open, more accessible, and more forthcoming when it comes to handling his customers and their requests. As an owner, he will be able to make immediate decisions and see to it that whatever needs doing is done and done now. Because he is the owner and the sole responsible entity, he can do this.

On the other hand, we have the operator. The operator of a casino may be a person, such as an appointee representing the owner, or this may be a corporation that operates the casino on behalf of the owner. For example, most of the tribal gaming enterprises are actually operated by casino corporations, or casino entities, for and on behalf of the tribe, which is the owner. The operator, therefore, has an entirely different agenda. Usually, operators of casinos work under a separate contract, which is finite. Often these contracts include performance clauses that state that a certain level of profitability must be maintained and achieved on an annual basis, or the operator's contract will be terminated or not renewed at the end of the term. Under such pressures, operators are usually less willing to accommodate changes, cater to their customers, or offer more liberal games, playing rules, and options.

These operators are normally very tight with everything, because their own interests take precedence over all others. If they don't meet their quota, or contract performance levels, they're out. That's it. Therefore an operator is likely to think of their customers both as a herd that must be maintained at a certain member number, and as a threat. Every time the head count of the herd falls below what its mean average should be, the operator starts passing bricks because this is a danger sign that things are falling below expectations and goals. Likewise, any time one or more of the herd wants something or starts to get better at gaming, they want to nip that in the bud. All the operator wants is for a steady stream of cattle to come and deposit their cash in their coffers so he can clean them out, and then get ready for the next herd, and so on. Such operators are, consequently, not very open to accommodating any member of the human herd to do better than the operators are willing to allow. This is a very large problem in many of the gaming centers outside of Nevada and Atlantic City, and this is largely why, for the most part, you won't find the better games in such casinos.

The top-echelon executive, by which we mean either the president, the chief operating officer (COO), the chief executive officer (CEO), or the chief financial officer (CFO), is virtually a combination of the owner and operator. On one hand, they are like an owner. In fact, most of them are part owners because they own stock or have stock options as part of their remuneration package. On the other hand, they are an operator because they usually work for a very large corporation (or a subsidiary of an even larger corporation) that is publicly traded and therefore has to maintain a certain level of performance to ensure shareholder value. This therefore becomes the classic dichotomy of conflict.

On one hand, playing the part of the owner, these top executives want to give the customer all they want. They want to be generous, provide the better games and rules, give liberal comps, and make the customers comfortable and happy. On the other hand, they are responsible to their corporate masters who, in turn, are responsible to the shareholders, and herein lies the gaping maw of a whole wide world of regulations and other kinds of governmental nonsense, all of which very often ties up many of these executives in knots from which they can only rarely escape. By having to play both the part of the owners and the part of the operator, most gaming executives are caught in a trap of give-and-take. As owners, they wish to give. As operators it's their job to take. The result is what's often called the "corporate syndrome."

This is particularly observable in casino gaming, and distinctly so in casinos that are controlled by publicly traded corporations, or are themselves such corporations. The corporate syndrome shows itself as *indecision*. No one wants to be the first to stand up and speak. No one wants to "rock the boat." No one wants to be the one on whom anyone else could pin the failure if the idea crashes and burns. No one wants to be the first to try anything, because if it didn't work they would be the ones singled out for punishment, which very often means loss of their very lucrative jobs. As a result, very little ever gets done. At least very little of what is actually needed, or actually useful to the daily conduct of the profitable business whose foundation is solely in the gaming customer. Everyone wants to "pass the buck." Decisions are made by committee, after endless meetings and nitpicking, additions, deletions, modifications, and so on and on. The old joke that says that a camel is a horse designed by a committee certainly applies here. Mostly these executives are like rats in a golden cage, running feverishly inside their spinning wheel, but, like the rat, never getting anywhere and winding up exhausted for no purpose. This may sound harsh, but I have witnessed this time and time again, and I see it happening among the major hotel corporations in Las Vegas every single day. The only thing that these executives actually do in unison is manage the company debt. If they didn't, the company would die, and they would be out.

The other major problem with these top-echelon executives is that they are not at risk for their own rewards unless something "bad" gets pinned on them, or they do something really stupid. It happens, and many executives and management teams have lost their jobs because they did. That's another part of the problem. If the executives make a mistake, they stand to be labeled as "ineffective," ostracized, and often publicly labeled as the ones responsible for the financial failure or corporate disaster. There is no second chance, and this mind-set does not warrant or reward inventiveness or flexibility. This also means that such people will want to protect themselves, and I don't blame them. If I had a job where I made $1 million to $5 million a year, and often more, with stock options often worth in the tens of millions of dollars, I wouldn't want to risk this for anything. If this were my world, why would I ever want to do anything to even remotely jeopardize this? That's the major problem. These people are human, like the rest of us, and they won't do anything that could possibly label them as ineffective or, worse, stupid. Why would they ever want to do anything that could publicly humiliate them and result in the loss of their nice, cushy lives? Of course they don't.

So anything that is done by these executives is done with the "consent of the board," or "consent of the executive committee." What this does is spread the potential risk among all the members of the board or the committee so that no single person can be blamed as the fall guy if whatever they are doing results in a disaster. It's what politicians call "plausible deniability." It's a built-in excuse or a built-in escape clause if anything goes bad. Well, when it does, none of these individuals can be blamed, and so it's all swept neatly under the carpet and the game goes on. If it's a success, then they start to posture around the table and hustle to get the most credit, like children in a sandbox, but that's how the entire world works. It's sadly so. The outcome of this mind-set, and corporate culture, is that it takes months, even years, and sometimes decades to get anything done. No one wants to commit to anything. Unless, that is, it is stamped with the "approved by the board" or "approved by the executive committee" label. To get those stamps takes too much time.

While all this posturing is going on, the customers suffer. The players can't get simple comps because the frontline employees get yelled at each time they write one. The customers can't get comfortable chairs, because this would have to be approved by all those committees, and this will take a few more years. The customers will be frozen like slabs of meat in the casino because the executives are afraid to turn the air conditioner down, while at the same time complaining about the costs of power. I have personally witnessed this gross stupidity over and over again, in virtually all of the casinos in the United States. It's mind-boggling that this would continue, but it does. Who are these "executives"? Why are they so dull and out of touch with reality? Well, I provided the answer above. Sadly, it is the customer who suffers as a result. It is the customer who cannot get the value for their patronage, the customer who is constantly underappreciated, and the customer who has to play in an uncomfortable environment. It is the customer who has been reduced to no more than a number in the herd of human cargo.

Yet it is the customer who feeds the casino, and pays for everything. Unfortunately, this does not seem to sink into the thick heads that unfortunately occupy most of the executive positions in the casino corporations. Most, but not all. There are some very notable exceptions in the casino executive community. Quite a few of them, men and women, are now actively working to break these chains that bind the abilities of those who occupy these positions. It is not my intention to say that they don't know how to do this. Many do, but don't do it. Unfortunately, there are even more who actually don't know and don't want to know. So the story goes on and the customer goes on bringing in billions of dollars every year and receiving less and less attention and less and less for their patronage.

For over a decade I have been personally involved in analyzing casino operations among most of the casinos throughout the United States. I have personally witnessed the ineffectiveness of the executive structure and the corporate dilemma. Right now, I can walk into any casino in the

United States and immediately boost their revenue by a minimum of 10 percent, and without undue costs to them. Why? Because each casino is making at least ten major mistakes in their operations, all of which cost them millions of dollars in lost revenue. With a simple fix, this can be overcome and the money flow substantially improved. This is almost like heart bypass surgery. The lifeblood of the casino is the money and happiness of the customers. These are both being choked by the buildup of accumulated apathy and executive ignorance. This can be resolved. The patient can become even healthier and produce more and more, with less and less expenses. Unfortunately, the casino executives don't want to know. If they find out, they don't want to do what needs to be done. Each time I walk into a casino in Las Vegas, I am saddened by the problems that loom bright and big all around me, but are always universally ignored by casino executives and management. It's painful for me to see this and realize that not only could the customers be better off, but the casino would make tens of millions of dollars more, and all with such simple solutions. Ahh, well—maybe someday they will finally let me tell them.

The second of our three categories is the employees, including the blackjack dealer who is dealing you the cards, the pit boss who watches over him and the game, and the other employees as well. These are the frontline people, the people you actually see when you go to the casino. They are the ones who will incur your wrath when you get upset, and they are the ones who do everything for you when you are their customer. They face "the public" on a daily basis and are continually exposed to the very best, and the very worst, of humanity. It's little wonder that they sometimes "lose it," as the saying goes.

To the employee, their job is a tedious, repetitive grind. They work mostly for minimum wage, and rely entirely on the tips—known as "tokes" in casino parlance—that the customers give them. Mostly, they share the tips among all of them on the shift, which is the case in almost all casino pit games like blackjack. Their minimum wage is hardly enough to live on, and they get taxed on almost all of it up front by the IRS, regardless of whether or not they actually make any tips for that day. So, many times, they work the whole day and get no tips, but the IRS still steals their wages. It's very unfair, and no politician has yet thought of creating legislation that corrects this.

So, next time you go to a casino and find a blackjack dealer who isn't smiling, or who, perhaps, is a little less than friendly, think of it in his terms. You have to come to work five days a week and go into a casino environment where the air-conditioning is so high that it blasts you with freezing cold air all day long, so that by the time you leave on your break, you are more like an icicle than a human being. You slave for minimum wages hoping that the players on your shift will tip well today so you can house and feed your family. You have surly bosses lording over you who all think you are meat to be ground up and they are God. You work in a corporate environment where everybody wants to stab everyone else in the back to climb over the bodies to the next level, so that at least they can get some breathing room and actually start making a living wage. You work under constant surveillance so whenever you so much as sneeze you are summarily carted off into the midst of the security dungeon where you will be subjected to humiliating comments, snide remarks, and psychological torture, then subjected to alcohol tests, drug tests, then suspended from work, and then have to defend yourself in front of some equally surly human resources people who look at you as some more meat to be butchered. Then you have to face your departmental boss who looks at you as some potential victim in his gallery of hunted trophies and, if you survive all this and get back on the job, you still have to face the slobbering public who think they can throw things at you and abuse you at will.

You think this is not so? Next time you go to the casino, look at how other people behave. Listen and watch how the public treats the dealers. Listen to how the bosses treat them. Talk to the dealers on their breaks. You'll see that even if I have described these events in colorful language, the real truth is that this *is* the real truth.

It's little wonder then that the frontline employees are often less than accommodating. Even more surprising, however, is that the vast majority of the frontline employees are actually very good at what they do and are very friendly and helpful. Despite the extreme conditions under which these people have to work, they still find time, and the energy, to smile, to help, and to answer your questions (even though they have heard these questions, and answered them, a million times before). They treat you as the only customer in the world, and go out of their way to make your stay a pleasant and enjoyable one. Why is this? Because the people who work there are generally nice people. Also, because once they have worked in the casino for a while, most of them soon develop a thick skin. As an employee of the casino you will soon stop taking things personally. If the customer has a problem, it may have nothing to do with you, even though you may be the unfortunate person who bears the brunt of this customer's frustrated tirade. So you listen, smile, and offer to help. It really does work that way, and that's the miracle of the casino. The workers can actually do this job and still make it fun, exciting, and rewarding for the customers. Never forget, as a customer, that behind this facade there are human beings whose lives are very much harder than yours.

Of course, none of what I have said here excuses poor performance, rudeness to the customer, or any other misbehavior by any employee. This also happens, but it is generally very rare. If it does happen, it is usually because that employee has reached a point of no return, a meltdown of their ability to withstand the abuse and the conditions. For these reasons, the casino frontline employees are likely to change jobs far more frequently than the national statistical average. Frontline workers are highly transient in casinos. This is also not necessary, because some very easy steps by management could prevent this and make the work environment much better. Because of the issues I have discussed in the section above on executives, these situations are being, thus far, likewise ignored. Again, someday they may ask me, and if they do I can show them a very easy way to overcome this. For now, let's tackle the last group, which is us.

We are the customers and the players of blackjack. So, how does all this neat mumbo-jumbo work for us? Why should we even bother about this? So what if the executives and the employees have problems? So do we. We get lousy service. We can't get simple comps. We aren't appreciated for our investment. Well, now, doesn't this answer the questions?

The reason that it's important for us to know how "they think" is that it helps us understand how "we think." As players of blackjack, we want simple things:

1. A good game
2. A fast game
3. Good rules and options
4. Nice dealers
5. Helpful staff
6. Recognition by pit bosses
7. Appreciation for our money
8. Comps
9. A comfortable environment
10. Enjoyment

Well, that's how *we* think. Why we often don't get many of these items is because of the reasons stated earlier—and because of the following.

We want a good game—that's simple, but what is it? To us, this means being profitable and easy. To them, it means players losing.

We want a fast game—we both agree on this, except to them, the faster the game, the more money the customers lose. To us, the faster the game, the less bored we are (and the more money we make if we know how to play well).

We want good rules and options—which are essential to us. To them, well, they're not really essential. They want bad rules, so that the pit makes money, so that the pit boss can tell his boss the pit made a profit, so that this boss can write a report to the executives that says they were in the black on his shift. Because if the shift loses money, all the managers and employees all the way down the line stand to get fired, because the executive can (and often does) blame them as the reason his bottom line suffered that quarter.

We want nice dealers—fine, the casinos also want nice dealers. In the old days, the dealers were told, "Shut up and deal," meaning that they were supposed to keep their heads down, their noses in the cards, and never talk to the customers. Now, the casinos encourage friendly dealers. Friendly dealers make customers feel more like a part of the family. This is better for everyone. The dealers, however, are human beings. They won't always feel like smiling, chatting, or being perky, particularly when they have to work in an environment where they are squeezed for their income from all sides, and still have to deal with unruly customers. Often it takes just one bad apple to spoil the whole day for these dealers. Don't be too harsh on them. As long as they deal you the cards and do that sufficiently well, leave them alone if they seem a little down that day. They may be entirely different the next day. Don't be stingy with the tips. When you are winning, share. You may actually be the one customer who will make this dealer's day, and influence a person who may have given up on humanity almost entirely.

We want helpful staff—yes, indeed, we want not just the dealers and the pit staff, but everyone to be helpful. People who actually know where the rest rooms are and which way to get to the buffet—or anything else. People who know the language and can speak understandably. We want just the very basics and nothing extravagant. That's how *we* think. They think as long as they've got the bodies, it's okay. The bodies think it's just another day. The joke among casino employees is, "Just another day in paradise!" It's meant sarcastically, because there's very little "paradise" in their daily grind.

We want pit bosses, and staff who recognize us. That's what we think. What they think is, unless the players splash money around and lots of it, it's a waste of time and effort. Small gamblers mean nothing. Big gamblers get all the attention. This is both good and bad. If you are a knowledgeable blackjack player, you want anonymity, up to a point. You don't want the pit boss breathing down your neck, watching all your moves, but you do want to be noticed for your patronage. *They* think, however, that unless you bet at a certain level (and that is usually at the very least $25 per hand minimum for four hours, or more, consistently, each day of your visit), then you are not worth the bother—and "bother" it truly is. To do anything for you, the pit boss and the entire pit staff have a mountain of work to do. They must log you and your information into their computers. This means everything about you, from your birthday, address, social security number, wedding anniversary, preferences, likes, dislikes, and so on and on. Then they have to create a file for you, which will be in the computer and accessible to the

casino marketing department, public relations, and everyone else so that no matter where you go in that casino you
will get the kind of treatment you deserve. This takes a lot
of work, especially since there are tens of thousands of such
customers to deal with. Often several thousand in a day. No
wonder they don't want to waste their time on someone
who bets only $10 and will be gone in two hours.

We want simple comps, and that's the thorn in everyone's side. *We* think we should at the very least get *something*. Some kind of appreciation for being a blackjack
player in that casino. Why not get a comp for the buffet, or
at least the $2.99 breakfast in the coffee shop? Well, not so
fast and not so easy. *They* think, well, that person is a $5
player, and plays about three hours a day. By the formula
that is used to calculate the comp value of that person, it
wouldn't even qualify. First, the executives send a memo to
the pit that says that only players who bet at least $25 per
hand and play for at least four hours per day will be entitled
to comps. So when we ask the pit boss, or employee, for a
comp, and we don't fall in that pigeonhole, they say "no."
So we get mad. We start telling stories of how we lost this
much and that much, and how we have been playing here
for hours, and go to that casino ten times a year, and so on
and on. The pit boss or employee listen, then they say,
"Sorry, but you didn't play at my table, at my pit, at my
station, and you don't bet enough so that we can track you."
(Or something like that.) So you get stiffed.

Where is the problem? It's not with the pit boss or the pit
employee. The problem is with the corporate culture and
the executives. The executive committee decided that only
certain kinds of qualifications will entitle a person to a
comp, and only if that person fits the formula and only to
the level stated and allowed for by that formula. Therefore,
the pit boss has no choice. He must refuse you, even if it's
only a small comp. Otherwise, he will have to explain why

he did this and can lose his job. I have often heard comments like this: "I'd love to write you this comp. I know you and I know you play more than many of the other players put together. But you don't fit the formula and I won't risk my job for a $2.99 comp!" (End of story.)

That is one of the two biggest problems in the corporate-run casino. Everything has been formularized, quantified, and defined. If you don't fit into those particular boxes, you will be ignored. You will get nothing—zip. You will be relegated to the "herd." It doesn't matter if you actually spend a million dollars per visit. If you don't do this exactly in accordance with these formulas, then you will never get any comps, or even be noticed. The fault here lies in the total, unending, and fastidiously numeric inflexibility of the decisions made by the executives. They have taken away from the very people who know best the ability to make judgments regarding the very customers upon whom everything depends. So now the vast majority of the customers get missed, are treated badly, are ignored, and, very often, are simply looked upon as no more than fodder for the coffers.

This is a very bad policy, yet it is being perpetrated upon customers in virtually all of the casinos. This does not mean that customers never get anything. As long as you do your gaming in accordance with their rules and formulas, you will get quite a lot. However, you have to use the Slot Club card, you have to bet the required minimum at the table, and you have to play for the required minimum number of hours per day. If you do you will get the "royal treatment." You will then be rewarded with whatever comps and perks you are entitled to, based on the calculated formula. Usually, the casinos will give you back about 10 to 40 percent of your expected value, which means they will give you back about 10 to 40 percent of the *expected theoretical loss* that your kind of action demonstrates. There's no need for you to keep mulling the details of this in your head. Suffice it to say that if you force yourself to conduct your gaming in accordance with their format and formula, you will get the comps and the perks. If you don't, you will be ignored. That's it.

Unfortunately, this is a very large problem. By doing it in this way the casinos are losing tens of millions of customers whom they would attract (and retain) if they went back to the way it was done before they started all this nonsense of "theoretical loss" and other such crap. In the old days, it was the host, or the pit boss, or the slot boss, or the casino boss who gave the comps. They were the people on the floor, the ones who knew you as a player. So what if you only play one hour on this table at $10 per bet, but then go to the other side of the casino and bet $10,000 and lose it in five minutes? Under the current formula, you won't get anything, because you didn't bet at least the required $25 per hand for the required four hours per day. So you get stiffed. In the old days, any action like this would have brought you the pit boss and the casino boss, who would both ask what they could get for you. First, all your rooms, food, and drinks would immediately be comped. So would your airfare (in most cases). From that point on, whatever you wanted was provided. *That* was customer service!

Today, you are more likely to be told that you didn't qualify for any complimentaries (comps). Oops, you casinos are letting a lot of big players slip right though your net, and all because you are so stingy you won't even allow your pit boss to write a measly breakfast comp. Shame on you.

We want comfort and enjoyment, and these last two categories go hand-in-hand. Comfort is the most important. It is a constant source of frustration for me to witness, on a daily basis, how casino executives allow their casinos to be structured in a way that seems to be specifically designed to make their customers as uncomfortable and as miserable as possible. They have short stools with no backrests, machines too high to reach, blackjack tables too close together so that customers can't get in and out and are constantly bumping each other, long waits between cocktails, lousy service, and dirt and ashes all over the place. The ventilation is so poor in some casinos that breathing Los Angeles smog would be infinitely preferable.

The most vile of all, however, is the freezing cold. Every casino is so refrigerated that being there is like being hung like a slab of meat in a meat locker. Customers and employees literally shiver. In some places it's so cold that your hands begin to stiffen so badly that you can't even hold the cards or pull the slot machine handle. Although the outside may be mild and nice, customers have to drag heavy coats and sweaters inside just to be able to sit in the casino for a few minutes and play. Employees have to wear body-length thermal underwear just to be able to come to work, plus their two layers of uniform clothing over that. Infections and bacterial contamination are spread like the plague, because everyone has a cold or the flu. Elderly customers, who already have poor circulation, fall off their chairs because the casino is so cold they become ill from it.

What do the casino executives do about it? Well, they go to the media and complain about the costs of power. In the summer of 2001, California had a lot of trouble with its power supply. So did Nevada. In Nevada, the power company has steadily increased its rates over the last decade, most notably in the summer of 2001, and then again in 2002. Casino executives were huddling in stark terror. What in the world would they do about this? It's so much extra money. Some casinos began to charge their customers a fee for power consumption. One executive, who shall remain nameless, was quoted in the Las Vegas newspapers as saying, "These power costs are just getting too high. We don't know what we can do about it."

Well, I have a solution for you—*turn down the air condi-*

tioner! Raise the temperature in your freezing casinos. Make the customers comfortable for a change. What a novel idea: Make it pleasant to be in the casino, and make the customers comfortable. Well, let's see, we will have them gamble longer, and we will make more money. They will feel better, so they will come back more often. We will sell more drinks—and, well, let's see, we will actually save on our power bills! Why, isn't that a fresh idea?

It is unfathomable to me that these casino corporations would be so oblivious to solutions so easily accomplished. Yet they are, and they continue to be. The problems still persist. That's how *they* think. Or, rather, in this case, *they aren't thinking*. We think differently. We can't figure out why it's all such a mystery. Why can't the casino have comfortable chairs for us to sit on? Why can't we get cocktail service regularly? Why can't the casino be nice and warm and comfortable? Well, read again the section on the executives, and you will find out.

Okay, this is how *we* think versus how *they* think. As the comedian Dennis Miller used to say, that's my rant, my opinion, and, of course, I could be wrong. Now, back to blackjack, but do keep in mind the serious differences in how they think as opposed to how we think, as customers. It will help you gain a better experience from all your gaming, and particularly from your blackjack. It's all part of the overall steps for blackjack profits.

The Big Secret

This is the chapter where we tie everything together and reveal how to make powerful profits from blackjack. It sure looks like a simple game, but as you have seen, there is a lot more to it than just the two cards dealt to each player and the dealer. This is a game whose apparent simplicity absolutely belies the complexities that collectively make up the whole game as a combination of rules, options, and wagers. As we have seen, by learning all that we have shown here we will gain enough knowledge about blackjack to be able to play any blackjack game anywhere, under any rules, and most of the time play it so well that we will be able to get what is essentially an even game. By using what we have learned, we can almost entirely eliminate the house edge and, under some circumstances, actually get an advantage over the house. What this means is further reaffirmation that the game of blackjack *can* be beaten, even though not easily—but from where do the profits come?

I will now take for granted that you have acquired enough knowledge of blackjack that we no longer need to keep referring to the basics, and that you now know how to play the game as it should be played, with all the mastery of the MBS and all the other principles and methods I have outlined thus far.

Some of the profits from blackjack, when played properly, come from the exploitation of player-favorable options. Options such as being able to double-down, split, resplit, and double-down after resplits. Also from the fact that blackjacks pay 3:2, a bonus for the two-card 21 in the standard game. These are tools that you can use, skillfully and under the correct circumstances, to gain a positive expectation from the game. The dealer cannot do this, because the dealer plays for the house under the strict house rules. It is this basic difference that provides you with the ability to get at the very least an even game, or at best, under the appropriately favorable rules, to be able to gain a fractional edge over the house. A mere fractional advantage, however, isn't much. It certainly will not do a whole lot for you during the course of your visit to the casino. Even if you play as a professional and use all the tools that can be acquired, you will still have barely more than 0.5 percent, or 1 percent, or at the very best maybe a 2 percent edge over the game. You would have to find a very, very good and liberal game to get any edge like that. So how *do* you make these profits?

WAGERING STRUCTURE AND BETTING METHODS

The answer to the "big secret," in part, is wagering differential. "Wagering differential," as I have called it, is the varying structure of a tiered series of bets. What this means is a consciously derived sequence, or structure, of raising and lowering the amount of your bets.

To derive the most profits that you can from the game of blackjack, you must employ a wagering differential in your betting structure. You must *bet more* when you have the opportunity to score *wins* (and bigger wins), and *bet less* when you have the *least* opportunity to win and more of a chance to lose. This may sound like the betting hierarchy often associated with card counting. To some degree, this is correct. However, since card counting cannot be done reliably, and even cannot be practiced in many games such as the machine-dealt games, your application of the wagering differential will have to fall under the main category of "opportunity," and under the sub-category of "tiered structure."

To understand this, simply place yourself in the position of being able to increase your wagers when the opportunity beckons. Taking advantage of double-downs, splits, resplits, and additional double-downs is part of that. Knowing when to split and double-down by using the MBS is another—and so on. For each and every instance where you have the opportunity to increase your bet by exploiting the favorable options of blackjack, under the most favorable conditions as indicated by the MBS, these instances will provide you with the *opportunity* to make the most of your profit potential. However, that isn't all, by itself.

In order for the wagering differential to be of maximum use, and for all these opportunities to be of maximum yield, you must also establish a tiered betting structure. In its simplest form, this means to vary your bet so that you do not always bet the same. Betting the same amount all the time is called "flat betting," and such wagers are often called "flat bets." Casinos love players who do this because they know that all flat bettors will lose. By making flat bets all the time you will be ground up by the house edge and the inevitable swings against you. At the very best, playing perfectly but making only flat bets, you will break even. Or it will cause you to suffer the small mathematical loss derived from the fractional house edge against you in many games. Even using the available opportunities will not allow you all of the profits to which your play entitles you. Therefore, we introduce another concept, called the "fractional differential."

The fractional differential becomes part of the wagering differential, in the category of "opportunity" and under the sub-category of "tiered structure." Fractional differential in wagering means to alter your bets in fractional increments.

There are many "systems" (but many other significantly more reliable "methods") that show various versions of a betting hierarchy. The most famous of all these is what is called the Martingale system. This calls for you to double your bet each time you lose. The rationale is that eventually you will win, and therefore recover all your losses up to that point plus the win of the initial starting wager amount. The first part of the fallacy of this is that such a system can reach staggering proportions. For example, if you started with a $5 wager, and then doubled your bet each time you lost, you could easy have the following situation:

WAGER NUMBER	BET	RESULT	
	(after each *loss*, the next bet is *doubled*)		
1	$5	loss	
2	$10	loss	
3	$20	loss	
4	$40	loss	
5	$80	loss	
6	$160	loss	
7	$320	loss	
8	$640	loss	
9	$1,280	loss	
10	$2,560	loss	
11	$5,120	loss	
12	$10,240	loss	
13	$20,380	loss	
14	$40,960	win	(*Phew, what a relief!*)

Okay, so there it is. Eventually, you did win. After thirteen consecutive losses, you had to risk $40,960 and for what? Well, actually you risked all that to win a mere $5. Do you think that this kind of a series of consecutive losses is unusual? Well, statistically, yes—but it does happen! I have personally counted several losing streaks of sixteen, eighteen, and even twenty-four hands in a row. Of course I wasn't playing at that table after a few hands like that, but I took a look at the protracted series just to see how far it went—and it went quite far. If you have to double your bet after each loss just to make the profit of the initial starting wager, a sequence of that many losers in a row will destroy you. Take a look at the above chart, and continue it for yourself into the series of sixteen losses, eighteen losses, and then twenty-four losses. Do you see how much you would have to risk in order to eventually win that $5? This kind of a "system" is pure bunk and a prescription for total disaster.

The second fallacy with this system is that eventually you will run up against the house limits. Each table posts a sign that indicates the minimum and maximum bets. So, if you sit at a $5 table, many times you will see that the maximum bet is only $200. On many games, the maximum bet on such a table may even go as high as $5,000, or even $10,000. There are several tables in Las Vegas casinos that offer this kind of a spread. Even this will not help you if you play with the Martingale system, or any of its derivatives. If you just use the example shown above, you will see that in the worst case, where the table maximum is only $200, you would already have run up against the table limit by hand #7. So, you would have lost your hand #6 wager of $160, and never gotten the chance to keep chasing your $5 win. It's similar for the other limits, which you can see for yourself. The point is that none of these "systems" will help because of the two inherent flaws in them: you can lose exponentially, and the table has betting limits.

There is, however, a big difference between something called a "system" and something called a "method." Generally, anything called a "system" is usually something like the Martingale system shown above, which usually means it's some kind of a gimmick. On the other hand, something called a "method" is usually a more thoroughly researched and mathematically sound application of an analysis of empirically derived evidence that leads to a series of structured suggestions. These suggestions may take the form of an advised sequence of events that, by such research, tends to indicate that a positive and useful result may be obtained most of the time under the correct sets of circumstances, which are also identified.

Methods and their derived applications are called "methodology." These are what I have called the wagering differential and the fractional differential applied to tiered wagering.

Instead of trying to win the house by betting the farm, you can more accurately exploit the opportunities presented to you in the game of blackjack by utilizing a betting structure that allows for the increase and decrease of the amounts of your bets in fractional increments. With card counting, this is usually accomplished in whole unit progressions, based on the positive expectations of the high PM and true counts. In these instances, which I wish to indicate are far from precise, you at least have a better-than-average guess as to what kind of a result you may expect. Based on this assumption, the betting structure advice indicates that you should increase your bets by the amount of unit increases recommended for that particular situation. Many books and texts that advise card counting as the main technique for blackjack play also advise a wagering structure that increases by what is usually called a 1-to-4 unit spread. This simply means that you increase your original bet, which is your 1 unit, by like unit amounts, up to a total of a

4-unit wager when the count turns very positive. And, of course, all the various smaller unit increases, as well as decreases, called for in this way. So if you start with a wager of $5, then each of your "units" has the value of $5. So, a 4-unit bet would be $20; a 3-unit bet would be $15; and so on. You get the picture.

Still others advise what is sometimes called the "regression" technique. This advice, also based in the mastery of card counting, means that you bet more than the minimum number of units as your first bet, and then take half of it back if you win and bet only a single unit thereafter. For example, this would mean that you would use, say, the $5 bet as your 1-unit equivalent. So, in this situation, you would wager $10 as your first bet, which equals a 2-unit wager, and if you won then you would take back the $10 win, plus also take back one of the two units you first bet, meaning one of the two $5 units. So you would have *regressed* your wager back to one unit ($5) for the next hand. The reason this is being suggested is that it assures you of a profit immediately—*if,* that is, you win the first hand. If you lose the first hand, well, then you have to do all sorts of other things to get back to where you started, and so you become immersed in an entire "system," the eventual outcome of which will be your loss.

Anyway, these are examples of wagering "systems" that at least indicate what is meant by a tiered approach to your wagering. It is true that several of these "systems" can in fact be called "methods" because some do have merit. However, most of these are vested solely in your ability to become an expert card-counter, and therein lies their featured fallacy. First, you must be *able* to be such a perfect card-counter. Second, you must be *willing* to be a card counter, knowing that what you are doing is already flawed (as I have shown earlier). Third, you must be able to actually find a game where you can still practice card counting to at least some degree of its proposed level of potential success. All of this is virtually no longer possible in the casinos of the twenty-first century. Even if it was, it still depends on far too many variables, your abilities, other associated skills, and availability of games, rules, and so on, all vested in something that already has holes in it even before you start using it. It's simply impractical in the real world of today.

A tiered wagering structure is, indeed, essential to make your profits in blackjack count for something. But what to do? How to do it? Well, here is what I propose. Read it, use it, analyze it. I leave it to you to determine whether it is any better than any of the other methods that are being circulated in blackjack literature.

METHODS OF PLAY TO MAXIMIZE THE MBS

You must remember that we are speaking about a tiered wagering structure, based on the principles of wagering differential and fractional differential. Wagering differential provides for the modification of your tiered betting structure, while fractional differential will allow for incremental variations. Rather than being limited to various per-unit variations, incremental or regressive, the principles that I am here recommending will allow you to structure your bets more accurately, with less risk, and with greater gain.

I will simplify this methodology for this example. The actual structure of the entire process is somewhat more complex and considerably more involved. For those of you who wish to know the entire process in all of its detail, and therefore are willing to invest some additional learning time to master this, I refer you to my book on Advanced Strategies.

In order to best exploit not merely the opportunities for profit already offered by the game of blackjack, but also the opportunities for added value of increased wagers, both in a tiered structure as well as the resultant higher-wager outcomes in situations such as double-downs and splits, we must first understand the frequencies of occurrence of blackjack events.

A hand in the game of blackjack is an "event." More than one such hand is a "sequence of events." When you take the game of blackjack and pool as many of the available events as possible, you will get a sampling of several million such events—in my case, nine million such events, played on my computer hand by hand over the past seventeen years, and several thousand additional events played by me personally in actual casino blackjack games. Add to that several thousand more "observed" events in actual casino situations. Together, these events form a pool of a statistical sampling upon which a certain set of reasonably accurate assumptions may be based.

In my research, as far as I, and I only, have been able to calculate and determine, all events at blackjack consist of the following:

80 percent of the time, a WIN is followed by a LOSS, and a LOSS is followed by a WIN

20 percent of the time, a *sequence* of WINS and/or LOSSES happen *consecutively*

What this means is this: When you have a win, expect that the next hand will be a loss. When you have a loss, expect that the next hand will be a win. This will be so for 80 percent of all events. This is what is usually referred to as the "push-and-pull" scenario. You win, you lose. You lose, you win. Push and pull.

Then, there is the 20 percent of the time when this will turn into a statistical anomaly. Both ways, mind you. There will be a sequence of consecutive wins, anywhere from two-in-a-row to as many as is statistically feasible, as well as a like sequence of losses (the longest consecutive sequence I have encountered in my samplings was eleven; the *average* of any consecutive sequence was about 3.83). As a general estimate, among the 20 percent occurrences of a series of consecutive events, either wins or losses, there will be, on average, about four such sequence events strung together. Therefore, in order to exploit them, we must use wagering differential and fractional differential. This means to increase our wagers proportionately in "win" situations, and decrease our wagers more aggressively in "loss" situations.

To simplify this, imagine yourself as a $5 flat bettor. In 80 percent of the events, you will win $5, and then lose $5, and then win $5 and then lose $5, and so on. This is the W-L-W-L-W-L scenario. You will neither win nor lose in such a series. Now, let us assume that you have a series of four consecutive wins, but you are still betting only the $5 per hand. So you have four such wins, which will be as follows: Win $5, win $5, win $5, win $5, lose $5. The four consecutive wins ended when the fifth event was a loss. So where are you with your money? Four wins in a row, *with flat bets* of $5 each, are as follows:

BET	WIN	GROSS	NET WIN	CUMULATIVE WIN
$5	$5	$10	$5	$5
$5	$5	$10	$5	$10
$5	$5	$10	$5	$15
$5	$5	$10	$5	$20
$5	0	0	0	$15

The fifth event is the loss, and that's where you lost your original $5 bet, after that series of wins. Your net cumulative win was, therefore, the $20 won, minus the original $5 lost, which equals a net win of $15.

Now let's assume that your very next series will be a series of an equal number of consecutive *losses*. This would play out as follows:

BET		LOSS	GROSS	NET WIN	CUMULATIVE LOSS
$5		$5	− $5	$0	− $5
$5		$5	− $10	$0	− $10
$5		$5	− $15	$0	− $15
$5		$5	− $20	$0	− $20
$5	Win	$5	− $15	$5	− $15

As you can see, this sequence of four consecutive losses was ended by a win, and therefore the entire series resulted in the net cumulative loss of − $15. So, before you had a net win of $15, and now you have a net loss of − $15. This leaves you even, square, and with no profit.

What if the situations don't always work out just exactly perfect like this? What if your sessions result in more consecutive *loss* events than consecutive win events? Well, if you were to continue to wager flat bets, as shown above, you would be losing overall, and losing a lot more than you should be. In fact, although the actual events will even out, statistically, in the long run, I have personally observed that the frequency of losing events in a row in my samplings occurred more often than winning events. I believe that this was so not only because, in my small slice of reality, I had not yet reached the statistical median, which will happen eventually, but also because my nine million–plus hands are still not enough for that to show up in that way. Actually, in my statistical samplings, I have had winning events only about 41 percent of the time. Yet I still made an overall profit for each session series. In fact, with the application of the entire methodology, it is possible for you to actually lose about seven more hands per session than you win, but still book a profit for that session. It all comes down to the intricacies of the wagering differential.

To accomplish this, you must use a tiered structure with a *fractional* differential. Increasing your bets by whole units will not work. You must fractionalize these in increments, and add and subtract in numerically higher or proportionately lower sequences. For the entire principle, I again refer you to my book on Advanced Strategies. Here, however, for the sake of simplicity, you can do this as follows:

1. Start with a 3-unit base.
2. After each WIN, expect a LOSS, so bet *two-thirds LESS*.
3. After each LOSS, expect a WIN, so bet *one-third MORE*.
4. If you have a LOSS *followed* by a LOSS, you are in a series of LOSING events; therefore REDUCE your bets by *two-thirds* each time, until you reach the table minimum 1-unit bet.
5. If you have a WIN followed by a WIN, you are in a series of WINNING events; therefore INCREASE your bets by *one-third* of your previous bet amount as long as you continue to have winning events; as soon as you have a LOSS, REDUCE your *next* wager by *two-thirds of your previous bet* and use *that* as your *starting unit base* and begin the process from #1 all over again, but this time you will use that *last amount* as your *starting unit base.*

If you continue to lose, then you are in the protracted losing series, and since this is covered in this plan because you always reduce your next wager by two-thirds after each such loss, you will eventually get back to the table minimum, and get there much faster than in the converse situation of incremental wager increases. Once you reach the table minimum, then treat that as your starting unit, and begin all over again from #1. This time, however, your #1 starting point will be only the table minimum 1-unit wager, and therefore the rest of the series of wagers will be as incremental as is possible under whatever the wagering units in that casino may be, such as in half-dollar increments, for example. In fact, every time you get a series of losses that take you back to the table minimum bet, you will always begin with #1 under these conditions.

Similarly, when you suffer the inevitable loss after a series of wins, your new starting base unit will be one-third of the previous bet (a reduction of two-thirds from the last wager), so you will begin the next series with a *higher* base-unit wager. In this way, you will always maximize your wins and always minimize your losses. If you do this correctly you will never lose, over your session sequences. Again, there are more details available in my book on Advanced Strategies, which also shows a sampling of the strategy events and their individual analysis.

Here you have an easy-to-use plan that will assure you of always having the biggest bet ready when the best opportunity presents itself, while always assuring you of losing less in bad situations.

Simple Strategy

Now that we have covered the wagering decisions, it's time to set aside a few rules of simple strategy that will allow you to play better, without having to remember everything about the MBS. However, I caution you that this example of a simple strategy is *only* intended as a *quick guide*, and in no way is meant to replace the full and complete mastery of the entire MBS. What I am presenting here in this simple strategy are some of the most important features of the entire MBS. This is intended as a *beginning* point for you, so that you can have a basis upon which you can build your complete knowledge of the MBS. These are only simple guidelines, but they will help in your decision making for profitable play. Again, these strategy suggestions are not meant as the complete answer to blackjack. They are only a guide. Keep that in mind.

1. Never split two 10-value cards. This hand is a total of 20, and it is a very good hand. The theoretical object in blackjack may be to achieve 21, but if you have 20 on the

first two cards dealt to you there is only one hand with which the dealer can beat you, and that is 21 (either as cards drawn, or as a blackjack hand). If the dealer has 20 as well, you push and don't lose. Any other combination for the dealer means an automatic winner for you. Many times I see players splitting two 10-value cards and winding up losing all their money and at the same time incurring the wrath of all the other players at the table. Doing this is financial suicide.

2. Never split two 5s. Two 5s equal 10, so double-down instead, and ask for "one card only, please." If you split the two 5s, and get two 10s, you made two bad hands out of a good hand, and would have had 20 if you had doubled-down. It's already hard enough to win, so when you have a chance to win double your initial bet, take it and don't play foolishly.

3. Never take insurance. Insurance is a sucker bet and is there as a means of making the players bet on whether or not the dealer has a blackjack when he has an Ace showing as the upcard. Most of the time the dealer does not have a blackjack, and it will cost you an additional 50 percent of your bet to find out something that will be determined any-way—without it costing you extra money. If the dealer does not have a blackjack, you lose the additional 50 percent bet you made, and then stand a good chance of losing the origi-nal bet you made. If the dealer does have a blackjack, tough luck. Swallow the loss, and play the next hand. You won't win every hand you play, but the extra 50 percent bet isn't worth spending on the off chance the dealer does in fact have a blackjack. Even if you have a blackjack hand yourself, don't take the insurance. You stand to lose nothing, since you will push if the dealer does have the same hand as you. If he doesn't, you will win at 3:2, and that extra money is what counts significantly in your overall ability to make powerful profits from blackjack.

4. If the dealer is showing a 7 card or higher, and you have a total of 12, 13, 14, 15, or 16, always take a hit and continue to hit your hand until you get 17 or better, or you bust. Any of these hands (12, 13, 14, 15, or 16) are automatic losers if the dealer has a 7 or higher showing, and 10 hiding. Dealer's 17 or better will beat any of the hands you hold, as shown here. You risk little by taking a hit, assuming the dealer has already beaten your hand, which will happen about 72 percent of the time (cumulatively). This is significant enough for you to take the hit and try to improve. To improve your hand is your only sensible option. This is especially true when you hold a soft hand. In this case you take no risk at all and have a terrific chance to make a winning hand out of a bad one. If you do not take the hit you will be giving the dealer a multitude of cards with which he can draw a better hand. Either way it's a bad situation, so hitting will cost you less overall. You won't win every time, and sometimes you will bust. Hitting these hands in these situations means that you will be preventing more of the dealer wins, and therefore lowering your overall losses. It is, consequently, a defensive play designed to save you money.

5. If the dealer shows an upcard of 2, 3, 4, 5, or 6, stand on any hand that is 12 or over, hit any hand that is 8 or less, and double-down on everything else. This is especially advisable, and often profitable, if the dealer has a 5 or a 6 showing. These are the worst dealer hands possible, since often the dealer will get a 15 or 16, and has to take another card, which makes it likely he will bust. If you have a soft hand, even soft 17, double-down. You are now playing both that you will improve the hand you already have, and that the dealer will bust. These circumstances are the best possible option for you to make money.

6. Always split two 8s, *except* as shown in the MBS. Two 8s make 16, and that is the worst hand in blackjack. By splitting the two 8s, you stand a better chance of making at

least one hand a winner, and thereby saving you money. If one hand wins, and the other loses, one pays the other and you lose nothing (assuming you bet the same amount on both hands, which is normally a rule requirement). If you draw a 10 to both hands, you have made two 18s, as opposed to one 16, and prevented yourself from busting out if you held the 16 and drew the 10.

7. Always split Aces. When given two Aces as your first two cards, you either have a total of 2 or a total of 12, both bad hands. If you split them, and get a 10 on each, you have two hands of 21, both winners (unless the dealer also makes 21, in which case your hands are a push, or the dealer has blackjack, in which case only your original bet will lose). These hands are *not* blackjack, a common mistake among casual players. After you split the Aces you will get only one more card on each of the two hands. The exceptions are in casinos that allow you to resplit Aces, so in these events if you get another Ace dealt to you, split it again, and you will now have three hands. Whatever the case, and whatever the dealer is showing as his upcard, splitting Aces will give you additional chances of winning.

8. Always double-down on 11, except as shown in the MBS. Any two cards equaling 11 are the best chance you have to make 21 with just one more card, or a great hand with almost any other card. Plus, you cannot bust out, making this double-down bet even better. This is also the only other edge you have against the house. By doubling-down you are taking full advantage of the favorable situation offered to you. This is like craps, where taking advantage of the passline, or come, full odds on any roll reduces the house edge to statistical insignificance.

9. Always double-down on any first two-card combination of 10, unless the dealer is showing a 10 or an Ace as the upcard. The principle here is the same as for doubling-

down on 11, and works in your favor to nearly the same extent.

10. Never hit a hard 17 or higher. If you are dealt a hard 17, stand no matter what. Any card higher than a 4 will bust you out, so your chances are better to stay and see what the dealer turns up. The dealer may be showing a 10 but hiding a 6, then drawing a 6 and busting out. If you hit your hard 17, that 6 as the next card out would have busted you, and you would have lost. This way you win. Whatever the dealer is showing, if you have 17, 18, 19, or 20 on the first two cards, stand. Of course, if you have 21, a blackjack, you win anyway, so why hit it? As strange as it sounds, people do make silly plays like this, even when holding an automatic 1.5:1 winner (3:2 as shown on the table layout).

In addition to these simple guidelines, there are many other options you can take depending on the value of your first two cards, and what the dealer's upcard shows. What I have offered here are the most basic of all the strategy rules pertaining to blackjack. Even if you have no further interest in reading about blackjack and blackjack strategy, the simple strategy I outlined here will help make you a better player, and give you a better chance of making your vacation gaming dollar count for more, and earn more, in your blackjack play.

THE ESSENTIAL MBS

To follow in the spirit of the above section on simple strategy, it occurred to me that some of the readers of this book may not wish to do as much brain work as may be required to master everything that I have shown so far. Perhaps all you really want from blackjack is to be able to feel more secure at the table, not feel intimidated, or look like a novice. Maybe all you want are some really simple (and short) guidelines to help you with your play.

If this is so, then perhaps if I simplify the MBS all the way down to the bare bones, this may help you do just that. So, here goes. This is the entire MBS, boiled down to a mere few rules that you should be able to learn almost instantly.

1. If you get two cards, and one is an Ace and the other any 10-value card, then this is the natural, the 21, the blackjack, and an automatic winner under the majority of conditions. *Stand.*
2. Two picture cards, or two 10s, or any 10 and any picture card, are all a total of 20, a very good hand. *Stand.*
3. If you get two Aces, *split* them.
4. If you get two 8s, *split* them.
5. If you have a total of 17, 18, 19, 20, or 21, *stand*.
6. If you have a total of 12, 13, 14, 15, or 16, *hit* until you get one of the hands above, or bust.
7. If you have an Ace with any of the following: 2, 3, 4, 5, or 6, these are called soft hands. *Hit*, and treat the new total as in accordance with the above indications for those totals.
8. If you have a two-card total of 10 or 11, *double-down*.

Well, that's it. That's about as simple as it can get. If you learn this, you will not know everything, and you will not be able to take the full advantage that your complete mastery of the MBS and the other principles and methods will allow, but at least you will be ahead of most of the people who play blackjack and know absolutely nothing about it. I caution you, however, that this is a *very simplified* version of the MBS, and therefore you cannot consider this as the entire base of your blackjack expertise. However, if all you want is to dive right in, this will allow you to float a little longer than you would otherwise. At least for that, it is a life raft—or, in the case of blackjack, a money raft.

GOOD RULES, BAD RULES, GOOD GAMES, BAD GAMES

Continuing in the spirit of simplifying some of the information that I have outlined in this book, here is a recap of some of the things to look for, and others to avoid:

GOOD RULES

1. Dealer stands on *all* 17s.
2. Double-down on *any* first two cards.
3. Split and resplit *any* pair.
4. Split and resplit Aces.
5. Double-down *after* splits and resplits.
6. Blackjack pays 3:2.

BAD RULES

1. Dealer must *hit* soft 17.
2. Double-down *only* on 10 and 11.
3. *No* resplit of like pairs.
4. *No* resplit of Aces.
5. *No* double-down after splits.
6. Blackjack pays anything other than 3:2.*

GOOD GAMES

1. Two-deck hand-held shuffled by a human dealer.
2. Four-deck shoes shuffled by a human dealer with at least 70 percent penetration.

* In some casinos, various promotional gimmicks may cause blackjack 21s to be paid at 2:1 or perhaps 3:1. This is usually done for games where some suited combination of cards will pay this extra bonus, such as, for example, the Ace and Jack of Spades. This, however, actually has a detrimental effect on your overall blackjack expectations, played in accordance with the recommendations in this book. Usually, this seemingly good extra payoff is countered by some other rule restrictions, which are often not easily recognizable. Therefore, if you see a game where blackjacks pay anything other than the normal 3:2, stay away, because you are likely to be caught in a gimmick game.

3. Six-deck shoes shuffled by a human dealer with at least 75 percent penetration.
4. Any of the above three that have the *majority* of the *Good Rules.*
5. Any one-on-one game, between you and the dealer, that have all of the above.

BAD GAMES

1. Any game shuffled by a machine.
2. Any game shuffled by a machine that is a continuous shuffler, or randomizer.
3. Any game that has less than 70 percent penetration.
4. Any game that cuts 50 percent or more off the deck, or decks.
5. Any game that has the majority of the *Bad Rules.*
6. Any single-deck game played with less than two-thirds of the deck and without all of the *Good Rules.*

This is your blueprint for knowing what kind of a game to look for, and what rules to play by. In all your blackjack play, you are looking for the best possible game with the best possible rules. This information should help you select the best possible game in whatever casino you may visit. Just take a few moments to look the games over, and see if they have at least the majority of the better options, as shown here. If they do, play. If they don't, go elsewhere.

DEVIATIONS FROM THE MBS

You may have read other books on blackjack. If you have, most likely you have found large sections, or portions, of these books dedicated to variations in Basic Strategy. These variations are usually described as refinements to your blackjack expertise, and are almost always described in direct references to some card-counting systems. Usually, by the time you get to these parts of these books you are expected to have mastered the card-counting system that is being described, along with the Basic Strategy as stated by those authors. Now, you are being asked to learn more details. These details are to be used in specific situations based on the running count, or true count, in conjunction with the various house rules for the specified games.

For example, you may be offered various deviations from the Basic Strategy based on the rule changes to the standard blackjack game made in different regions of the United States. The best examples that can easily be shown are the most visible basic rule differences between blackjack games in Reno and those in Las Vegas, Nevada. In the Reno (and Lake Tahoe) blackjack games, the dealer must hit soft 17. In Las Vegas, dealer must stand on all 17s. Although there are casinos in both locations where the opposite may be found, these are the most widely recognizable differences between the rules of the game of blackjack in two very distinct gaming regions. The Reno/Tahoe game is, therefore, often referred to as the "Northern Nevada" rules, and often even as the "Reno/Tahoe" rules, while the Las Vegas game is often described as the "Nevada Rules," or "Nevada Game," or "Vegas Rules." I mention this because these are the best examples of what many books often cite as the necessity for making various changes to Basic Strategy.

With gaming spreading across the nation, there are now many different gaming centers, and therefore many more differences in the rules of the game. Blackjack is no longer divided only between the "Vegas Rules" and the "Reno/Tahoe" rules. The direct effect of all of this has been that the sections within many blackjack books that detail the various alterations to the Basic Strategy have become so complex that it is hard to keep track of it all. There are rules for this, and other rules for that, and if this, then that, but not if this or that, and so on. It just gets a little too much, and all for very little gain.

I do, nevertheless, realize that some of the readers of this book may wish to explore further into the depth of the various theories of blackjack, and may even wish to invest the additional time to learn the variations to blackjack Basic Strategy. I have therefore designed a condensed version of the various refinements to blackjack Basic Strategy, and structured them to fit as well as possible within the boundaries of my own version of blackjack Basic Strategy, which I have called the MBS—Modified Basic Strategy—throughout this book. These refinements for my MBS are intended only for those readers who wish to try to fine-tune their game for the various gaming regions, or various rule situations, for the game of blackjack as played in different casinos in the United States.

I caution all other readers not to consider these refinements as the complete answer to MBS situations. These are only *refinements*, based on the specific situations for which they are intended. I further caution all readers not to instill in these refinements more value than they offer. Even these refinements provide only a minimal gain to your overall game as played with the MBS. In fact, any of these refinements will add only about 0.05 to 0.6 percent to your game. If you play MBS perfectly, as written here, you will already have virtually negated the house edge in almost all casinos and games. By adding these refinements, you assure yourself of only a small additional edge. However, since I have always stated in this book that any knowledge is better than no knowledge, learning these can be a useful exercise in the mastery of the game. For this reason, if no other, they are worth the effort. What follow, therefore, are the various refinements to the MBS, as these apply specifically and only to the situations as specified.

Las Vegas Rules Single-Deck Game

As I mentioned several times, it is virtually impossible to find a single-deck game where you can play blackjack with most of the available player-favorable rules and options. However, there are some games that use the Las Vegas rules for single-deck games, and if you are able to find one where you can play more than one or two hands before the dealer shuffles, then you would refine your MBS for these situations as follows:

- Split a pair of 7s versus a dealer's upcard of 8.
- Split a pair of 6s versus a dealer's upcard of 7.
- Split a pair of 4s versus a dealer's upcard of 5 or 6.
- Split a pair of 3s versus a dealer's upcard of 2 or 3.
- Split a pair of 2s versus a dealer's upcard of 2.

I would also like to mention the refinements for surrender, but since this is virtually extinct, there's little reason to do so. As an exercise, just remember that if you did have early surrender, you would surrender a hard 16 against the dealer's Ace, and also surrender a hard 15, hard 16, and hard 14 (including 7,7) against the dealer's 10. There's little chance you will ever need this information because surrender is all but dead and gone, just about everywhere.

Reno/Tahoe Single-Deck Games

The following are MBS refinements for the Northern Nevada type of game.

- Always split 8,8 and A,A.
- Always hit 8-9, 4-4, A-2, A-3, A-4, A-5, and A-6.
- Always double 11.
- Double 10 only against the dealer's 2, 3, 4, 5, 6, 7, 8, or 9. Hit otherwise.

Nevada Shoe Game

Applicable to most shoe-dealt games, regardless of in which region they may be found, as long as they use the majority of the rules as played in shoe games in Las Vegas.

- Double a 9 against the dealer's 2, 3, 4, 5, or 6.
- If you have a 6,5 (11), double against the dealer's Ace.
- If you have a 9,2 or 8,3, only hit against the dealer's Ace.

If your shoe game also offers surrender, then the following will add a few extra tenths of a percent to your game:

- Surrender hard 16 against a dealer's 9, 10, or Ace.
- Surrender hard 15 and hard 16 against a dealer's 10 or Ace.

Atlantic City Shoe Game

These refinements are applicable to all shoe games that use the Atlantic City rules. Caution—these do not apply to machine-dealt games!

- Double-down on 9 against the dealer's 3, 4, 5, 6, or 7.
- Double-down on A-2, A-3, A-4, A-5, and A-6 against the dealer's 3, 4, 5, 6, or 7.
- Double-down on A-7 against the dealer's 2, 3, 4, 5, or 6, stand against 7 or 8.

These refinements to the MBS are all you will require in the event that you find games where such opportunities, or requirements, present themselves. I have streamlined these on purpose, because it is my opinion that any further complexities are unworkable and, frankly, quite useless in the real world. Further refinements are possible, but they are of so little usefulness that even their purely theoretical or educational value is lost. I will again advise you not to overvalue any such refinements to the MBS. If you properly apply the MBS, then that is all you will need in the real world of casino blackjack, and you will not require these refinements, although you can use them if you wish—but correctly, please, or they will detract from your proper MBS play.

The Quiz Show:
Know Your Blackjack

This is where we all get to have some fun. Here we have a short quiz to find out how much we have learned. I don't expect you to get everything correct the first time—or even the second or third time. The beauty of this quiz is that you can take it over and over again, and keep taking it until you become so familiar with the questions (and the answers) that you will have mastered the major portion of your blackjack playing knowledge. I am not interested in answers pertaining to theory. These questions are designed to have you think about answers that are workable and applicable to the actual conditions of playing blackjack in the casinos of the twenty-first century.

The scoring structure is +10 points for each correct answer, and −10 points for each incorrect answer. There is a balanced number of questions, so that if you get half of them correct and half of them wrong, you will wind up with a "0" in the end. That's not as bad as it seems. As the optimist said, the "glass is half-full." By getting a "0," this means that you got half the answers right. Now all you have to figure out is which ones you got right, and which ones you didn't. Then you can work on improving your knowledge on the ones where you didn't do so well. The same goes for all the other possible combinations of plus-minus scores. When you get the maximum possible score, then you have answered all the questions correctly, and this means that you have mastered the most basic and important aspects of playing blackjack in a real casino. Don't be hard on yourself if you don't get the best score right away. The point of making this quiz available is that you can keep taking it over again, even after some time has passed, or even after you have played in the casinos for a while. This is meant to be a tool to help you always. So come on down, the game is about to begin!

QUIZ QUESTIONS

QUESTION 1
Do the mathematics of blackjack show that the game can be beaten?

ANSWER
A. Not really, not in the real world of actual casino play.
B. Only when dealt first-card-to-last.
C. Theoretically, yes.
D. Only when you are a skilled card-counter.

QUESTION 2
Can blackjack be beaten for financial profits?

ANSWER
A. Only if you are an expert card-counter.
B. Only if the rules allow it.
C. Only if you learn the proper Basic Strategy and playing strategies, such as the MBS.
D. Only if you play MBS correctly and use all your knowledge of the game.

QUESTION 3
How do you identify a "good" game?

ANSWER
   A. One where lots of players are yelling and screaming and having a great time.
   B. One where the dealer busts a lot.
   C. One where there are fewer decks, with deep penetration, and most of the favorable rules.
   D. One where you win a lot of hands.

QUESTION 4
Which of the following are the "good" rules and options?

ANSWER
   A. Double-down on 9, 10, and 11.
   B. Split Aces and 8s.
   C. Dealer hits soft 17.
   D. None of the above.

QUESTION 5
Who developed Basic Strategy?

ANSWER
   A. Edward O. Thorp in his book *Beat the Dealer* in 1962.
   B. Julian Braun, the IBM mathematician who programmed blackjack into the computer.
   C. Authors on blackjack who took the results from Thorp and Braun and created it.
   D. Casino dealers who found out how to beat the casinos.

QUESTION 6
How can financial profits be made from playing blackjack?

ANSWER

A. By learning the MBS and playing with the wagering differential tiered betting method.
B. By learning Basic Strategy.
C. By learning the MBS.
D. By learning Basic Strategy, or the MBS, and counting cards with the PM count and true count.

QUESTION 7

Which of the following represents the *worst* game?

ANSWER

A. Two decks where dealer hits soft 17.
B. Single deck where dealer hits soft 17.
C. Single deck where dealer hits soft 17 and shuffles after each one or two hands.
D. Any shoe game where more than 50 percent is cut off the decks.

QUESTION 8

A blackjack game shuffled by a machine is better, because:

ANSWER

A. It helps to prevent cheating.
B. It helps to speed up the game, giving you more hands and therefore more winners.
C. It shuffles the cards so well there's no chance of getting a series of losing hands.
D. It's the worst possible kind of blackjack game that can ever be found, and there's absolutely nothing good about a game shuffled by any machine.

QUESTION 9

Dealers get more blackjack 21s than players, because:

ANSWER

A. Both players and dealers have an equal chance of getting a blackjack 21.

B. Dealers play by house rules and therefore get more blackjacks.

C. Dealers get more blackjacks because the house doesn't get 3:2.

D. Dealers are more skillful and therefore deal themselves more blackjacks.

QUESTION 10

Can casinos cheat at the game of blackjack?

ANSWER

A. Yes, they can, but would never allow this to happen because that would risk their license.

B. Yes, they can, but would never try it against the regular players who only bet small.

C. No, they can't, because they are watched by cameras all the time.

D. Yes, they can, but not very often because big players would get wise and stop playing.

QUESTION 11

You should tip the dealer well, because:

ANSWER

A. When you tip you will get better cards.

B. You realize that dealers work for minimum wage and rely on tips for their income.

C. Dealers need the tip money to replace the money they lose to the customers.

D. When you tip, the dealer will sometimes pay you even on losing hands.

QUESTION 12
You should always take the "insurance" bet, because:

ANSWER
A. You will save yourself a lot of money by saving the bets when the dealer has a blackjack.
B. It is simply a very good bet.
C. It saves you money by saving the bets on bad hands.
D. You should not take the "insurance" bet ever, because it is never a good bet.

QUESTION 13
You can win big in blackjack, because:

ANSWER
A. When you bet big, you win big.
B. By applying your knowledge and skill your wins will accumulate.
C. Gamblers who bet big are always welcome.
D. Players who make big bets are the only ones allowed to win big.

QUESTION 14
Card counting is the best way to win consistently at blackjack, because:

ANSWER
A. It's the only surefire system ever developed.
B. It's the only way to know the exact cards in the deck, or decks.
C. It's only an estimate, but better than nothing.
D. It's not the best way to win, but is one of the better ways available, although not perfect.

QUESTION 15

Every blackjack player must learn the Basic Strategy, because:

ANSWER
   A. Without knowing this, the player can at best only hope for a win, and has no idea what to do with whatever cards he gets.
   B. It provides a framework upon which to build blackjack playing skills.
   C. It lets you formalize various decisions so that you always know what to do.
   D. All of the above.

QUESTION 16

The Modified Basic Strategy (MBS) is just as good as Basic Strategy for blackjack, because:

ANSWER
   A. It is actually better, because it applies to all blackjack games and does not require refinements or modifications to be of best usefulness under the majority of playing conditions.
   B. There's not much of a difference; therefore it is just as good as any Basic Strategy.
   C. It helps to put everything together at the same time.
   D. Basic Strategy allows for a large variety of modifications for a whole lot of different conditions, and therefore the MBS is not as good.

QUESTION 17

When you have a hard stiff, and the dealer shows a 5 or a 6, what do you do?

ANSWER
   A. Run for cover, then yell for help.
   B. Immediately visit your pastor, priest, or rabbi and beg forgiveness.
   C. Make your decision in accordance with the MBS.
   D. Start crying and beg for half your money back.

QUESTION 18
You should never split any pair against the dealer's up-card of 7, 8, 9, or 10, because:

ANSWER
   A. It depends on the pair, and what the MBS says you should do in that situation.
   B. If you split, you will lose twice as much.
   C. It's never a good idea to split pairs against dealer's cards that can make him a winning hand.
   D. The dealer is more likely to already have a better hand, or even a blackjack, and therefore hitting a pair is better.

QUESTION 19
You should always double-down on all soft hands against the dealer's upcards of 5 or 6, because:

ANSWER
   A. These are dealer's "bust" cards, and you therefore have the best chance to win twice as much.
   B. Not all soft hands should be doubled against these cards, only some.
   C. Soft hands cannot be busted, and therefore it's always a good idea to put twice the bet in play against these dealer's cards.
   D. Soft hands are trouble, and therefore we should only hit them at all times.

QUESTION 20

You should always split pairs of 5s and 10s, because:

ANSWER

- A. These are the best opportunities of all blackjack plays to make the most money.
- B. Doing this assures you of making two good hands out of just one.
- C. You can't bust by splitting, and therefore have more chances for better profits.
- D. You should never do this unless you want to be called a blackjack bonehead.

QUIZ ANSWERS

Q. 1. The answer is C. In theory, yes, the game can be beaten. In reality, the best that can be achieved is virtually an even game. In some games, the house edge can be as low as 0.01 percent, and for these reasons the game is so advantageous, as compared to other house-banked casino games. By playing the MBS, you will face a house edge of around 0.01 percent to 0.5 percent, depending on where you play, how many decks, what the rules are, and so on, as has been explained throughout this book. By using the wagering differential, tiered betting structure, and fractional differential, along with taking advantage of the best rules and options, and incorporating your skills over all aspects of blackjack, you will actually beat the game for profits, even though you are playing what is in reality an unbeatable game. Don't confuse this with the *theory* of the game, which shows easily that the game can be mathematically beaten. By applying the mathematics to the game as it is theoretically structured, and using the principles of empirical sciences that lead to these mathematical conclusions as commonly used in most blackjack texts, then the game can be shown to be beatable.

But in reality, under the actual playing conditions of the real world, blackjack as so offered in the casinos *always* has an in-built house edge. Although very tiny, nonetheless it is an edge and therefore the game has to be considered *realistically* unbeatable, although *theoretically* beatable.

Q. 2. The answer is D. I'm certain there will be several critics who will dispute this, citing the card-counting systems as a means of entirely eliminating the house edge and consequently making the game beatable. In some instances, this can be considered a valid position. But, as I have shown, this is based on incomplete information, and hence is largely unreliable. But, by using the principles that I have shown here, I have likewise demonstrated that it is possible to play a game where the house edge is against you, but yet beat the game for *financial* profits. And that is, after all, the point. So the answer to this question is D, because the game can be beaten only in theory, as based purely on the laboratory mathematics. But the game can also be beaten for *profit*, by using the principles I have described.

The difference that has to be identified is between the beatability of the game *theoretically*, and being able to beat the game for *profit*. Although both are intended to arrive at the same conclusion, namely that we make money from the game, the truth is that the theory excludes the profit when considered within the restrictions and confines of the real world of actual casino play, while the profit, by like reasons, excludes the theory.

Q. 3. The answer is C. A good game can include all of the other features of the other answers, but the main point is that you want a game containing as few decks as possible, all the way down to a two-deck hand-held game, with deep penetration, and with most of the better rules and options. These games can be found, and therefore are called "good," because here you have most of the opportunities to make better and more consistent profits. This is not meant to exclude the six-deck shoe games, or the four-deck shoe games, because if that's all you can find, this answer still applies.

Q. 4. The answer is D. None of the above. Answer A is restrictive. If you can't double-down on soft hands, and are limited to the 9, 10, and 11, you are giving up a substantial portion of your profit potential to the house. These are very bad rules. In answer B you have something that is offered in all blackjack games, and is therefore not a "rule," but an option that is universally available. Consequently, it doesn't factor in your knowledge of what the "good" rules are. Answer C shows a very bad rule that again adds to the house edge against you, further diminishing what should be your ability to make profits. Therefore, none of the above is the correct answer.

Q. 5. The answer is B. Although it was Thorp who first recognized that a system could be created for beating the game, it was Julian Braun who first recognized that blackjack is a game that can be beaten by the use of a series of *standardized* rules. He programmed the IBM supercomputer in the mid-1960s with the rules of blackjack, and came up with a series of decisions that the players should make, as based on the information available from the dealer's exposed card. This then quantified the best decisions to make under the specified circumstances, and assigned each a percentage of success value. From this a chart was developed that showed what these decisions should be under each and every playing situation. These quantified decisions were so structured to show the best possible option under the circumstances. Later, this was developed further and became known as the basic strategy for blackjack.

Q. 6. The answer is A. Surely I will have plenty of critics who dispute this. Actually, you can make profits from each of the answers. Particularly from answer D, when you use these counting systems. It is possible, but not practical under real-world conditions, as I have explained. Rather, for consistency in making profits from blackjack, it is my opinion that mastering my Modified Basic Strategy, playing blackjack perfectly each hand in accordance with this MBS, and then adding the mastery of my wagering differential, tiered betting, and fractional differential principles, all these together, done well, will result in more *noticeable* profits within the finite exposure of each player to their own individual and independent short-term series of events.

Q. 7. The answer is C. Actually, all of these are pretty awful games. But a single-deck game where the dealer will hit soft 17, and then shuffles each time one, or a maximum of two, hands are dealt, is a game so bad that I'd rather give up blackjack entirely than sit at something this terrible. In a game like this, you will be better off just to hand your money to the casino and go home, and save yourself the prolonged agony of losing it hand by hand. This is the worst kind of game you can ever get, and if the casino offers this game then their other rules are likely to be equally bad.

Q. 8. The answer is D. The answer explains it all. If you didn't pick this answer, go back to chapter 7, and read again the section on shuffling machines. Playing blackjack on any table where one of these shuffling machines is used means you will be losing your money at so much the faster rate that you will get dizzy from how fast it disappears. Stay away from these games!

Q. 9. The answer is A. If the game is fair, and there's no cheating, both the dealer and each of the players all have the same and equal chance of getting the two-card 21 hand known as blackjack. This is true for all the major casinos. No such casino would ever allow such cheating to jeopardize their gaming license. Therefore, all players have the same chance to get a blackjack, and so does the dealer. Neither gets more blackjacks than the other by some design. It's all equal, and all chances equally available.

Q. 10. The answer is A. Yes, of course they can. Cheating

is a skill, and it is possible by anyone who has that skill. However, and this is a very big however, *the casinos would never, ever, allow this under any circumstances* because they would immediately risk losing their gaming license. For example, the casinos in Las Vegas make more than $4.7 billion per year. Yes, that's *billion*, with a "B." No casino that makes that much money would ever even *think* of risking all of this in order to cheat at blackjack, no matter how big a bettor they may have. In fact, casinos prize big bettors, known as "whales" in the casino industry, and they want them to come and play. Some of these "whales" can bet, and win or lose, over $22 million at a time, and even more. If they so much as *suspected* that any kind of cheating were going on, they would not only leave, but they would sue the casino for billions of dollars for fraud. Therefore, no known major casino in the United States will ever cheat you in blackjack, *under any circumstances.* Casino games and casino gaming are among the most regulated, and the safest, of any kind of business anywhere. Period. The casinos are justly proud of this fact, and so should you be as their customer. A business so safe and so secure is hard to find. The casinos are to be complimented for their diligence in making certain all their games are free from cheats, and are always fair under their rules.

Q. 11. The answer is B. All casino dealers start working at minimum wage, and most of them will stay at that level for their entire career. I know of many dealers who have been dealing for more than twenty years, and who are still paid only the minimum wage. Casinos don't pay dealers any more because they know that dealers will get tips, so the casinos figure it's not worth the added expense to pay their dealers as other companies would ordinarily pay their employees. Although there are some very rare exceptions to this, most dealers never get a pay raise. What they get in tips is what they live on. Their small wages are usually taken by the IRS and applied to their income tax liability. Even when they make no tips, the dealers are still stuck with paying taxes because the IRS formula assumes that they get tips to a specified amount every day. This is not so, but it remains as a law, so the poor employees who are among the lowest-paid are also stuck with the biggest tax bill. For these reasons, if no other, you should always be generous. If you get a nice dealer, and you are winning, share your fortune. By all means, if you get a surly person who is not nice, well, then maybe tip small. Remember, in all games other than live poker, the dealers share their tokes. So, even if you don't like that particular dealer, but do like some others, remember that your tip will help them as well. In live poker, all dealers keep their own tips, so it's even more important not to forget them, as they work very hard.

Q. 12. The answer is D. The "insurance" bet in blackjack is a complete sucker bet. It is there only to entice you to make additional side wagers on the unlikely possibility that the dealer may actually have a blackjack 21 hand, when he shows an Ace as the upcard. The dealer will, in fact, have such a hand only about 21 percent of the time, so 79 percent of the time you will lose that insurance bet, and then still have a good chance to lose your original bet. This is especially so when you have a really bad hand, such as a hard-16 stiff, for example. As strange as it may seem, I have seen people take insurance on this lousy hand, lose the insurance bet, and then lose their original hand. So now these players have lost 1.5 times their investment, and this one bad decision alone negates the time they got paid 3:2 on their blackjacks. Doing this all the time will cost you 79 percent more losers than by not taking the insurance, and therefore you should never, ever, take it. (There is only one exception, and that is if you are tracking cards, counting cards, or counting or tracking 10s. Even though I have, hopefully, demonstrated that these systems are flawed, nevertheless they can be used to a minor degree of assistance, if done properly. Under these situations, if you *absolutely know* that there are a lot of 10-value cards in this part of the deck, or decks, then and only then, *and only very rarely*, you may wish to consider taking insurance. However, I personally will refuse this no matter what, because I know that for each one of these instances where I successfully guess and make that one insurance bet pay off, I will subsequently suffer seven more, on average, where I will be wrong, and so I will have lost more money than I made. But I will leave this up to you to decide, if you want to take me to task with this suggestion. Overall, for most players, I will recommend *never* to take insurance.)

Q. 13. The answer is B. While it is true that a big bet will make a big win, it can also make a big loss. However, by learning to play blackjack well, with skill and knowledge, and applying them to your regular and consistent play, your wins will accumulate. Unless you are already a very wealthy player, most likely you will never win as much in one hand as some fool gambler who walks up to a table rolling drunk and slaps $10,000 on the table and mumbles, "Let's deal some cards!" or something like that. He then gets a hard 17 against the dealer's upcard of 6, and yells, "Hit me!" and then draws a 4 for a perfect 21, while the dealer turns over a 16 and draws a 4 to a 20, and the drunk wins, and yells and yelps and hollers like a banshee, all proud of himself. What you don't see is that he's most likely going home in a bus. There's the old gamblers' folk tale of the man who came to Las Vegas in an $80,000 Mercedes-Benz, and left in a $200,000 bus. Well, you get the picture. The point is that by playing with all your knowledge and skills, your wins will soon accumulate far beyond any one lucky win by some foolhardy gamblers. You can be justly proud of yourself because you're not one of them, not a "gambler." You are a "blackjack player," and there's a big difference. Gamblers take foolish risks. Players like you play knowing what to do and when to do it, and how to make more money when the going is good, and lose little when the going is bad.

Q. 14. The answer is D. Card counting is *one* of the ways that can be used as a means to make more educated guesses as to the composition of the remaining deck, or decks. But it is not the best way to win, or the best system, and certainly not perfect. It is, however, one of the better ways available. Nevertheless, you must realize by now that counting cards is very hard, and that even if you learn all of those systems perfectly, you are still working with imperfect and incomplete information. Therefore, the best you can ever achieve is a little better guess. These card-counting systems are still being touted as the ultimate answer to blackjack profits, in virtually all the books on blackjack that I have been able to find. The trouble is that all of these systems are based on two very flawed premises:

a. That the person doing this actually can learn all of it and actually do it perfectly at all times in the real-world casino.

b. That the rules of blackjack, and the way it is dealt, will allow a sufficient degree of accuracy for the card-counter to have anything close to the kind of theoretical advantage that the *theory* of counting cards allows.

The first one can be overcome if you are a person who can learn so much and then also be able to put it to actual practice, with constant perfection at all times and under all conditions. The second, however, cannot be overcome. The reality of the game today is such that none of these card-counting systems can ever make any significant-enough difference to your limited exposure to the blackjack playing experience to have any positive effect on your ability to win. It's just not possible in the real world, under these conditions and limitations. The only time this can actually work is either under laboratory conditions, where the theory of the system is allowed to play itself out without any of the real-world restrictions and encumbrances, or if you are able to master it so well, play every day like a job, and still be able to find a game where you can make the theoretically viable 1 percent or 1.6 percent advantage. And even then it's frankly very little money for a whole lot of effort, and huge risk.

Q. 15. The answer is, of course, D. All of the above. Basic Strategy for blackjack is essential. Without it, you are playing in the dark, and only making guesses, and not even educated guesses. Without Basic Strategy for blackjack, you just have nothing upon which to base any of your playing decisions. You are, therefore, a certain loser. However, learning the Basic Strategy will provide you with all of the best information available, and give you a framework designed to offer you a series of decisions for every possible option and occasion, which you can memorize and therefore always know what to do under any and all conditions of the game.

Q. 16. The answer is A. It is actually better, because it applies to all blackjack games and does not require refinements or modifications to be of best usefulness under the majority of playing conditions. That's about it. The problem with the standard Basic Strategy, as usually described in many books and texts about blackjack, is that it mostly requires a slew of side modifications and refinements for various other conditions. Because there are so many different games of blackjack now available, with so many different rules, numbers of decks, and so on, the various alterations and refinements to the standard Basic Strategy wind up being overwhelming and so cumbersome that learning all of it makes everything extremely confusing. Rather than making blackjack simpler, these situations make it far more complicated. Even a knowledgeable player can become confused by the proliferation of the various "extra" side modifications to the basic strategy, as it was originally developed and as these various texts now show.

The main problem is that when Basic Strategy was first developed, it was developed in a laboratory environment, under the most theoretically viable conditions. Then it was refined and applied to the actual playing conditions. However, these were the playing conditions of casinos in the 1960s and 1970s. Such conditions no longer exist. There are new conditions. Therefore, the need for all these "extra" modifications. But that defeats the purpose for which the Basic Strategy was originally intended, which was to *simplify* the game and make it easier to beat for profit. Therefore, when I developed the MBS, I chose to select those aspects of the game of blackjack that are the most universally applicable, under any and all conditions, rules, and options. By learning the MBS, and then combining it with the other information here presented, you will be able to play simply, with fun, and for profit.

Q. 17. The answer is, of course, C. Whatever situation you are facing, the MBS provides the answer. You should know what to do by the time you go to the real casino. If you don't, then refer to the easy-to-carry chart, which is made available to you in the next chapter. Crying at the table and begging may get you sympathy, but won't help you with the hand. Running for cover and yelling for help will most likely get you arrested and placed in a padded room. However, praying, or seeking guidance from your minister, can't hurt (it will likely not have the immediate effect that you desire, so try adding the use of the MBS).

Q. 18. The answer is A. It simply depends on the pair, and then the decision is covered by the MBS. None of the other answers apply. It doesn't matter what the dealer has, or can make. The proper and correct play simply depends on what the pair is, what the actual dealer's upcard is, and what the MBS indicates as the correct strategy for that situation.

Q. 19. The answer is B. Only some of the soft hands are the correct candidate for a double-down opportunity against these dealer's upcards. The MBS shows which ones. While it is true that putting more money in play under the most advantageous conditions is to your benefit, it is not true that doing so only for the sake of adding bets will also benefit your profits. These situations are designed to be useful under the *specified* circumstances, and these circumstances only. Just because a dealer shows an upcard of a 5 or a 6 does not mean that this is the occasion to double-down on all soft hands every time. It is important to always know what the MBS indicates, and then play accordingly, no matter what your instincts may push you to do.

It is a common misconception that 5 and 6 are the dealer's "bust" cards. There is no such thing. While it is correct that the dealer will bust more often with these cards than with 10s and Aces, and while it is also true that, under the correct conditions, you can increase your bet in a proper double-down or split situation against these dealer's upcards, it is not correct that doing this will always assure you of twice the win. The dealer will make standing hands more often than busting hands. The reason that double-down opportunities on certain soft hands are advantageous is that you can't bust that hand with the draw of just one card to your specified soft hand, while the dealer may in fact bust, or draw a card that will force him to stand on a hand whose value is worse than yours, and therefore you win. Consequently, only the properly identified soft hands should be doubled against these dealer's upcards, and for those you should always refer to the MBS.

Q. 20. The answer is D. But don't be too hard on yourself if you didn't get it. You don't have to be a bonehead, because these situations are the most common mistakes made by novice players, or players who have forgotten some parts of their basic strategy. Splitting a pair of 5s simply means you will make two bad hands out of a good one. This is a double-down opportunity instead. Whenever you get a pair of 5s, this is the time you treat this as a total of 10, and therefore use this as a double-down opportunity as indicated in the MBS. As for a pair of 10s, well, here you have a total of 20, which can be beaten only by a dealer's 21, and therefore you have a made winner most of the time. Splitting these 10s is indeed a very bad play, and if you ever do this you are certainly entitled to be called a bonehead. No disrespect intended. This is just a means of making the point sink in. Don't do it! It's a no-no, a really bad thing.

SCORING

So here we are, at the end of the quiz. How did you do? Score +10 points for each correct answer, and −10 points for each incorrect answer. Your total indicates one of the following:

Score 60 or less
You need a lot of help. Try reading the book again, and make notes. You must have missed something.

Score 70–90
Not too bad. You are close, but must have missed a lot of details at some point. I suggest you go and start the book from the top, and take some notes.

Score 0
This is the 50-50 spot. If you scored 0, then this means you got half the questions right, and half of them wrong. Find out which ones were wrong, and why you answered them the way you did. Then go back through the book and

find out why you chose those answers, and take the test again. You should do better the next time.

Score 110–120

Pretty good! You are well on your way. But you need some extra help, so try to find out why you answered some of the questions the way you did, and learn a little more.

Score 130–150

Very good! You are close to becoming a good player. Just keep working.

Score 160–170

You have done very well indeed! Now find out where you answered incorrectly, and try again.

Score 180–190

You are really, really good! I'm proud of you! Just a little more and you've got it.

Score 200

Wow! A perfect score! You are the expert. Now go to the casino and make some money.

The MBS Card

The design on the next page is the MBS compressed to a small chart that can be used as a pocket guide. If you photocopy this page and then cut out the chart, you can laminate it and it will become your pocket strategy guide. This way you will be able to refresh your memory any time you go to a casino, and will not need to purchase another strategy card. The use of this strategy card is not illegal, and in most casinos you will be allowed to refer to it at any time. Although it's very rare, in some casinos you may be asked to keep it in your pocket and not let it lie on the table. Either way, this will be your guide in case you forget some decisions while you are in the heat of the blackjack battle.

Pocket Guide MBS

YOUR HAND	2	3	4	5	6	7	8	9	10	A
5-8	H	H	H	H	H	H	H	H	H	H
9	H	H	D	D	D	D	H	H	H	H
10	D	D	D	D	D	D	D	D	H	H
11	D	D	D	D	D	D	D	D	D	H
Hard Hands 12	S	S	S	S	S	H	H	H	H	H
13	S	S	S	S	S	H	H	H	H	H
14	S	S	S	S	S	H	H	H	H	H
15	S	S	S	S	S	H	H	H	H	H
16	S	S	S	S	S	H	H	H	H	H
17-21	S	S	S	S	S	S	S	S	S	S
Soft Hands A-2	H	H	H	D	D	H	H	H	H	H
A-3	H	H	H	D	D	H	H	H	H	H
A-4	H	H	D	D	D	H	H	H	H	H
A-5	H	H	D	D	D	H	H	H	H	H
A-6	H	H	D	D	D	S	H	H	H	H
A-7	H	H	D	D	D	S	S	H	H	H
A-8	S	S	S	S	S	S	S	S	S	S
A-9	S	S	S	S	S	S	S	S	S	S
A-10 (BJ)	S	S	S	S	S	S	S	S	S	S
Pair Hands A+A	Sp	Sp	Sp	Sp	Sp	Sp	Sp	Sp	Sp	Sp
2+2	H	H	Sp	Sp	Sp	H	H	H	H	H
3+3	H	Sp	Sp	Sp	Sp	H	H	H	H	H
4+4	H	H	H	H	H	H	H	H	H	H
5+5	D	D	D	D	D	D	D	D	H	H
6+6	Sp	Sp	Sp	Sp	Sp	H	H	H	H	H
7+7	Sp	Sp	Sp	Sp	Sp	Sp	H	H	H	H
8+8	Sp	Sp	Sp	Sp	Sp	Sp	Sp	Sp	H	H
9+9	Sp	Sp	Sp	Sp	Sp	Sp	S	S	S	S
10+10	S	S	S	S	S	S	S	S	S	S

H = Hit   **S** = Stand   **D** = Double-Down   **Sp** = Split

Odds and Ends

In this chapter I will include various points and comments that either did not fit anywhere else, or required some additional thoughts or explanation. There is no particular order to these items, but if they refer to some specific section of the book, this will be so identified.

COMPUTER PROGRAMS

In several sections of this book I encouraged you to practice, either for gaining a better mastery of the MBS, or for learning the various strategy aspects of the game of blackjack. Mostly, I recommended that you use real cards and deal out actual hands of blackjack just as they will be dealt in the real casino. This helps you tremendously because you get the actual feel of the cards and the game. However, I do understand that many of you may prefer to purchase some of the better computer programs that play blackjack on your home computer.

If you wish to practice by buying a computer program

that plays blackjack on your PC, I wish to warn you not to rely on the strategy advice that usually comes with such programs. Many of these programs contain very limited strategy advice, or help features, and when they do, these are very often misleading and incorrect. These programs are usually written quickly and the advice for strategy they offer is mostly made up from bits and pieces of "standard" strategies, such as those that have been widely available in many books since the 1960s. The programs mostly have an icon, or a button, which enables the advice option. This program then flags you each time you make a "wrong" decision. These "flags" are often themselves in error, and therefore any reliance that you place in the accuracy of your decisions based on these programs will also be in error.

My best advice is to completely *disable* any such "help" or "strategy advice" part of the blackjack software, and play the game only and solely with reliance on the MBS that I have presented in this book. In this way you will be able to use the computer program to help you practice your blackjack mastery, while not becoming corrupted by the flawed and incorrect strategies found in these blackjack computer software programs and games.

TOO MANY BLACKJACKS

Although the discussion that initiated these thoughts had to do with the double-deck game, in the section to which this initially applied, the point actually focuses on the seeming incongruity in the number of potential two-card blackjack 21s in a single deck of cards. This point was first mentioned to me by my friend and fellow gaming columnist and author, John Grochowski. John and I had an interesting discussion regarding this during several e-mail messages. As a result, I have given considerable thought to this and have come up with some material that I think is worth discussion. First, however, let us explain what the actual issue is in this matter.

In a single deck of fifty-two cards, there are sixty-four blackjacks. Hmmm. How is it possible, you may ask, that in a deck that has only fifty-two cards, we can have sixty-four natural 21 hands? Well, it works as follows. There are four Aces in a deck of fifty-two cards. Then, there are four Kings, four Queens, four Jacks, and four 10s, all of which are called the 10-value cards. Any one of these cards, combined with any Ace, makes a blackjack 21 hand, the natural. Now, common sense would seem to indicate that with only four Aces, there can only be four blackjacks, right? Well, not according to the way this particular format of mathematical thinking allows. Here's how that breaks down.

Since there are four Kings, Queens, Jacks, and Tens, this means that there are a total of sixteen 10-value cards in the deck. And since there are four Aces, this means that *each* Ace can combine with *each* 10-value card to make a blackjack 21 natural. First you have the sixteen 10-value cards combining with the Ace of Spades. Then you have the sixteen 10-value cards combining with the Ace of Hearts. Then with the Ace of Diamonds and, finally, with the Ace of Clubs. So, we have $16 + 16 + 16 + 16 = 64$. So that's how we arrive at the sixty-four blackjacks per fifty-two-card deck.

Now this may not seem very important. In fact it isn't, in the general sense of what we, as casual players of blackjack, can expect as profoundly meaningful. Its meaning is largely academic, or perhaps interesting only from the perspective of the overall mathematical analysis of the game of blackjack. As John wrote to me in one of his e-mails, the main meaning in this is as follows:

> For anyone interested in calculating the odds of the game, the percentages of initial two-card hands that result in blackjacks and the effect on the house

edge, it is important to look at the possible two-card 21s as 64 unique hands. We can calculate that there are 1,378 possible two-card hands using a fifty-two-card deck. If we know that 64 of those hands are two-card 21s, we then can calculate that an average of one in 21.5 hands will be a two-card 21. A little bit more calculation, and we find that the 3:2 payoff on black-jacks trims the house edge by 2.3 percent. If we see the two-card 21 possibilities as only four hands instead of 64, we'll be far, far off target when we compute the house edge on the game.

This becomes substantially more important when we consider some of the various "bonus" payoffs for the game of blackjack, such as games where *suited* two-card 21s pay at 2:1, or at 3:1. Since in the standard game of blackjack, the suits of the cards do not matter, this calculation has far more meaning when applied to those few bonus-type games where some alterations to the standard rules of the game have specified that the *suits* of the cards do, in this case, matter.

But what of regular blackjack? The game where the suits of the cards do *not* matter, and do *not* affect the overall game, its standard rules, or the principles of playing. How does this help us win money?

Well, actually, it doesn't. Trying to think of a fifty-two-card deck as having sixty-four blackjacks is a seemingly mind-boggling exercise in intellectual futility. If indeed there are sixty-four possible blackjacks made up of the four Aces and the sixteen 10-value cards, so what? The real-world truth is that you can only ever get four blackjack hands, and that's it. Since the suits don't matter, the fact is that all the sixteen 10-value cards are all together, simply one clump, a block, identified only as a chunk of sixteen cards whose numerical value is 10. So it doesn't matter how much we twist our minds in cogitating on the theoretical number of possible combinations of 21s, when the simple truth is there are only four such possibilities.

My problem with this kind of thinking has nothing to do with John, or his position. In fact, I am very grateful to John for his notes on this issue. If it had not been for his thoughts, I would have never focused on something that has become, at least to my mind, a very interesting exercise in conceptual perspectives. In his thoughts, John correctly follows the principles of applied mathematics in the research into the frequency of occurrences of two-card 21 hands in a deck of fifty-two cards, composed as understood by the values that have been established for the rank of the cards. As this is done in accordance with these established protocols and principles, and with the standardized approach to theoretical analysis of applied number theory in probability calculus, this position is absolutely correct. Well, "absolutely" is a relative term, and in fact there is no such thing as an applied "absolute." An algebraic or numeric "absolute" becomes wholly impotent when it comes to producing anything that can become meaningful, or meaningfully applicable.

My issue with this is actually vested in the very foundations of what forms the framework of such mathematical thinking. This example of the sixty-four blackjacks merely serves to illustrate the point. Such numerical thinking is vested in a series of assumptions that form the basis of all mathematical theorems. These are in themselves vested in further assumptions based upon empirical observations, which are then quantified under other sets of assumptions under the auspices of conceptual rationalism. This is again vested in other assumptions, the ultimate result of which is indefinable and inherently flawed. Anyway, there is a whole body of discussion of these subjects, but we can leave that for another time. The point I am trying to make is that the calculations that are offered to justify the concept of sixty-four blackjacks in a single deck are fundamentally in error. I will attempt to illustrate with an example.

Let us postulate that we have fifty-two candles. Among these, there are four red candles and forty-eight blue candles. Our task is to make as many two-candle combinations of a red candle and a blue candle as possible. So we pick up a red candle, and look at the rest of the candles. We now have three red candles and forty-eight blue candles. So we pick out a blue candle, in no particular order since they are all equally blue candles, and place this candle next to the red candle. We now have achieved the first goal of making a two-candle combination of a red candle and a blue candle. We put this aside. Then we pick up the next red candle, and repeat this process. And so on for the third and fourth red candles. In the end, we have set aside four combinations of red-and-blue two-candle pairs. Our goal has been achieved. But what of all the other blue candles that have been left over? Should they somehow be also included in our task of making as many two-candle combinations of a red candle and a blue candle as possible? Well, we try again.

We mix up all the candles again, and look at what we have. We now have four red candles mixed in with forty-eight blue candles. Since our goal is the same as before, we pick out any red candle and then any blue candle, and put these aside as our first combination of a red-and-blue candle pair. Now we stop to think for a moment. Should we try to combine that one red candle with all of the blue candles? After all, each red candle should be able to combine with each of the blue candles to make such a two-candle combination of a red-and-blue candle pair. So we put that blue candle back with all the other blue candles, and pick out another blue candle. But wait. How do we know this was *another* blue candle, and not the same one? Since we cannot differentiate between the blue candles, since they are all equally blue, then how can we? We can't. There is simply no way of telling which blue candle is which, or how many times it had been used in combination with any of the red candles. We could go on forever with this, and would never, ever, end up with a definitive answer. Each time we make a combination of a red-and-blue candle, we would then have to repeat the process and this would never end. We would be caught in an infinite and futile exercise of trying to match up all the blue candles with the red ones. In the end, we would have to give up, and in order to gain anything meaningful out of this exercise, we would have to simply pick out four blue candles and combine them with the four red candles, and so we would actually have a *workable* result of four combinations of red-and-blue candle pairs.

So, what does all this mean? Well, a whole lot if you think of the underlying principles that govern the thinking in blackjack. Think of the blue candles as all of the 10-value cards. Instead of forty-eight candles, we now have only sixteen. Our task is to take the four red ones and make as many combinations of red-and-blue candles out of these as possible. As in the above example, the results are the same. You cannot make more than four. Otherwise you will be forever trapped in a meaningless infinite exercise of switching and swapping. And therein lies the fallacy of the kind of mathematical thinking that brought about the discussion of how we arrived at the sixty-four-blackjacks. We can only arrive at the sixty-four-blackjack conclusion if we *artificially* ascribe to the sixteen 10-value cards *other* principles, features, and meanings, *other* than their inherent value as being all 10-value cards. In our second example, the sixteen 10-value cards are all the blue candles. And it makes no difference what kind of cards they are. They are all the same. Only if we choose to treat these sixteen cards as somehow different, then and only then does that sixty-four-blackjack calculus come into play. But then we are no longer calculating the original issue, and that's my point.

In a deck of fifty-two cards, where all the 10-value cards are the same 10-value, and where there are only four Aces, there can only be four *events* of a combination of any 10-value card with any Ace. Same as in the candle example. There can be only four possible combinations of a red and blue candle, regardless of how many blue candles there may be. The point is that they are all blue candles, and therefore only four of them can ever be used to make the two-candle combination of a red-and-blue pair. In the blackjack example, there can only be the four two-card combinations of any 10-value card and any Ace. Anything else invalidates the very principles of what blackjack is, and, therefore, any other analysis does not apply to the game of blackjack as it is commonly understood, but rather to something else that has been introduced as an additional element (such as when considering blackjack hands in suits).

It is this kind of thinking that leads to a lot of misconceptions and problems in a multitude of what we all have come to understand as "common concepts." Our thinking has been perverted, and segmented, into compliance with incorrectly defined parameters, and equally corrupted by methodologies that we have become accustomed to glossing over, or bypassing, or entirely ignoring facts and principles that are requisite if the desired result is to be achieved not merely with theoretical, but also with *functional* accuracy. Theoretical accuracy is a gross misnomer, because there is no such thing. What good is it if it is theoretically accurate? No good at all, because most of the time even that theoretical accuracy is inherently pliable and results in functional inaccuracies and imperfect applicability.

The point is that in a finite universe, in a finite and applied game of blackjack, at the table, in the casino, in the few hours you are playing, there is simply no way in which you can make sixty-four blackjacks out of four Aces. And I don't care what the figures seem to indicate, because the very foundation of such thinking is grossly in error. What you've got in the reality of your casino blackjack game are four blackjack possibilities for a single deck, eight for two decks, sixteen for four decks, and twenty-four for six decks. And that's it. Period. End of discussion. Anything else is simply moot, as it applies to your finite exposure to the *real* game. Thinking of those concepts isn't going to make you any more money. And that's the point of this discussion. Our goal in playing blackjack is to beat the game for *financial profit*. To achieve this, all we need to know is that we have this many red candles, and this many blue ones, and that we can only make this many two-candle pairs. And that's all that matters. Cash in hand.

For those of you who now have a large headache from all this thinking, I offer my regrets and a bottle of aspirin. Don't let any of this become an issue for you. Your desire is simple, and so is mine—to make money from the game. To that end, all that we have here said is so directed. And so we bid farewell to such cogitation and remove ourselves back again to the far more interesting world of casino blackjack.

MULTIPLE-ACTION BLACKJACK (MAB)

Multiple-Action Blackjack (MAB for short), is an imaginative innovation on the game of blackjack. The game was invented by a casino executive for the Four Queens Resort in downtown Las Vegas, and is now licensed to many casinos nationwide.

Blackjack has been such a good game for both players and house alike for so many years that the temptation of "don't fix it if it ain't broke" has kept the game virtually unchanged for decades (other than some rule alterations, but that didn't change the game itself).

Multiple-Action Blackjack is an innovation that allows the player to play up to three hands with the same set of cards. The rules are the same as for regular blackjack, with the exception of how the dealer plays (and whatever other rules for blackjack happen to apply in the casino where you may be playing). The game of MAB begins when the player places bets. In the case of regular blackjack, the player can make only one bet, then stand, double, split, or hit as the cards dictate (unless he plays more than one hand, but then to do so the player must play additional spots, thereby preventing other players from being able to join in the game; in addition, playing more than one hand on a standard blackjack game often requires that each bet be a multiple of the other, so that on, say, a $5 minimum table, a player who wishes to bet three hands will have to bet $30 on each of the three spots). In Multiple-Action Blackjack, the player can make three bets on the *same* hand, prior to receiving his first two cards, and (in most casinos) these bets do not have to be the same amount. Players can bet $5 on the first hand, $50 on the second, and, say, $20 on the third. Once the bets are set, the dealer deals two cards to each player, just as in regular blackjack, and then only one card, face up, to himself. On an MAB table, the dealer has three boxes in front of him marked 1, 2, and 3.

On the first hand the dealer will place his one upcard in the #1 box, signifying that hand #1 will now be played. Whatever the dealer's first card is, the dealer will keep this first card for all three hands. After the dealer deals the players their cards, and then deals himself his upcard, the players go through their normal choices: stand, double, split, or hit (there is no "surrender" on most MAB tables). After the players have made their choices, the dealer then deals himself a second card, or third, fourth, and so on, as the house rules dictate. Depending on what cards the dealer gets, he will either stand or bust, according to house rules.

Whatever the outcome, the dealer will then pay winning hands and collect losing bets on the first hand only. Then the dealer will discard all his cards except the original first upcard. He will move that upcard to box #2, draw a set of new cards for his hand, pay winners and take losers for hand #2, then move the original upcard to the #3 position and repeat the process. When three hands are so played, a new game begins.

Throughout this process, the player keeps his original cards; however, the player has a choice to stand, hit, double, or split *only* on the *first* hand. Whatever value hand the player achieved on the first hand remains the same for hands #2 and #3. If the player busts, he loses all three bets. If he makes, say, 19, and stands, his 19 will play for all three hands against the three hands made by the dealer.

Because the players can lose all three hands if they bust on the first hand, the tendency among players is not to hit bad hands, and this fact significantly increases the house win percentage. Of course the advantage for the player is that he can win three times the amount on one hand, and even if dealt a bad hand, may in fact win one or two of the three hands wagered because the dealer may bust on dealer's hands #2 and #3. Splitting, doubling-down, resplitting, and all the other player options (as allowed by the house rules) are also determined by the player for his three hands prior to the dealer completing his first hand. Whatever decisions the player has so made, these also stand for all three hands.

OTHER BLACKJACK-TYPE GAMES

Since MAB was introduced, many other variations on blackjack have been introduced and continue to appear in casinos, mostly in Las Vegas, which is a traditional proving ground for new games. There are so many new blackjack games now available, and continually being introduced, that listing all of them would be nearly impossible. However, a few of them warrant short descriptions. You'll get the idea very quickly, and if you are in a casino where you see one of these games, or any other variation, my suggestion is to find out what the game is, read the available brochure, and then watch the game a while before trying it out.

The most important strategy advice I can give you for all these blackjack variations is that you should watch out for too many deviations from the standard way of playing the game. Often these new variations look interesting and profitable, but are not. The reason casinos like so many new variations on the game is not only that the standard blackjack game is somewhat passé (although still enormously popular, and rightly so), but also that casinos are constantly looking for ways to make their winning percentage higher.

On standard blackjack, for example, the average house withholding percentage is about 6 percent—higher or lower depending on some rule variations. With expert play, on many standard games, this percentage can be substantially minimized, and even eliminated completely, giving the very skilled player an edge over the house. Casinos don't like this, and so the newer blackjack games are attractive to them, because these games often hold upward of 20 percent for the house. So be careful. Find out, apply the principles of gaming knowledge that I have outlined in this book, and you'll be able to make intelligent choices no matter what kind of blackjack variation you may encounter on your casino visit. Now, some of the newer games:

Over-and-Under-13

Over-and-under-13 is a blackjack game originated at Caesars Tahoe, and features a side bet on a standard blackjack game. The side bet is on whether the player's first two cards will equal over or under 13, and pays even money for winners. Decisions are made and paid before the remainder of the game takes place. This side bet can be of any amount from the table's minimum to maximum betting limits. This is not a very good game for the player.

Super 7s

Super 7s is another blackjack side bet game. While the over-and-under-13 side bet can be any amount up to the table limit, this side bet can be a $1 bet only. The player bets whether the first two or three cards dealt to him will be 7-value cards. Three 7s suited (three 7s of Clubs, Diamonds, Hearts, or Spades) will pay $5,000, while three 7s mixed will pay $500, the first two cards of suited 7s will pay $100, first two 7s in any suit will pay $50, and first seven, any suit, will pay $3.

Of course, this game can be played only with multiple decks; otherwise the winning combinations would not be possible. If the dealer has a blackjack, a player making this side bet will still be dealt a third card if his first two cards are 7s. All other rules play the same as regular blackjack and the game continues as standard blackjack after all side bets are decided. In this game the advantage to the player is quite minimal, and the payoffs do not warrant the risk, even if it is just another dollar. In more than twenty years of playing I have only seen three 7s dealt twice, and these were not suited. There is little benefit here for the player.

Royal Match 21

Royal Match 21 is a game where a side bet is made on whether the player's first two cards will match in suit. Any two face cards in any suit (two Hearts, two Clubs, and so on) generally will pay 3:1, while a King and Queen suited will pay 10:1. This is one of the better new blackjack innovations, and therefore the only one that I would recommend (although I generally advise you to stay away from most of these blackjack innovations).

Progressives

Recently, several "progressive" versions of blackjack have been introduced in many casinos. These differ slightly from game to game; however, the basic principle is the same. For an extra side bet (usually $1), which is placed in a mechanical slot (like Progressive Caribbean Stud, for example), the player has a chance to win all, or part, of a metered progressive jackpot—as well as a series of smaller "bonus pays." What these are and in what amounts depends on the game and the various payoffs such a game offers. If you see one of these games in the casino where you happen to be, ask about it, read the brochure, which is usually available right at the table, and then apply the playing principles and knowledge you have learned in this book. You can then make your own informed decisions on whether or not this particular version of the blackjack game is worth playing.

Postscript

I took some chances in this book. I did something that most writers about blackjack usually don't do—I rocked the boat. I spoke truthfully about the fallacy of the single-deck game, as it is now played in the casinos of the twenty-first century. This is not the good game it is often touted to be. I spoke truthfully about the problems with counting cards, and the fact that card-counters in today's casinos can do very little to win consistently, and for the kinds of profits that they were able to achieve in years past. I showed that even with counting cards, the financial results are mostly not anywhere near the kind of successes that others claim for this kind of approach to blackjack. At best, card-counters use incomplete information based on flawed thinking and are therefore able to make barely better guesses than other players. Better, yes. Consistently profitable, well, maybe. I just don't think that card-counting is possible anymore to any degree of accuracy and consistent profitability.

I spoke the truth about the shuffling machines that are eventually going to kill the game of blackjack as we now know it if they are allowed to spread further. I also suggested that my Modified Basic Strategy can be applied to the vast majority of casino blackjack games, without the need for the pages and pages of various alterations and modifications and refinements. Here too, no doubt, I will have critics who will cite specific and individual examples to point out my folly, while, in so doing, ever so subtly reaffirming my point that the MBS was designed for the overall *general* game, and not for any one specific situation. Finally, I went out on a limb and suggested a method of tiered and fractional wagering, which is mostly contrary to any kind of wager-structure thinking in most blackjack books.

I did this because it was time for a different kind of book on blackjack. Just about all the books I have read that have been published since the 1970s are the same. All of them show the Basic Strategy, then show the variations that are required by the changes in playing rules, options, and dealing conditions in various casinos and expanding gaming jurisdictions. Then they all talk about how card-counting is the complete and only answer to winning, which then inevitably leads to the author's one or more "pet" systems or suggestions. Fine, I have read most of these, and have also used them in play. They mostly work—up to a point. The writing and the suggestions are very good in most of these books. Many of my friends and fellow columnists, whom I have known for several years, have also written such books. These are also fine books and worth reading.

However, in all of this I have not found anything new. Not since Thorp, Braun, Wong, Uston, Patterson, and others throughout the 1960s and 1970s, has there been anything that could be called "revolutionary." By this I mean that little or no innovation in the way we look at blackjack has been offered. At least not that I have been able to find and read, or that is actually useful and applicable to the game as it now exists. Perhaps even this book may one day be viewed as merely the instructional manual that it is, indeed, intended to be.

However, I still wanted something more. I wanted to present something different. Something that can be actually used by the average player, the vacationer, and the weekend warrior, to a level of success previously reserved for only that small fraction of 1 percent of professionals who have so

mastered the game that it is their entire life, and their *job*. I
wanted my readers to be able to master blackjack quickly,
and be able to hit the game for profits immediately—*now*—
not after years of study and practice. However, I do recognize the need for such study and practice and do, in fact,
recommend that this also be included as part of the overall
approach to the game.

Nevertheless, I wanted still more. I wanted to leave
something for discussion. I wanted to present something
that would provoke debate and further thoughts. To stimu-
late the blackjack debate so that, perhaps, something even
more profound can be born from these steps. So I presented
not just my MBS, but also my principles of "keys to winning," and, mostly, my "wagering differential," "tiered wagering," and "fractional differential" principles, and their
method of application.

There is a whole lot more to all of this than I was able to
include in this book. Even though I have simplified all of it
to fit within this instructional book designed to teach the
game quickly and profitably, the methods I have described,
even in such brevity, are those that do actually work. At
least such has been my experience, as I am able to detail at
the time of this writing. Nothing is infinite except infinity
itself. That in itself can also be considered sophistry. What
I have proposed may, some day, become different. Nevertheless, I do believe that anyone who has read this book,
understood what I have discussed, and learned all that I
have stated as the requirements for success, will become a
profitable blackjack player. If you do this correctly, you can
win only 41 percent of the time, but still have a *profit* in
the end. This does not buck the casino's edge in the game.
It merely shaves it to an almost even point, where the advantages of the game's own inherent rules, along with the
principles that I have outlined, combine under all the conditions of correct and knowledgeable play as I have listed

it, to provide the end-result profitability. It's really not that hard to do, but it is essential that the light first dawn, and when it does, the rest will be yours for the taking.

I do wish you the best of luck, and success. To have one you need the other. The knowledge you have found in this book is the fuel for that ride.

"If tomorrow should never come,
today is the best day of your life"

Index

DON'T MISS

THE NEXT BOOK IN THE

POWERFUL PROFITS

SERIES . . .

Powerful Profits from

♣

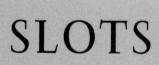

SLOTS

♣

COMING FROM CITADEL

IN MARCH 2003

Table 91/322

MBS — MODIFIED BASIC STRATEGY

- Double down

- HIT ~ draw — scratch
                the card

- STAND = waving hand = palm
              down

Hit 62 — Break M○○ Bust
                one

  TIE OR PUSH — draw

CRAPS   single deck
game ←   2 deck
              shoe or
              ATLANTIC city
              Las Vegas
              Reno Tahoe